AF615976

BURIDAN'S MULE

BURIDAN'S MULE

by

Kenneth Coe

PHILOSOPHICAL LIBRARY
New York

Library of Congress Cataloging in Publication Data

Coe, Kenneth.
Buridan's mule.

1. God--Biblical teaching. 2. God--History of doctrines. I. Title.
BS544.C63 231.7 81-82692
ISBN 0-8022-2392-3 AACR2

200 West 57th Street, New York, N.Y. 10019

Manufactured in the United States of America

Overseas distributor: George Prior Ltd.
52-54 High Holborn
London WC1V 6RL England

For Mary Louise,
Edmund,
Eleanor,
Edna, and
Eunice.

Contents

Preface

This book is a layman's overview of man's changing perceptions of God, derived from the luminous Biblical insights and the church creeds and dogmas.

"Why were God's commands to the ancient Hebrews, more often than not, cruel, blood-thirsty and devilish than Godly?" "Once you are gone you are gone—no heaven or hell." "You cannot go by the teachings of Jesus in this competitive day and age." "God said this or that to Moses. What does it mean?" These are but a few of the endless modern remarks.

No matter how each reader may take these modern comments, undeniably there are widely different Christian perceptions of God and correspondingly varying attitudes toward the church and religion in general. Do the Christians today believe in one and same God?

Many of the church creeds and dogmas, which had originated for one reason or another, have been practiced for centuries and have acquired factual authority: they were integral parts of Early and Medieval Christianity. The modern scientific atmosphere and proliferation of information, however, place all traditional beliefs under scrutiny, scientific or otherwise, and place the value of religion itself in question.

Timeless spiritual and moral principles, deeply embedded in the traditional Judeo-Christian faith, are being obscured not only by diverse truths advanced by modern philosophical and scientific theories but also by the creeds and dogmas, the mysticism of the Ancient and the Medieval Ages and the human yearning for millennium. Therefore, this book has the sole purpose: a matter of fact probing in the reverent aspects of the Judeo-Christian faith without adhering to traditional a priori constraints, or skirting around the touchy religious issues, or glossing things over.

A reader of the Bible may find a wide discrepancy between the church creeds and dogmas on one hand and the religious subjects contained in the Bible. A church-goer may find a gulf between the religious yardstick of right or wrong and values and morals required of the socio-economic and political realities of modern life. Each generation of the ancients, the medievals, and the moderns, has lived through the guilt complex of many different kinds. This book sorts out the religious principles amid baffling religious mysticism and perplexity and helps any reader see why and when the sources of the modern guilt complex originated.

The personal beliefs and convictions of the author inevitably creep into such a book as this; nevertheless, efforts have been made so that the main thread of the vital religious themes may not be distorted in any way.

This book is partly addressed to the church authorities with deep sympathy for the growing pains and difficulties of bringing about theological consensus on the Christian creeds and dogmas. The world today comprises all sorts of societies which range from primitive to modern and combine voodooism, shamanism, or other superstitious native beliefs with Christianity; accordingly, religious consensus is easier said than done, if varying stages of human progress in Africa, Asia, Latin America, and the Western countries are taken into consideration.

This book is written in a direct and simple way, and bypasses the unnecessary details, including the Eastern Orthodox faith, which are not relevant to the purpose of this book. The aim is to avoid a trifling analysis but to clarify the general approach to understand the religious principles contained in the Bible so that each reader may do a study for himself; accordingly, this book aspires to simplify and clarify rather than to delve into obscure items.

Needless to mention, there cannot be novel scholarship to demonstrate in restating the spiritual and moral values embedded in the Bible. It is my hope that this book will be of some help to the readers of the Bible who want to doubt and know before believing and to put the teachings of Jesus back into modern life.

Kenneth Coe
Belmont, Mass.
1981

BURIDAN'S MULE

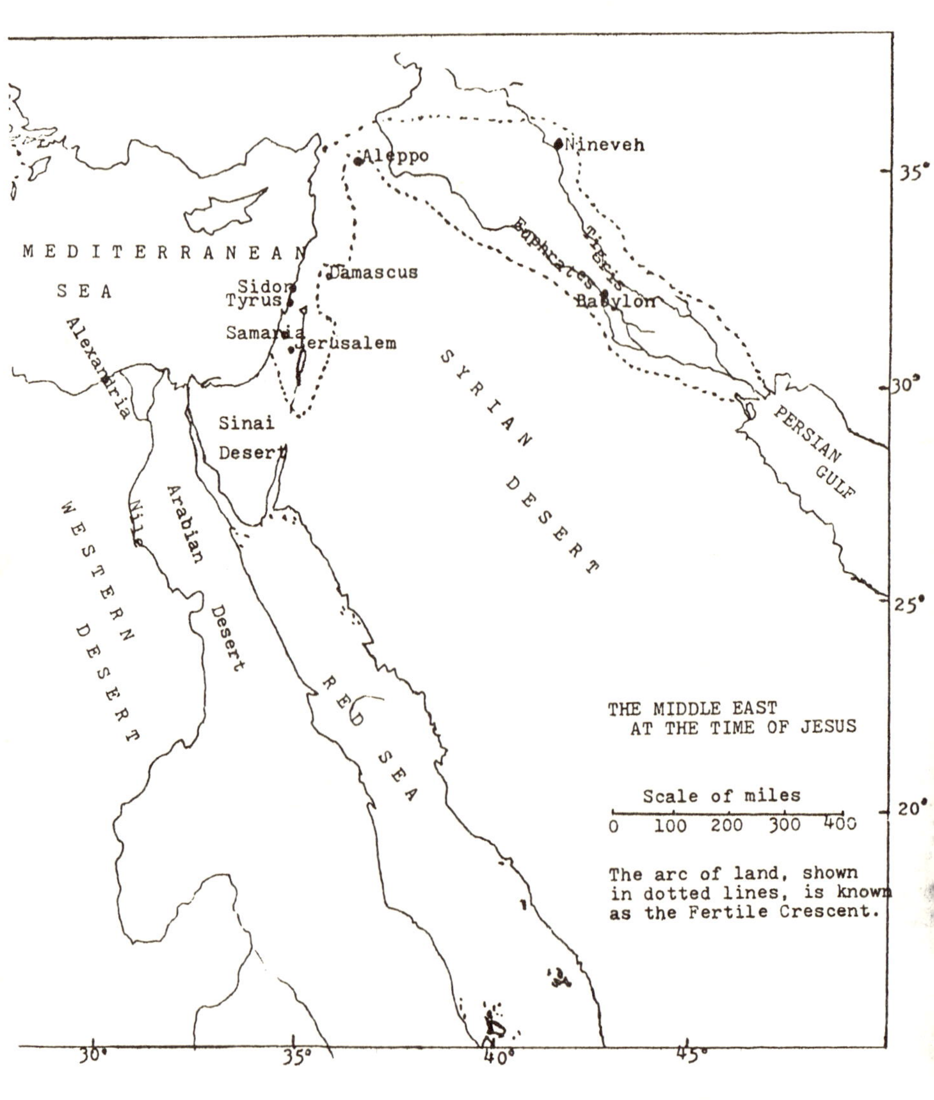

Nineveh
Aleppo
35°
MEDITERRANEAN
SEA
Damascus
Euphrates
Tigris
Sidon
Tyrus
Babylon
Samaria
Jerusalem
Alexandria
SYRIAN
DESERT
30°
PERSIAN
GULF
Sinai
Desert
WESTERN
DESERT
Nile
Arabian
Desert
25°
RED SEA
THE MIDDLE EAST
AT THE TIME OF JESUS
Scale of miles
0 100 200 300 400
20°
The arc of land, shown
in dotted lines, is known
as the Fertile Crescent.
30°
35°
40°
45°

CHAPTER I

Vision for an Ideal Jewish Society

This chapter traces the ancient Hebrew life by depicting the events leading up to why, when, how, and where the greater part of the Old Testament came to be put into writing. The Babylonian exile marks the turning point in the ancient Hebrew religious life and there is no better starting point.

BABYLONIAN EXILE

The lands of the Bible or the ancient Middle East in this book cover, from west to east, roughly the land areas of modern Egypt, Israel, Jordan, Lebanon, Syria, Iraq, and Saudi Arabia.

Looking at the map opposite one should forget for a moment it is God's gift, but see how stingy, inhospitable, cruel, savage and wasteful nature can be. Focus attention on the massive deserts, from west to east; all of Egypt is desert except the Nile Valley; then, the Sinai, Negev and Syrian Deserts.

Look at the rivers: the Nile in Egypt and the Euphrates and Tigris in Mesopotamia (modern Iraq), as if they are faulty cracks on the perfect sandy surface of the Middle East. A narrow range of mountains, plateaus and hills stretches like a protective bank along the eastern shore of the Mediterranean Sea as if to shield and preserve the deserts from the waves of the Sea. This Syrio-Palestine region barely connects the Egyptian and the Mesopotamian river valleys, extending in a great arc, and this arc is known as the Fertile Crescent.

In the days of foot travel and caravan trades it was an enormously difficult and risky task to traverse the desert from one fertile region to another. One's attempt to shorten the journey too much would bring him too deeply into the desert and to death. Rare water holes along the path meant life or death for travelers and their animal companions, and no one could afford to make mistakes about the exact locations of such holes.

The expanse of arid empty deserts, however, could not deter ambitious kings from conquering and expanding. In the ninth century B.C. the warlike Assyrian city-state in northern Mesopotamia became a strong military power by subjugating the neighboring cities and tribes. The Assyrians improved the battering rams and siege engines, and crossed the Syrian Desert into Syria and the ancient Hebrew Kingdoms of Israel and Judah.

Initially Assyria was content to extract periodic tributes from Syria, the Phoenician city-states of Tyre and Sidon, and the Kingdoms of Israel and Judah.

Tiglath-Pilesar III, known as Pul in the Bible, became the King of Assyria in 745 B.C. Shortly thereafter, he abolished the age-old practice of flaying, impaling, and massacring defeated peoples, and established the new imperial policy of deporting and resettling the vanquished within the Assyrian domains. The policy was to annex as many territories as possible, to make Assyria the melting pot for the conquered peoples, and to break their national or tribal consciousness and traditions of their political independence so that they would become loyal to the king of Assyria.

In 729 when Pul, the King of Assyria, also proclaimed himself the King of Babylonia, consisting of the city-states in southern Mesopotamia, he completed the consolidation of the entire Mesopotamian region, and made Assyria a nation of truly imperial proportion even by modern standards.

At this critical moment in the history of the ancient Middle East two ancient Hebrew Kingdoms were bitterly engaged in battles against each other. Pekah, the hawkish King of Israel, allied with the Syrian King, attempted to subdue Judah. The Syrian army took captives from Judah, and the Israelites killed men of Judah by the thousands and took captives, the sons and daughters of Judah. The Edomites invaded Judah and so did the Philistines. In desperation, Ahaz, the King of Judah, burned his son as an offering to whatever god might help him. He took all the treasuries of the Temple and the palace, and sent them as tributes to the King of Assyria for help.

Taking advantage of the situation in the Syrio-Palestine region the Assyrian King subjugated Syria. In 722 the Assyrian armies took Samaria, the capital of Israel, after having besieged the city for three years. Witnessing the Assyrian attack on Israel, Isaiah, a prophet of Israel, wrote:

> He [God] will raise a signal for nation afar off,
> and whistle for it from the end of the earth;
> and lo, swiftly, speedily it comes!
> None is weary, none stumbles, none slumbers or
> sleeps,
> not a waistcloth is loose, not a sandal-thong broken;
> their arrows are sharp, all their bows bent,
> their horses' hoofs seem like flint,
> and the wheels like the whirlwind.

Their roaring is like a lion, like young lions they
roar;
they growl and seize their prey,
they carry it off, and none can rescue.
They will growl over it on that day, like the roaring
of the sea.
And if one look to the land, behold, darkness and
distress;
and the light is darkened by its clouds.

(Isaiah 5:26-30)

The Assyrian armies expelled 27,000 Hebrews as captives to northern Mesopotamian cities for resettlement. Then, Assyria brought the defeated peoples from five different places of the Assyrian domain for relocation in Israel, and each of these peoples had gods of their own, and adopted the God of Israel as well. The Assyrian Kings were ruthless in war but more so in social engineering: They shifted the peoples around and imposed impersonal cosmopolitanism upon the clannish tribal peoples.

The Assyrian Empire had well-organized central and local administrations; on the surface, it seemed the empire would remain strong for centuries. In the latter part of the 7th century B.C. Nabopolassar, the Chaldean Governor of Babylon in southern Mesopotamia, proclaimed himself King of Babylon in an uprising against the Assyrian King. He gradually enlarged the rebel domain, and finally, in alliance with the Medes, captured Nineveh, the Assyrian capital, and ended the Assyrian Empire by defeating the Assyrians in the battle of Carchemish.

The Babylonian Empire replaced Assyria as the new master of Israel. The Kingdom of Judah used to be nominally independent by paying heavy tributes on time and submitting completely to Assyria. Judah became hopeful over the rise of Babylonia.

Judah had every reason to believe that the Chaldean King of Babylonia would be favorable to Judah because the Chaldeans were one of the Aramaean tribes closely related to the Hebrews in kinship. In the Bible Moses claimed himself to be an Aramaean. (Deuteronomy 26:5) But the Chaldeans of Babylonia could not care less about kinship and conquered Judah in 597. Judah's King and his family, the nobles, 7,000 warriors and 1,000 craftsmen and smiths were taken to Babylonia for resettlement.

The Babylonian King handpicked Zedekiah as the King of Judah. In 586 when Zedekiah, soliciting the Egyptians for aid, rebelled against Babylonia, the Babylonian armies destroyed the towns in Judah and besieged Jerusalem. Thousands of Hebrews, young and old, crammed into the walled city of Jerusalem with mules, horses, donkeys, and camels, watched the Babylonian soldiers circling the city, and listened to the noise of the battering rams without knowing how long the wall would withstand the breach. In sheer terror numerous Hebrew fighting men as well as the multitudes of the Hebrews deserted to the Babylonians rather than starve or fight to death.

The Babylonian armies razed Jerusalem after the eighteen months of siege. The Old Testament writers vividly depict, as curses upon the Hebrews for disobeying the will of God, the horrible experiences of the Hebrews: panic-stricken confusion; raping; unsanitary conditions causing all sorts of sickness; prolonged starvation leading to insanity and cannibalism and driving each man and woman to hide and withhold any scrap of food from even spouse and children; and the utter despair of parents helplessly watching their children being dragged into captivity. (Deuteronomy 28)

"Then they [Babylonians] captured the king [Zedekiah], and brought him up to the king of Babylon at Riblah, who passed sentence upon him. They slew the sons of Zedekiah before his eyes, and put out the eyes of Zedekiah, and bound him in fetters, and took him to Babylon." (2 Kings 25:6f.) About seventy top leaders of Judah, including the chief priest, the army commander, the king's advisers and civil administrators were put to death at Riblah.

Once again the remaining leaders of Judah were carried off to Babylon. Some fled to Egypt taking with them the prophet Jeremiah. Only the poor peasants were allowed to remain on their land. Prophet Jeremiah wrote:

> Thus says the Lord:
> "Behold, a people is coming from the north country,
> a great nation is stirring from the farthest parts of
>   the earth.
> They lay hold on bow and spear,
> They are cruel and have no mercy, the sound of
>   them is like the roaring sea;
> they ride upon horses, set in array as a man for
>   battle, against you, O daughter of Zion!"
> We have heard the report of it,
> our hands fall helpless; anguish has taken hold of
>   us,
> pain as of a woman in travail.
> Go not forth into the field, nor walk on the road;
> for the enemy has a sword, terror is on every side.
> O daughter of my people, gird on sackcloth, and roll
>   in ashes;
> make mourning as for an only son, most bitter
>   lamentation;
> for suddenly the destroyer will come upon us.
>
> (Jeremiah 6:22-26)

The Hebrew priests and the intellectuals were led to Babylonia from Jerusalem. Horses, asses and camels helped to transport the sick and their few possessions which the captives needed on the way and at the unknown destination for an uncertain life. A customary four-month foot travel along the edge of the arid and empty Syrian Desert makes Babylonia "the farthest parts of the earth." Day after day a baking sun assailed the desert for weeks without rain. The temperatures of well over 100°F. by day and freezing cold by night and the dusty winds followed the journey of the terrified Hebrews. Their fear in anticipation of the uncertain life in exile was no less painful than the quick stab of death.

BIG CITY LIFE IN BABYLON

When the Hebrew captives traversed the inhospitable desert and finally arrived in the capital city of Babylon, they found a dazzling, prosperous urban life. Babylon stood on both sides of the Euphrates River (near Baghdad, the capital city of modern Iraq). The city had two sets of surrounding walls, 10 to 12 feet thick and about 60 miles in length. The fields between two sets of walls were to provide food during a long siege by enemies.

Babylonia had a few dozen cities, including the Assyrian cities in northern Mesopotamia. Some of them perhaps had the population of as many as a quarter of a million. The city of Nineveh, in northern Mesopotamia, is described as "an exceedingly great city, three days' journey in breadth." (Jonah 3:3)

Each city was surrounded by farming villages. Both the Assyrians and the Babylonians inherited such a metropolitan way of life and socio-economic and legal systems from the Sumerians and Akkadians who preceded them. The urban way of life had proved so effective that it spread to all of Mesopotamia.

Babylon was the most prosperous metropolis in the world then. There were luxurious temple buildings and towers in every street block, and the palaces with "the Hanging Gardens," designed to simulate mountain scenery to please a homesick Median princess. The ancient Greek travelers called it one of the seven wonders of the ancient world. Perhaps the Hebrews initially had to work in building, repairing and maintaining the walls of the city, pagan temple buildings and palaces.

The Hebrew captives found a large Hebrew community. The descendants of the Hebrews, deported during the destruction of Israel in 722 B.C., made up a thriving colony of their own. The Hebrews were made to feel secure in Babylon, due to the eight-feet-tall pillar-code of the ancient Babylonian King Hammurabi. When the Hebrews arrived in Babylon, the Hammurabi code, the most advanced legal code then, was already 1500 years old. (This pillar-code was unearthed by a French archaeological team at the turn of this century and is now in the Louvre Museum of Paris.)

King Hammurabi, in its epilogue, said that he received the code from the Babylonian sun-god and god of law, Shamash, whose children are Justice and Right. He credited himself for guarding the weak, the orphans, and the widows from oppression by the powerful. The pillar, with the laws inscribed for all to read, stood at the temple gate of Shamash.

The Babylonian law recognized three classes of people: the priestly upper class freemen; freemen; and slaves. A freeman might be reduced to slavery as punishment for certain crimes or debts. A debtor could turn over himself and his family to a creditor for slavery for a period of less than three years. A slave had the right to engage in business, and become a freeman by paying the master about 20 shekels of silver. A mule or a horse did cost as much as a male or female slave then. As long as one parent was free the children were born free. It was relatively easy for the slaves and the captives to become freemen.

Furthermore, it was the imperial policy to treat the captives well. They were king's subjects, and were left in peace as long as they paid taxes and did not rebel; besides, no one could think of an uprising against the world empire then.

In the urban atmosphere of Babylon, where the peoples from every corner of the Middle East congregated, there were no distinctions between Babylonian citizens and aliens. The Hebrews, the Egyptians, the Syrians (Aramaens), the Phoenicians, and various peoples from the Aegean Sea coast and southeastern Mediterranean coast rubbed shoulders in the busy streets of Babylon. The men of means and knowledge spoke in Aramaic, the international language of the ancient Middle East.

Everyone was the king's subject. The captives who had arrived earlier in Babylon were the natives, but the status of being a native amounted to nothing legally or socially. The distinction was whether one was a freeman or a slave. The freemen, like slaves, had no part in the political life of the city or the Empire because the government and its administration was carried out by the priestly governors, and the priestly mayors and elders, all king's appointees. Governors and mayors and elders dispensed justice.

Political unification over a wide area prompted trade on an unprecedented scale. The Phoenicians of Tyre and Sidon, the notable ancient maritime traders, set sail throughout the Mediterranean coastal areas, traded their famous jewels, glassware, and gold and silver vessels for goods of other peoples, and enriched the commercial activities in Babylon.

Babylonia had well-standardized weights and measures and a money economy. The bars of silver and copper were stamped and the weights and quality of metals were guaranteed by the Empire. Merchants had to haggle over the price but did not have to bicker over the weights of metals or suspect that silver was debased with lead. Barley as a dry measure of value was not only bulky but also unreliable because barley in a measuring jar, if shaken, shrank in its quantity.

The roads which had been used for military purposes and for relocating the tribes from one end of the Empire to the other came to be used for transporting goods for trade. Horse-relayed messenger services also helped commercial communications. River channels connected cities and towns in Mesopotamia, and boat trading was as common as trade by land routes. Larger ships were facilitating more than ever the traffic between the Syrian coast and the Mediterranean Sea ports.

The temples were used to monopolize a banking system in Babylonia. But commercial and trading activities required prompt short-term lending for often risky ventures, which the temples could not readily facilitate. The private banking firm of Jacob (or Igibi) conducted a highly successful banking business.

The ideas in commercial law and legal instruments were similar to modern ones: promissory notes payable to the bearer, loans, sales, bills of lading, agency, brokerage, partnership and others. Opportunities were presented to the Hebrews, who became peddlers, merchants, artisans, moneylenders, and cattle raisers. In Judah, the Hebrews were poor and hard pressed by the invasions of the Edomites and the Samaritans; in Babylonia, however, they were prosperous and secure. In Judah they always lived in fear, but in Babylonia they readily took commercial risks which were minor compared with their life experiences in Judah.

All was, however, not well with the Hebrews in Babylon in spite of a materially rich life. The Babylonian Empire atomized average freemen and slaves. Each man was alienated from the tribe, and the native town where he had lived.

Men had to learn to live alone in large cities, like Babylon, Nineveh, Calah, Kish, Nippur, and Lagash, as they had never done before. Various peoples of the Middle East, the Greeks and even the Persians (modern Iran) mingled with one another and distrusted one another.

In their native lands and communities one's significance depended on his status, the reputation of his family or his social functions. All the freemen, congregated in Babylonian cities, had played significant roles in their native lands. In the large cities of Babylonia even a freeman could hardly think he had a function except making a living and looking after himself: he was no longer a significant being.

The Hebrew priests and intellectuals no longer had an active share in the city's or the Empire's political and social life. A status of being a nobleman or an intellectual or a priest in his homeland amounted to nothing in Babylonian cities.

The inner feelings of the Hebrews in Babylon varied from one individual to another. Some Hebrews preferred the rich Babylonian life, and many of them simply broke off their past as Hebrews and became assimilated into the main stream of Babylonian life. But the Hebrew priests and intellectuals were not readily adaptable to the unscrupulous double-talking life of street vendors and traders in the commercial world of Babylon, and perhaps they were not too successful in the dazzling Babylonian Empire. They refused to be integrated into Babylonian life.

All the material splendors of Babylonian civilization with a wide discrepancy of wealth between the affluent and the impoverished went against the traditional principles of the Hebrews. Many Hebrews were climbing the social ladder in major cities of Babylonia, and some, like Daniel, became a royal adviser, but Babylonian theocracy kept an upward movement basically within the wide range of middle-class freemen rather than from the status of freemen into the priestly upper-class freemen. Whatever the inner feelings of the Hebrew priests might have been, their longing for the homeland of Judah and the way of life there were uppermost in their minds.

BABYLONIAN"GODS"

It is a matter of conjecture how the Hebrew priests might have felt when they saw Babylonian temples built on a massive scale. A temple, built as tall as 300 feet high with numerous stairways leading up higher from one level to the next, was known as a ziggrat or "mountain top." The Old Testament writers referred to one of the temples as the tower of Babel, "a tower with its top in the heavens." (Genesis 11:4)

Temple buildings and city walls and even houses in Babylonia were constructed with the sun baked bricks made of straws and clay. Perhaps the Hebrews in Babylonia were forced to make such bricks since, in the Bible, the Hebrews in Egypt at the time of Moses were so coerced. (Exodus 5:7f.)

At the time of the Hebrew exile in Babylonia there were more than fifty temples in the city of Babylon alone. High priests, sacrifice priests, priestesses, lay sisters, singers, musicians, dream-interpreters, and a host of other temple assistants conducted rites and ceremonies. Such a ceremony culminated in an orgiastic ritual of marriage between the Priest-King and a temple priestess in the temple sanctuary. Sexual intercourse with either priest or priestess was considered essential to mystic communion with gods. Priestesses were not allowed to bear children. The husband of the priestess could have children by slave girls, presented by the priestess-wife.

Babylonians believed in innumerable gods or demons, supermen-like but invisible. If there were no pestilence, droughts, earthquakes, and wars but abundant foods, peace, and good life for everyone, and one could live as long as he wanted, religion would not have originated. In anticipation and fear of the uncertainty and the unknown beyond death the ancient peoples came to believe in the existence of beings whose power was superior to that of mortal men. (Even today the saying goes, "There is no atheist in a fox hole.")

Plague, floods, droughts, earthquakes or defeats in wars were considered bad miracles caused by spiritual beings. Men everywhere began recognizing the limitations which nature placed upon them. The ancient peoples could not make distinctions between powerful forces of nature or natural courses of events on one hand and miracles on the other, because, in the pre-scientific age, such distinctions were not possible. All that modern scientific men take for granted as natural order of events were miracles or acts of spirits to the ancient people. The harsher the life was, the closer the demonic spirits were to ancient men. A show of superpower or force was a sign of spirits, and normal events were disregarded.

Each Babylonian god had his domain: heaven, earth, sun, a river, a city or town, a rock, wars and so on. Each spirit had a name, and was believed to rule his domain according to well-laid eternal plans. Babylonians assigned a status to each god: the god of a certain city acquired an exalted position if the army of that city were victorious in a war. Such a warrior god was more a ruthless, blood-thirsty, and treacherous being. At the head of these gods the national god, Marduk, was considered to have created the universe and everything in it.

Each Babylonian had a personal god. Each man could hope and wait for the time when his personal god might become stronger and might be kind to him, bring blessings to him, and eventually raise him higher on the social and economic scale. If a family became prosperous, the god of that household commanded a higher esteem.

Each of the important gods had a large or small temple, depending on the status of the god. Religious practices were based on the hierarchical social system: the Priest-King offered sacrifices to the national god, local priest-mayors to local deities, and individual families to household gods.

The Priest-King, temples and priests owned most of the land just outside of each walled city. Temple revenues were raised from land, money-lending and offerings.

Each temple had a school, which taught arithmetic with fractional quantities and multiplication, geometry, astronomy and other subjects. The position of stars at the moment of a child's birth was considered as dictating his good or bad future. The astronomers observed and recorded the courses of the stars, and the top of the temple towers was a logical place for Babylonians to set up observatories. Astronomy was merely for astrology to determine cosmic orders and peer into the future.

On the other hand Babylonians, like their predecessors, Sumerians, used medicines for various ailments, and practiced even minor surgeries, for which doctors were held liable if they failed.

The Hebrew priests were hardly impressed by Babylonian gods and their temples, but they were by the temple schools. In their yearnings for their Temple of Jerusalem and their way of life, the Hebrew priests organized the prayer meetings or the synagogues in which the Hebrew religious ceremonies, civic affairs and educational sessions were conducted. They were immersed in discussing their common ancestry, background, tradition, and the common destiny of the Hebrews as a nation and a people.

It was at such prayer meetings in Babylonia that Ezekiel, the Hebrew priest and prophet, preached that the destruction of Judah came about not because the Hebrew God was weaker than other gods but because "she [the Kingdom of Judah] has wickedly rebelled against my [God's] ordinances more than the nations, and against my statutes more than the countries about her [Judah], by rejecting my ordinances and not walking in my statutes." In fact God's execution of a severe judgment drove the Hebrews to starvation, death and cannibalism. (Ezekiel 5:6-10)

The Hebrews recalled and pieced together the messages of the Hebrew prophets who had preceded Ezekiel. At the same time Ezekiel stirred the hope of the Hebrews to return to the homeland, rebuild the Temple in Jerusalem in due time according to the well-laid plans of God, and establish a theocratic society guided solely by priests according to the meticulously detailed plans he envisioned. (Ezekiel 40-48)

The Prophet Jeremiah, who had been allowed to stay in Jerusalem at the time of exile, kept writing letters to the Hebrews in Babylon with words of hope and encouragement: "For thus says the Lord: When seventy years are completed for Babylon, I will visit you, and I will fulfill to you my promise and bring you back to this place [Jerusalem]. For I know the plans I have for you, says the Lord, plans for welfare and not for evil, to give you a future and a hope." (Jeremiah 29:10f.)

Education at the synagogues became an indispensable part of the Hebrew religion. The Old Testament writers wrote:

> Hear, O Israel: the Lord our God is one Lord; and you shall love the Lord your God with all your heart and with all your soul, and with all your might. And these words which I command this day shall be upon your heart; and you shall teach them diligently to your children, and shall talk of them when you sit in your house, and when you walk by the way, and when you lie down, and when you rise. And you shall bind them as a sign upon your hand, and they shall be as frontlets between your eyes.
>
> (Deuteronomy 6:4-8)

Simply stated each Hebrew must regard his individuality in its relation to one God, who represents the whole Hebrew people. The message sounds highly nationalistic and encourages an inculcation rather than an education. For now, the important spiritual meanings of the message should not be overlooked: One has to have the spiritual perspective on the meaning of his life as frontlets between his eyes and the utmost importance of the educational process for each Hebrew is to learn love of one God and His people.

The prayer meetings inspired the Hebrews with the sense of helping one another without reservations to lead their common destiny and welfare. The Hebrews were no longer the vanquished but were regaining their self-esteem and emotional security by sharing responsibilities for their well-being in Babylonia and alleviating the helpless sense of lonely and alienated feelings. They were in Babylonia but their hearts and souls were in the homeland of Judah.

"LAND FLOWING WITH MILK AND HONEY"

The Old Testament writers, writing in the affluent city of Babylon, described their homeland as "the land flowing with milk and honey." It was a nostalgic cry for the homeland where they were not allowed to return and the way of life they used to know.

Their homeland is "a land of hills and valleys," barren, suitable mostly for pastoral nomadic purposes and limited agricultural cultivation: vines, fig trees, olive trees, and wheat and barley. The soil is generally poor, and water supply limited, and the rainfall unevenly distributed.

The homeland is a narrow strip extending between the Mediterranean Sea coast on the west and the Jordan River on the east, which flows from Mt. Hermon in the north to the Dead Sea in the south. It is about 150 miles long, 20 miles wide in the north and 80 miles in the south.

The narrow strip is further divided into three narrower strips. The first strip is the maritime coastal plain of Sharon, consisting of steep rocky coast, swamps, vegetation areas and sand dunes. It was occupied by the Philistines then. The term Palestine was derived from the name of the Philistines.

The central strip forms a chain of folded limestone mountains: from north to south, Mt. Hermon (about 9,000 feet high), Mt. Tabor, Mt. Gilboa, Mt. Ebal, Mt. Gerizim, Tell Asur (about 3,300 feet high), the highland of Jerusalem, Mt. Hebron (about 3,400 feet high) and Negev Desert. Steep dry riverbeds or wadis run between mountains and most of them remain dry except during the rainy season. This hill country was the nucleus of the two ancient kingdoms of Israel and Judah.

The last strip is the Jordan River valley, which varies from 3 to 14 miles wide. The River itself runs at the sea level at Lake Hula in the north but about 700 feet below sea level at the Lake of Galilee and 1300 feet below sea level at the Dead

Sea, in the south, which is the deepest land depression below sea level in the world. Consequently, the hills facing the Dead Sea are humid, salty, and hot waste lands.

The east of the Jordan River is a strip of Trans-Jordanian plateau (Jordan of today) with the Jordan River Valley on the west and the Syrian Desert on the east. The Trans-Jordanian plateau was occupied, from north to south, by the Aramaeans, the Ammonites, the Moabites and the Edomites. This strip of highland was also occupied rather precariously by the Israelite tribes of Manasseh, Gad and Reuben, scattered among the native tribes.

The homeland is a land of contrasting weather. The winter season of November to January is continuously rainy and the summer season of May to October is continuously hot and dry.

The geographical features of Palestine, broken into fragments by the natural barriers of hilly plateaus, and its location brought to the Hebrews the fortunes and misfortunes: the fortune of being located at the crossroad of caravan trading routes connecting two great ancient civilizations, Egyptian and Mesopotamian in times of peace, and the misfortune of being at the crossroad of ambitious military expeditions—Egyptians, Hittites, Assyrians, Babylonians, Persians, Greeks, Romans, Crusaders, Saracens, Mongols, Frenchmen, Germans, Austrians, Turks, and the British.

Each hill, with a small defending army, was able to defend against a relatively larger attacking army, and mountains and a perilous coast guarded against attack by land or sea. On the other hand, each hill encouraged the people to remain fragmentarily independent and stand against the unity of the Palestine region as a whole. Each tribe, fiercely independent, continued a pastoral nomadic life with emphasis on austere egalitarianism but also encouraged the Hebrews to remain clannish and isolationist right on the fringe of two great ancient civilizations.

Each hill and mountain was uninviting as a battle ground unless an attacking army was numerically well superior and had a compelling reason to conquer, because the defenders had a better chance of defending their rocky hills and hide-outs.

To use a modern term, Palestine was the buffer state, a natural stage for the meeting and clashing of big powers. Palestine became the frontier in times of war, the trade route in times of peace, and a no-man's-land when the big powers were in the hands of less ambitious or less capable rulers. To make the matter worse, the internal clash, due to the lack of unity among the peoples making homes in various parts of Palestine, made the area a ceaseless battleground.

Palestine, a poor or a rich land, was not only the homeland of the Hebrews but also the land of their ancestors since the days of the legendary patriarch, Abraham—that is, since time immemorial. Jacob in Egypt pleaded with his son Joseph: "Do not bury me in Egypt, but let me lie with my fathers; carry me out of Egypt and bury me in their burying place." (Genesis 47:30) When Moses led the Hebrews out of Egypt he took the bones of Joseph with him; "for Joseph has solemnly sworn the people of Israel, saying, 'God will visit you: then you must carry my bones with you from here.' " (Exodus 13:19)

Jeremiah expressed the sentiment of the Hebrews in Babylon:

> Weep not for him who is dead nor bemoan him;
> but weep bitterly for him who goes away,
> for he shall return no more to see his native land.
>
> (Jeremiah 22:10)

MISTAKES OF ANCESTORS

The unshakable belief of the prophets that God would eventually deliver the Hebrews out of the Babylonian Empire to their homeland, perhaps appeared even to many Hebrews a wishful dream rather than a hope. It was unthinkable for any one to return home by rebelling against the world empire or any other human efforts and means. But a group of hard-core Hebrew nationalists stuck to their belief. A psalm epitomized their feelings:

> By the waters of Babylon, there we sat down and
> wept,
> When we remembered Zion.
> On the willows there we hung up our lyres.
> For there our captors required of us songs,
> and our tormentors, mirth, saying,
> "Sing us one of the songs of Zion!"
>
> How shall we sing the Lord's song in a foreign land?
> If I forget you, O Jerusalem,
> let my right hand wither!
> Let my tongue cleave to the roof of my mouth,
> if I do not remember you,
> if I do not set Jerusalem
> above my highest joy!
>
> (The Psalms 137:1-6)

To this group of the Hebrews in Babylon, the question was not whether or not they would return home but how to rebuild the Temple in Jerusalem and plan a perfect Hebrew society in the homeland and the welfare of the people as soon as the period of exile should come to an end. They busied themselves in planning their ideal society.

This period of exile, which extended from the Assyrian destruction of Samaria in 722 to 539 B.C., the end of the exile, provided the Hebrews with a unique opportunity to collect all the tidbits of information about the Hebrew God, and the Law as His will, and the stories of the ancestors.

The Hebrews in Babylon came from the Northern Kingdom of Israel where Gods (in plural) were called Elohim, and the Southern Kingdom of Judah where God was called Yahweh. They had stories to exchange with one another. The stories were the ancient folk traditions concerning their legendary ancestors, Abraham, Isaac, and Jacob, and Moses, and the customs of rituals and offerings at the Temples at Dan and Bethel in Israel and those at the Temple in Jerusalem.

There were numerous prophets who preached in Israel and others in Judah. Most "true" prophets lived just before and during the period of exile. The Hebrews compiled the preachings of these prophets and the customs which the Hebrews lived under before the exile.

It was a monumental amount of work to collect and compile all the materials on the national saga, and put the customs into the written legal code. Who was intelligent and trained enough to accomplish such a complex task of digesting the vast materials and reducing them to writing? If there were persons so qualified, would they be ready to toil on the noble duty for life without being paid, and would their children take over their fathers' chore and keep laboring?

The priests defined their functions and codified religious laws in the book of Leviticus. There was another small group of people, among the Hebrews in Babylon, uniquely qualified and willing to the task. They were known as the scribes.

The profession of scribes was traceable to the time of King David. David created a cabinet consisting of several top officers, one of whom was Recorder or the chief scribe. Scribes were in charge of compiling the official records, preparing King's communications with foreign nations, and keeping records on tax and fiscal matters and provisions for the armed forces and the Temple. Initially their function was insignificant clerical work, but their influence gradually grew because they were the ancient intellectuals and as record keepers came to know the ins and outs of the Temple as well as the life of the royal palace. They valued their trade secrets and had their own guilds.

Scribes had come from the house of Rechab and were descendants of Judah just as King David was. The families of scribes used to live in one town (1 Chronicles 2:55) before their exile, and the job training for future scribes was limited to a closed circle of the Hebrews entitled as a matter of inheritance. They exercised the administrative power and were considered Hebrew nobles. In Babylonia some of the priests became scribes, and the priests and scribes shared the religious and civic leadership and the responsibility for educating the Hebrews in Babylonia and their children, and transmitting the national saga to future generations.

Scribes were not professional historians. They were not writing a matter-of-fact history, an economic or psychological or sociological interpretation of their ancestors' life, or any other interpretation, but the national saga centering around God and His attributes as affecting the lives of the generations of their ancestors.

God and His attributes as perceived by these Old Testament writers were different from those known by their ancestors. At times, the Old Testament writers narrated the attributes of God as their ancestors understood, and other times as the writers themselves perceived. They were writing the religious lives of the ancestors rather critically from their viewpoint: their ancestors lived in a way quite displeasing to God and invited God's wrath.

The dynasty of King Saul did not last long. What did Saul do to displease God? Somehow the ancient Hebrew Kingdom was divided into two kingdoms after the death of King Solomon. What did Solomon do to kindle God's anger? Above all, why did the exiles have to go through the terror-stricken experience? There had to be some explanations for every event. Their luminous thoughts ran over their future planning as well as over the past lives of their ancestors.

In order to plan an ideal Hebrew society in the future, the Old Testament writers were discovering the past mistakes of the ancestors in recalling their lives. In writing the Law as the will of God they invoked the voices of their ancestors to reinforce their foresight and to have their future plans accepted by the contemporary and future Hebrew generations. Their spiritual viewpoint linked the past, the present and the future generations of the Hebrews in the books destined to become the Old Testament.

The Hebrews in Babylon were nurturing the fertile crescent of the Hebrew history, and for that matter, of the history of mankind. Babylonian exile marked the end of the political independence of the ancient Hebrews, except for a brief period more than four centuries later.

Now, let us turn to the national saga, in the Old Testament, concerning the life of the ancient Hebrews and their shortcomings.

CHAPTER II

National Saga

"GOD"

Ancient Hebrew priests and scribes who contributed to the writing of the Book of the Law (the first five books of the Old Testament) just before, during and right after the Babylonian exile were the founders of Judaism. Priest and scribe Ezra and priest and prophet Ezekiel stand out among them. In this and subsequent chapters these founders of Judaism will be called simply "the writers," or "the writers of the Law."

There are numerous religious themes embedded in the Old Testament. How and why did the Law in such minute details come to be identified with the will of the willful God? How and why did Judaism come to stress self-righteousness and exclusivism? No one today knows exactly who developed each religious theme of Judaism and when or whether or not the writers borrowed from other peoples. The writers attribute most of Judaic religious themes to Moses.

Fragmentary facts in the Old Testament are important not because of their historicity but because of the myth, i.e. the spiritual perspective with which the writers looked back on the life of their ancestors and attempted to provide the answers to the needs and desires of the Hebrews in the postexilic Judea.

One cannot help noticing how briefly the writers stated the creation of the universe and everything in it, in only two short chapters of Genesis. God has no wife, children, divine friends or foes. God as the Creator is depicted as all-powerful and almighty, as capable of creating the world in one flashing bang. (One could claim the world is only several thousand years old by adding up the life span of each generation of the Hebrews in the Old Testament, or others could guess scientifically the world is 20 or 30 billion years old, or there is the question of a curious child, "Who made God?")

The writers were not interested in laying down the origin of the awesome universe which neither they nor any of the modern physicists could understand exactly, and which the writers could do nothing about.

God is portrayed as the sole cause (not first or primary cause) for all effects to follow in the world. Here God is perceived as the sole Being who causes, or "I AM WHO I AM."

God, as the almighty creator, has many attributes of little gods or demons in whom the ancient Hebrews and other Semitic peoples believed. The ancient peoples were fascinated and often terrified by the constantly changing natural objects of the world. A steady flowing river changes to a turbulent flood at times because the living god of rivers is kindled to anger. Green pastures turn to desert because of drought or locusts sent by little gods.

To the ancient peoples nothing in the material world was constant and stable. Earthquakes, floods, drought, pestilences, and other phenomena seemed to behave as whimsically as though guided by invisible and live spirits. (It should be noted that the ancient peoples in Mesopotamia, Greece, and Rome all believed in the gods as the causes of all things in nature and judges of human destiny; such a belief or mode of thinking was universal in the ancient world.)

Knowledgeable people of those days of little gods were witches, sorcerers and priests, who were supposed to be endowed with supernatural psychic receptivity to communicate with and to know hidden knowledge about gods, and they urged the people to build bigger altars and temples and make offerings, including burnt children, pleasing to gods.

The answers to human petitions came from gods in dreams, the entrails of the animals offered, the activities of birds and horses and other ways. No one would dare to undertake a war or any major effort unless it was determined that the auspices were favorable. Confronted by life and death situations man sought to peer into the future by whatever means and to interpret the nature and will of gods. Such human efforts seemed to calm down angry gods at times and failed at other times.

The ancient peoples did not question their beliefs. They inherited them from their ancestors; accordingly, sacred beliefs were common to them and their ancestors. If they deviated from the beliefs of their ancestors the worst afflictions might strike them.

The only important matter for the ancient peoples was to communicate with gods, and to find out the will or nature of gods, and to do whatever was pleasing to them. It became apparent to the ancient peoples that it was not enough to build big houses for gods and provide gods with offerings to calm down and please them. Certain human activities seemed to be pleasing to gods and other activities went against the will or nature of gods.

The ancient peoples inquired what human activities were pleasing to gods and what others offending to gods. The ancient peoples did not have the standards of measuring what was right or wrong and what was just or unjust. They came to identify those activities pleasing to gods with what was right and just. They perceived that gods have the power to determine what was right or just in times of bloody tribal wars and in times of peace. Customs developed and customs were regarded as prescribing those human activities acceptable to or least offending to the national god or gods.

The moral gods also had many attributes of little gods. The ancient peoples perceived such moral gods in the image of man with the bodily form, intelligence and emotions of jealousy, anger and love. The people in each city-state of ancient Mesopotamia claimed to have received the law from one of the gods of the city-state.

In Egypt it was believed that more than forty little gods, presided over by two gods of Justice, interrogated each human soul upon his death and passed a judgment on him with respect to his activities on earth. Each soul had to swear he did not steal, murder, falsify the measure of grain, oppress the orphans, the widows, etc. The unfavorable verdict cast out the dead to such demonic executioners as the Eater of Entrails, Bone-Breaker, etc. Endless was human ingenuity: One could buy the favorable verdict from the priest before his death.

Superpsychic claims made by sorcerers and witches were outrageous even to the ancient peoples. When the predictions of sorcerers and witches did not come to realization, some of them were put to death. To the astonishment of the ancient peoples little gods did not retaliate for putting sorcerers or witches to death.

Be that as it may, the perception of gods as moral creatures was not unique to the ancient Hebrews. The city-states in Mesopotamia had been putting the sorcerers to death who had claimed to be endowed with supernatural psychic powers to communicate with gods for more than one thousand years before the Babylonian exile.

In Egypt there were attempts to do away not only with sorcerers and priests but also with little gods. Such an attempt was vainly initiated by King Amenhotep IV, in the 14th century B.C. (who was the husband of Nefertiti, whose beauty is still famous through her celebrated portrait bust).

The writers did not have to go back to antiquity to observe that little moral gods also failed to keep their city-states in peace and prosperity. Ashur, the national god of Assyria, and Ishtar of Nineveh could not defend the nation and the city-state against Babylonian armies.

The writers came to perceive God as the formless Being, the sole source of righteousness. (No one could dare to damn God for harsh punishments inflicted upon the preexilic Hebrews or the unrighteousness of God for inflicting starvation, death and sufferings on the young and old. God was only to be praised for righteousness and His will was considered inscrutable by the multitudes of the Hebrews.)

The writers believed in men's ability to strictly adhere to the will of God and chart a future course for their lives, setting aside the fatalistic attitude which was inherent in the beliefs about little gods' roles in human affairs and the mysterious natural objects of the material world. The writers were planning a perfect society in the homeland as soon as the life of exile should end, and God was the sole driving force for the establishment of such an ideal society, in which the well-being of the Hebrews was to be based on the strict adherence of every Hebrew to the Law, the will of God.

One's intelligence and emotions should properly flow from God, the sole source of moral righteousness. That was the proper state of Hebrew wisdom, mind and will. If one disobeys the will of God, he is no longer deriving his intelligence, mind and will from the proper source, and should be excluded from God's community.

The writers depicted God as the willful Being, who obstinately and persistently demanded that the Hebrews absolutely obey the Law. God was to judge individuals, tribes, nations, human institutions and the course of human history:

God reveals His pleasure or displeasure in historical outcomes. Here God was not the formless sole Being but a stern judge with the attributes of a little god. The writers did not discard the attributes of little gods but superimposed many attributes of little gods on the sole moral Being.

(Centuries later, Jesus said, "No one sews a piece of unshrunk cloth on an old garment; if he does, the patch tears away from it, the new from the old, and a worse tear is made. And no one puts new wine into old wineskins; if he does the wine will burst the skins, and the wine is lost, and so are the skins." [Mark 2:21f.])

The writers recognized as inevitable the wide discrepancy between their perception of the moral God and His attributes and the demonic characteristics of God understood by the multitudes of the Hebrews. (The conviction of the writers that the Jews should set aside fatalism and reshape their future, and the perception of the multitudes of Jews that God knew and dictated future, were logically inconsistent but were reconciled in the Old Testament.) For this reason, the writers meant that God, portrayed in the Old Testament, should remain rather blurry. For the same reason too the writers did not see the need to separate miracles and extraordinary phenomena from ordinary events.

LORD OF HISTORY

God as the Lord of the national saga or history does two things. Firstly, God shows the Hebrews right or wrong in the light of the on-going historical and social reality: God reveals His will in the vision of such personalities as Abraham, Moses, the Kings, the prophets, so on. Secondly, God judges individuals, families, tribes, nations, and human institutions and dictates the course of human history itself.

More often than not the ancient Hebrews were engaged in

battles to secure land, and the concepts of right or wrong in the Old Testament reflect greatly the ongoing bloody reality of the ancient Palestine.

The story of Adam and Eve points out that Adam disobeyed God's command and ate the fruit of "the tree of knowledge of good and evil." The writers express the foresight and theme for the postexilic planning in this statement: No man has the right to determine what is right or wrong according to his own views, and if anyone attempts to usurp such power of God to determine what is right or wrong he shall die. (Genesis 2:17) The story also shows that human curiosity and intelligence are vulnerable to temptations to determine right or wrong on their own and disobey God's commands.

The writers, however, were not looking into the mind of men or examining human nature from a psychological point of view to conclude that human nature is either innately depraved or good.

Why did the writers feel that anyone who attempts to determine right or wrong on his own should be put to death? The answer to this crucial question is essential in understanding the development of Judaism and will be treated in the later chapters.

What is right at one time may not be right at other times because God determines what is right or wrong in the light of ongoing historical and social circumstances, and God's will is inscrutable. The writers scoff at the Babylonian attempts to communicate with gods and find out the will of gods by building and climbing up the tall tower of Babel (Genesis 11:1-9).

The writers trace the ancestry of the Hebrew people to a legendary figure named Abraham. About 2000 years B.C. Abraham, a farmer with cattle, lived in the land of Ur of the Chaldeans, about 150 miles south of Babylon. Then, successive waves of immigrations of the Semitic peoples were sweeping through the Fertile Crescent. Into Egypt, Palestine and Mesopotamia came the Semitic peoples from the vast Arabian desert. The land was free for the grabbing as long as the occupying tribe could retain and defend it. The Chaldeans were driven out of Ur.

A group of the Chaldeans, including Abraham, walked about 600 miles to Haran (in the southern edge of today's Turkey) in northern Mesopotamia, and came to be known as the Aramaeans. But Abraham and Lot, Abraham's nephew, and their families parted with their people and moved on to Canaan, i.e. Palestine.

It was the age of little gods of nature. The spirits were perceived as hiding behind the rocks, mountains, rivers and the tent of each household. But Abraham rejected the traditional beliefs of his ancestors when he refused to burn Isaac, his only child, and offer to the god (Genesis 22). He had been torn between his ancestors' traditional belief in the nature god of terror, and his equally strong belief in his perception of the personal household God who was supposed to love and favor him and his household.

The people living around Abraham believed that gods would put you and your family to starvation, plagues, or other worse troubles unless you pleased gods by offering the first-born son as a burnt offering. Abraham discarded little gods, laid down his own life and the lives of his entire family for his new faith in the loving God. Abraham's call by God to become the ancestor of God's chosen people points to that new religious direction in the history of the Hebrew people.

The writers then delineate the chosen people as the righteous people who obey the will of God. Ham [Canaan] one day saw his father, drunken and sleeping naked in his tent. Ham told his brothers Shem and Japheth, who took a garment and walked backward and covered their father without seeing their father's nakedness. When Noah awoke and knew what each of his sons had done to him he said:

> "Cursed be Canaan;
> a slave of slaves shall be to his brothers."
>
> "Blessed by the Lord my God be Shem;
> and let Canaan be his slave.
> God enlarge Japheth,
> and let him dwell in the tents of Shem;
> and let Canaan be his slave."
>
> (Genesis 9:20-27)

The writers portrayed Noah as if he himself had the power of a little god. The Canaanites, descended from Ham, are African peoples; the Semitic peoples are descended from Shem; and Indo-European peoples or the white peoples are descended from Japheth (Genesis 10). Mundane as this story might sound, this legend underscores the process of election whereby God chose certain individuals, families and tribes on the merits of righteousness for God's community, and excluded the unrighteous. This story, however, is somewhat confusing, because Canaanites–including the Moabites, and the Ammonites, and the Edomites–are not African peoples but Semitic peoples, related to the twelve Hebrew tribes.

Lot, Abraham's nephew, had incestuous union with his two daughters and became the father of the Ammonites and Moabites. Hagar, Abraham's Egyptian concubine, unrighteously tried to act equal to Sarah, Abraham's wife. Ishmael, Abraham's son by Hagar, became the father of the Arabs. Jacob's twin brother Esau, who had unrighteously sold his birthright to Jacob for a price of one meal, became the father of the Edomites. Jacob's twelve sons became the fathers of twelve Hebrew tribes.

(Of the ancient twelve Hebrew tribes ten tribes were excluded from God's chosen community soon after the Babylonian exile, because the ten tribes disobeyed God's commands more than the tribes of Levi, Judah and Benjamin.)

A famine in Palestine forced Jacob and his sons to move to Egypt where their descendants increased in numbers. The writers skip the four hundred years when the ancient Hebrews stayed in Egypt.

The account of Joseph's life in Egypt is noteworthy because it fits well into the analytical and legally minded background of the writers, who narrate it so vividly as if it were a modern legal fiction. At the time, Joseph was serving as an overseer of the house for the Pharaoh's captain of the guard:

> Now Joseph was handsome and good-looking. And after a time his master's wife cast her eyes upon Joseph, and said, "Lie with me." But he refused and said to his master's wife, "Lo, having me my master has no concern about anything in the house, and he has put everything that he has in my hand; he is not greater in this house than I am; nor has he kept back anything from me except yourself, because you are his wife; how then can I do this great wickedness, and sin against God?" And although she spoke to Joseph day after day, he would not listen to her, to lie with her or to be with her. But one day, when he went into the house to do his work and none of the men of the house was there in the house, she caught him by his garment, saying "Lie with me." But he left his garment in her hand, and had fled out of the house. And when she saw that he had left his garment in her hand, and had fled out of the house, she called to the men of her household and said to them, "See, he [her husband] has brought among us a Hebrew to insult us; he came in to me to lie with me, and I cried out with a loud voice; and when he heard that I lifted up my voice

and cried, he left his garment with me, and fled and got out of the house. . . ."

And Joseph's master took him and put him into the prison. . . .

(Genesis 39:7-20)

MOSES

In the 13th century B.C. Moses, the major actor of the drama of Exodus and what follows in the Old Testament, emerges as the founder of the Hebrew nation and the originator of the ancient Hebrew religion.

In reading the Old Testament one does not know when he is crossing or straddling the line which separates history from prehistoric legends. There is no evidence to indicate that Moses is a historic, rather than a legendary, figure.

One day when young Moses saw an Egyptian slave master beating up a Hebrew slave, he killed the slave master, discarded the privilege of being an adopted son of an Egyptian princess and fled. Eventually he joined the wandering Midianite tribes, and married the daughter of the priest chief of the Midianites.

One day God appeared to Moses on the slopes of Mt. Sinai, and commanded Moses to lead the enslaved Hebrews out of Egypt to the promised land of Canaan, which God had pledged to Abraham, Isaac and Jacob. Inspired by the Godly vision the determined Moses returned to Egypt and led the Hebrews out of Egypt to Mt. Sinai, at the foot of which Moses taught the Hebrews their new religion and the individual and social responsibilities based on God's commands. This divine-human drama climaxed when the Hebrews entered into the covenant with God to obey the will of God in return for a glorious future in the promised land.

Moses' religious and moral messages, however, are inconsistent and confusing because the writers attribute to Moses all the spiritual and legal principles which are on the surface consistent but in fact diametrically opposed to one another.

It is appropriate to divide Moses' messages very roughly into two categories: firstly, the Decalogue and the Laws of the Covenant (Exodus 21-23), which is a compilation of the customs found in the land of Canaan and is the earliest written Hebrew customs; and secondly, all other laws in the Book of the Law, which consists of the complex religious, civil and criminal laws drafted and codified by the writers. Customs illustrate the preexilic Hebrew norms of conducts, whereas the codified laws represent the postexilic Jewish code of behavior. The differences and the conflicting principles underlying them will be treated in the ensuing chapters.

The writers look back to the Sinai covenant as the point of inaugurating the new Hebrew nation. About two million Hebrews left Sinai and journeyed in the wilderness under the leadership of Moses. Even if the number of Hebrews were two thousand, the logistical problem of providing necessities for them at that time could not be an easy matter.

Moses was an outsider to the enslaved Hebrews in Egypt and was not even a tribal chieftain or a patriarch, but he emerged as the leader. He quickly won the confidence of the people, not because he was a great speaker, but because he was a moral giant who could inspire and mold fiercely independent, ill-disciplined and "stiff-necked" nomads into a people capable of subordinating the tribal interests to that of the whole as a nation and a people. He kept appealing to common fears and biases as well as to common purposes and goals.

Moses, an awe-inspiring leader, was forceful and willful enough to discipline the tribes and flexible enough to seek their consensus. The personal characteristics which the writers so vividly attribute to Moses were "Godly" and were those qualities required of the leader desperately in demand at the time of Babylonian exile.

The Hebrews under Moses' leadership spent forty years wandering as a nomadic people in the wilderness south of Canaan. Moses died in the land of Moab where he sighted the land of Canaan, the promised land, "but no man knows the place of his burial to this day" because God buried Moses in the valley in the land of Moab (Deuteronomy 34:5f).

JUDGES

The writers narrate as if all the twelve Hebrew tribes, in a marching formation, moved into Canaan toward the end of the 13th century B.C., and the Hebrews were a close-knit nomadic community on the basis of religion. Such a description must be viewed in the light of the awakening national consciousness about the time of Babylonian exile.

Several Hebrew tribes moved into Canaan well before the time of Moses. The Joseph tribes (Ephraim and Manasseh) under the leadership of Joshua, the successor to Moses, crossed the Jordan River and moved into the central part of Canaan. Three Hebrew tribes of Judah, Levi and Simeon were the last ones to move into Canaan and occupied the extreme south, the poor part of Canaan where a limited precipitation made pastoral and agricultural life difficult.

Canaan was a no-man's-land when the Hebrews moved in. No-man's-land meant anarchy. Assyria in Central Mesopotamia was not yet strong enough to extend its influence in Canaan; the Mittanni Kingdom in northern Mesopotamia disappeared because of Assyrian attack and conquest; and Egypt was declining because of the internal dissension over religious beliefs. Therefore, no big power was in a position to extend its influence over Canaan and maintain order.

No-man's-land was a prey for the lesser powers: the Aramaeans from the north, the Philistines from the west and the Hebrews from the south. There were also native Canaanites, including the Amorites, the Moabites, the Edomites and the

Ammonites. Each of these Canaanite peoples was a loose confederation of numerous, backward, petty, clannish tribes. So were the Hebrew tribes.

The Hebrew penetration into Canaan from about 1200 to 1000 B.C. was a long and slow process, locked up in life and death struggles for domination with other peoples. When Joshua died a minimum unity among the Hebrews also disappeared.

The Hebrew tribal chiefs were called "Judges." Local battles against other peoples went on constantly under the leadership of these Judges. At one time the Moabites dominated over the Hebrew tribes for 18 years. At another time Jabin, King of Canaan, "had nine hundred chariots of iron, and oppressed the people of Israel cruelly for twenty years." (Judges 4:1-3) The Midianites also ruled over the Hebrews for seven years. The native resistance against the Hebrews was fierce. Chariots and innumerable camels sent a wave of fear and terror into the hearts of the Hebrews. The victors took loot, passed judgments in the name of God or gods, killed the defeated people, or spared and took the virgins for wives or concubines.

Warfare was waged not only against other peoples but also among the Hebrew tribes. The tribe of Benjamin was nearly exterminated in a civil war and was reduced to a weak tribe of no military significance.

UNITED KINGDOM

The most formidable enemy of the Hebrews in Canaan was the Philistines, who had come from Greek isles in goose-billed sailing ships and settled on the seacoast of Canaan about the time when the first waves of the Hebrew tribes were moving into Canaan. Hard-pressed by the aggression of the Philistines and the Ammonites, the Hebrew tribal chiefs resolved to take a united stand against enemies, accepted the monarchical system, and chose by lot Saul their King.

Saul quickly won a spectacular military victory against the Ammonites in Jabesh-Gilead and legitimated his kingship in the eyes of most of the Hebrews. As the memory of his victory faded, Saul became a victim of tribal jealousies and was in no position to maintain legitimacy of his kingship in the eyes of the tribe of Judah.

Saul was a Benjaminite, a member of the least strong tribe of the Hebrews. The tribe of Judah, in a civil war, had spearheaded the attack and nearly exterminated the tribe of Benjamin, and made the weakened tribe of Benjamin a part of Judah. Judah, the strongest tribe, therefore, had the tribal grievances for choosing Saul as the King by lot. Saul was jealous of David, a member of Judah, who carefully waited for the opportune time to become the king.

When Saul died in battle his son, Ishbaal, nominally ruled over the northern tribes for seven years while David was King of Judah at Hebron. An assassination removed Ishbaal, and David became King of Israel in addition to being King of Judah.

King David (998-961 B.C.), an able military leader and a talented statesman, conquered a Jebusite town, Jerusalem, and enlarged the fortress by building up a new surrounding wall. He expanded and consolidated the occupied territories of Canaan against the Philistines, Moabites, Ammonites and Edomites. The Hebrews came to have the Kingdom of Israel and Judah, united for the first time, and came to hold the land more extensively than ever before or ever after in the history of the Hebrews.

A stable government, a United Kingdom, and a secure country offered the Hebrews the first opportunity to engage in an agricultural way of life in addition to traditional nomadic life, and resulted in a prosperous economy. A military conquest is one thing, and a consolidation, peace and security of the occupied land is another. In peace with the natives the process of assimilating or being assimilated into the native peoples took place. The tribe of Asher was nearly lost among the Phoenicians. All Hebrew tribes intermarried and assimilated the natives.

The Hebrews learned from the natives the skills of making and repairing woodwork, pottery and metals. They engaged in agriculture, readily adopted the harvest feast, unleavened cakes and other agricultural festivals as an integral part of the Hebrew way of life. The Hebrews perceived the Hebrew God as the national god rather than the unique moral Being. There were no theological distinctions for the Hebrews to be able to understand the national God of the Hebrews and the Baals differently, except that the Hebrew God was the sole Being and those of the Baals many beings.

An agricultural way of life in a secure land meant larger houses for the rich and a larger royal palace for the King and his family. David had a steady source of income from tributes from the Hebrew tribes as well as from the defeated natives. His royal court life differed markedly from that of King Saul, who lived in his own little house.

Saul's simple life style might have been due to his nomadic and democratic sensibilities or due to the fact that he ruled over a confederation of the tribes and lacked a steady source of income. Nevertheless, the Davidic dynasty made the first sharp departure from the Hebrew nomadic traditions by introducing the luxurious royal court life, the norm of agricultural societies.

The writers detail, with a remarkable objectivity, David's personal life. He had an affair with Bathsheba, the wife of Uri'ah, the Hittite. He arranged for Uri'ah to be killed in a battle and took Bathsheba as a wife.

David had many wives and concubines, which meant many royal children who plotted for succession to the throne. All children of David enjoyed royal pomp, privileges and benefits far above those of average Hebrews. Ammon, one of David's sons, raped his half-sister Tamar; consequently, Absalom, Tamar's brother, killed Ammon. Subsequently Absalom, in alliance with the northern tribes of Israel, attempted to overthrow his father from the throne and nearly succeeded. David's experienced generals put down the uprising and put Absalom to death.

Court intrigues and plots for succession to the throne became intense as David got older. Solomon, with the help of his mother Bathsheba, gained the support of David, and became the King.

King Solomon (961-933 B.C.) ruthlessly put to death his rivals and their supporters, and discharged and banished Abiathar, the priest. Solomon was the first Hebrew King who had never experienced the nomadic life. Being a great judge and an able administrator, he was anxious to build a truly United Kingdom by replacing tribal loyalty with national loyalty: he divided up the country into twelve administrative districts, intentionally disregarding tribal boundaries, and imposed direct taxation and forced labor upon the people.

He built the Temple at Jerusalem, which became a symbol of the Hebrew glory as one nation, the royal palace, government buildings in the administrative districts, and expanded the city wall of Jerusalam.

He also constructed chariot cities and forty thousand stalls of horses for his chariots and maintained domestic and external peace by a show of force. At the same time he made profits by buying horses in Egypt and selling them to Hittites and Aramaeans in the north, and undertook commercial trading by land and sea.

Solomon lacked his father's military ability but shrewedly built up alliances with Egypt and other neighboring peoples by marrying their princesses. He came to have a harem of nearly 1000 wives and concubines. Each foreign princess was accompanied by a group of ladies-in-waiting, singers, harp players and slave girls. Whatever Solomon's intentions might have been his sybaritic way of life served political purposes as well: many wives were political hostages as well as tokens of alliances.

Each of Solomon's wives brought with her a god of her own. Solomon not only allowed the worship of many gods but also built high places for Chemish, god of the Moabites, Molech, god of the Ammonites, and other gods, and made burnt offerings to little gods. Both Kings Saul and David were tolerant of other gods and they named their children after Baals.

The Bible does not say, at this stage of the Hebrew religious development, to what extent the Hebrew religion differed from other Canaanite religions.

Canaanites believed in El, just a common-name "power" or "god." So did the Hebrews believe in El, "God." The Canaanite El had the wife Asherah. Canaanites believed in Baal or Lord who was the storm god, and his wife Baalath or Lady, whose name was Astart, the fertility or vegetation cycle goddess. As each locality had its Baal and Astart there were many Baals and Astarts.

Each of the Canaanite tribal nations had a national patron "warrior" deity: Yahweh for the Hebrews, Chemosh for the Moabites, Milcom for the Ammonites, and so on. The God and little gods the Hebrews as well as the Canaanites were worshipping had their nature and attributes under various names and with different rituals. Each national patron deity was the invisible leader guiding his people in wars and other crises.

Canaanite deities were worshipped where they were supposed to reside—in temples, near aged trees, on numerous hills or high places and in the mountains. Each of these nature deities had his chief priest, priests, sacred prostitutes, wailing women and other assistants.

In anticipation of a big war or other calamity Canaanites had to please gods by offering burnt children. The rites of child sacrifice were not altogether extinct even among the Hebrews. Jephthah, judge of Gilead, offered his only daughter as a burnt offering to God (Judges 11). King Manasseh of Judah (694-642 B.C.) not only rebuilt high places for Baal and Asherah but also offered his son as a burnt offering to gods.

In ancient Palestine, the crossroad of trade and conquests, hundreds of different beliefs rubbed with one another; accordingly, it was difficult for the ancient Hebrews to advance the Hebrew God as the only God. As the Hebrews were often defeated in tribal wars they were skeptical about the strength of the Hebrew God just as other peoples of the region were about their national patron deities. In ordinary times animal sacrifices were considered sufficient to please or calm down gods or demons. The writers made the distinctions between the attributes of demonic little gods and those of the moral God only retrospectively.

The Hebrews sought after little gods throughout the Hebrew history up to the time of the Babylonian exile. The ancient Hebrews perceived the Hebrew God as the national god, and did not think they were vulgarizing their religion by going after other little gods. The Hebrew religious traditions in Canaan and native Canaanite traditions blended together and the Hebrews had no reason to make theological distinctions about God and other gods and could not care less.

As the Hebrews came to engage in agriculture they could not ignore Baal and Astart because they were gods of agriculture and the harvest, and the erotic ritual was merely a prayer to insure fertility and the plentiful harvest. Hebrew women became sacred prostitutes for Baals' high places or wailing women. The Hebrews not only tolerated but embraced Canaanite gods. Holiness, ethics, and purity as attributes of God mattered little to the Hebrews. Victory in war, peace, plentiful foods, health, rain in agricultural seasons and other worldly blessings mattered, but it made little difference which gods or God would provide them.

On the surface, Solomon's reign brought about a zenith of peace and economic prosperity and seemed to reinforce the foundation of a United Kingdom of Judah and Israel. But tribal jealousies and grievances for exalting the tribe of Judah above others were there even before the death of Solomon. Solomon's reign reduced the tribal chiefs to the lesser roles of elders, and imposed heavy taxation and forced labor. With Kings David and Solomon, able and strong, at the helm, discipline seemed to overcome the tribal clannishness of the Hebrew tribes. Solomon, however, underestimated tribal clannishness and moved too rapidly to turn a confederation of fiercely independent tribes into a strong United Kingdom.

In 933 B.C. when Solomon died, the ten northern tribes of Israel seceded from the dynasty of David and crowned the rebel leader Jeroboam as the King of Israel, leaving the tribes of Judah, Levi and Benjamin under the rule of Rehoboam, Solomon's son, as the King of Judah. Almost from the beginning of the Hebrew settlement in Palestine there was an observable cleavage between northern tribes led by the tribe of Ephraim and the tribe of Judah in the south, and upon Solomon's death this cleavage became permanent. The period of the United Kingdom lasted less than a century.

DIVIDED KINGDOM

The Kingdom of Israel (933-722 B.C.), a loose confederation of ten northern tribes, became the kingdom of assassinations and coups. Four kings who followed Jeroboam met violent deaths. Nine dynasties came and went in about two hundred years of its existence. Each new dynasty invariably passed judgments in the name of God or gods and put to death all the royal male members of the preceding dynasty.

Omri, a capable king, fortified Samaria as the capital of Israel. Two temples were built: one at Dan for the god of Dan in the north and the other at Bethel for the god of Bethel in the south. They were collectively called Elohim, the gods in plural form. The priests attending these temples were not the Levites.

The Phoenician god Melqart was worshipped during the twenty-two-year reign of King Ahab because Ahab's wife Jezebel of Tyre believed in her native god, and had 450 prophets of Baal and 400 prophets of Asherah at the royal expense.

While Israel was establishing its separate kingdom and building a new capital in Samaria, Assyria campaigned against the Phoenician city-states of Tyre and Sidon, gained access to the Mediterranean trade routes, overcame the Aramaean tribal kingdoms in Syria, and began looking for further conquests. The Assyrian army attempted to subjugate Israel in 853 B.C., but withdrew after receiving tributes.

Israel also had to engage in a violent struggle against the Syrian Kings from the north, and Judah and Egypt from the south. Assyrian influence, siding with one or another side, determined the outcome of the contests. Assyria not only collected tributes but also appointed the kings of Israel. It was the defection of King Hoshea, who had been appointed by Assyria, that resulted in the Assyrian siege and capture of Samaria in 722 B.C. and the exile of Israelite leaders.

The Kingdom of Judah (933-586 B.C.), reduced to a tiny kingdom in land and population, was poor, confined to the highland of Jerusalem and the wilderness of Judah. The ten northern tribes of Israel held the fertile part of Canaan. The tribes of Levi and Benjamin in Judah were of no military significance and did not challenge the Davidic dynasty. Only Queen Athaliah (841-835 B.C.) tried to usurp the throne by putting to death all the males of direct Davidic royal line. Only a baby, Joash, survived, and Jehoiada, the priest, led a coup which put Joash on the throne, thus maintaining the Davidic line.

Shortly after the northern tribes of Israel broke away, the Pharaoh of Egypt, Shishak, invaded Judah and Jerusalem and "took away the treasures of the house of the Lord and the treasures of the king's house; he took away everything." (1 Kings 14:25f.) Every nation claimed lordship over Judah: Egypt, Israel, Syria, Assyria and finally Babylonia. The Moabites and Edomites warred against Judah.

King Ahaz paid tribute to Pul of Assyria with the silver and gold treasure from the Temple and the king's house in 734 B.C.. Judah maintained its nominal independence under Assyrian suzerainty, and survived precariously over a century after Israel was made a domain of Assyria.

When the Babylonian Empire replaced Assyria as the new master, and imposed upon Judah the intolerable burden of tribute, Judah attempted to ally with Egypt and shake off the yoke of Babylonia, and this resulted in Babylonian siege and destruction of Jerusalem and subsequent exile in 586 B.C.

PROPHETS AND FALSE PROPHETS

Thousands of prophets, false or true, began preaching when both Israel and Judah became overshadowed by the rising Mesopotamian powers of Assyria and Babylonia and were eventually led to the loss of political independence. Retrospectively, only a small number of them are considered as true prophets.

Isaiah and Jeremiah are regarded as "major" prophets, and Amos, Hosea, and Micah are a few of the "minor" prophets of this period. There were hundreds of prophets and prophetesses at times in the history of Israel and Judah, and no one would dare guess how many prophets lived in the history of the Hebrews. Some of them were for Baals, and others for

God, but the distinction between Baals and God was not clear even to most prophets.

Of thousands of prophets and prophetesses in the history of the Hebrews the four major and the twelve minor prophets are singled out as prophets, distinguished from all other false prophets. What makes one a prophet and others false prophets?

Prophets at times predicted the future events. Some of their predictions came true and others did not materialize. So did false prophets' predictions. Did prophets have unique abilities to "see" or "be in close fellowship with God or gods" or "be in communion with God or gods"? Quacks, soothsayers, seers, and sorcerers everywhere claimed to be endowed with such abilities and clairvoyant powers as to communicate with God or gods–which the ordinary multitudes did not have. The books of prophets in the Bible were written and edited by the followers of each prophet well after the events each prophet foretold, and their predictions have no spiritual meanings.

Even the moral tone of the major and minor prophets varies from one prophet to another. Some were more intent in predicting God's punishments of an enemy nation or nations; however, others preached that God was merciful even toward the Assyrians and non-Hebrew peoples as well as toward the Hebrews. Some perceived God as a national god, but others more as "the God of the whole earth." (Isaiah 54:5)

To some prophets the coming of the day of the Lord is the day of judgment for all nations, filled with God's wrath and vengeance; nevertheless, the Prophet Hosea stressed that God was wonderfully loving and forgiving. Hosea's wife was a prostitute for Baal's temple, and Hosea drew an analogy between the faithless Israel and his own wife.

Some prophets had doubts about the Lord of history, for the righteous nation seemed to suffer and the wicked nations prosper: Each enemy of the Hebrews was conquered only to make way for a more ruthless overlord who in turn made captives of the Hebrews.

Some prophets were pessimistic enough to predict the end of the world, but others predicted the bright future that God had in store for the righteous Hebrews.

The background of major and minor prophets varied considerably too. Amos was a farmer and shepherd from a small village who was certainly not an intellectual by any standard, but Isaiah, a statesman and preacher, was an intellectual of his time. Some were from the priestly family but others were not.

Prophets as well as false prophets seemed to be concerned with prediction and telling the people what was the way or will of God or the gods. In his last battle against the Philistines, King Saul was afraid of the superior force of the Philistines and "when Saul inquired of the Lord, and the Lord did not answer him, either by dreams, or by urim, or by prophets" (1 Samuel 28:6) then Saul turned to a medium at Endor for divination. Then the dead judge and prophet Samuel, who had anointed Saul as the first king of the Hebrews, made an appearance to the witch of Endor and forewarned that the war would be lost. The prophecy of the witch came true and Saul and his sons lost their lives in the war.

Prophets were, however, invariably outstanding men of moral integrity who deeply shared the sufferings of their contemporaries and cared about their wants and desires. Their understanding, both in intellectual and emotional ways, flowed from their spiritual views of life. Their viewpoint, from which they observed critically the world around them, came closest to "Godly" moral perfection. Thus, the dialogue between God and a prophet was neither a matter of supernatural sense perception nor a literary format between an animated God and a prophet, but a living experience of each prophet.

The prophets spoke for God. It should be kept in mind that each prophet was in competition with numerous false prophets who claimed the supernatural psychic sense to communicate with gods, the ability to predict, and so on. Each prophet claimed he spoke for God because he clearly perceived God as the sole moral source and his own spiritual perspective of life as the sole cause for his wisdom and emotions.

Prophets were determined to bring up the standard of social righteousness and the moral order of the Hebrew society to a higher plane, and they were ready to lay down their lives for that cause. They were fearless in fearsome crises: they were not afraid to speak out against the kings, priests, popular but false prophets, and other political or religious authorities. The miracle was that the preachings of major and minor prophets survived the loss of ancient Hebrew political independence which swept away with it the voices of thousands of false prophets.

The question, however, remains: What was the spiritual perspective of life which prophets held onto steadfastly, and why did the ancient Hebrews of all peoples come to have such a perspective? No one today knows exactly when true prophecy originated, although the writers traced its origin to Moses as the first prophet, who became indignant over the cruel treatment of the enslaved Hebrews in Egypt.

The Prophet Nathan challenged the powerful King David for having an affair with Bathsheba and taking her as a wife after having her husband killed in a battle action. Ahijah prophesied against King Solomon for worshipping Baals. Prophet Elijah denounced King Ahab for killing Naboth and robbing him of the vineyard Ahab coveted. Perhaps such stories of ancient Hebrew prophets as handed down orally were adding on a new dimension to the Hebrew tradition of prophecy, which culminated in the awakening of social conscience invoked by major and minor prophets, and the writers of the Law.

In addition to the common spiritual perspective nearly all the major and minor prophets urged the Hebrews to go back to God's law, ordinances and statutes. It was their prophetic belief in God's fiery judgments or God's way of reminding the Hebrews of absolute obedience to the will of God, expressed in God's law, ordinances, and statutes. God led the Assyrians and the Babylonians to plunder Samaria and Jerusalem with sword and death because the Hebrews went astray, and the Assyrians and Babylonians were the tools of God.

Just what is the common spiritual perspective of the prophets and what is the will of God, expressed in His law, ordinances and statutes, can better be understood by first taking into account the pre-exilic Hebrew way of life, based largely on the customs spelled out in the Decalogue and the Laws of the Covenant, which the writers of the Law considered degenerate.

PRE-EXILIC HEBREW LIFE

In Palestine the ancient Hebrews took over fortified towns and villages which had grown up centering around the water wells or established new fortified towns. Caravan traders stopped by water wells to satisfy their animals' thirst as well as their own. The water wells were shared by men and cattles. It was an important function of women to keep water jars filled at home for home consumption. Water wells were the social centers for women where they gossipped and exchanged information. Water wells were also the breeding grounds for communicable plague which traveled as fast as gossip.

Palestine was much richer than the old desert world but was scarce of natural resources. The Hebrew nomads, breeding goats and sheep, began cultivating the land for wheat, barley, corn, grapes, olives, and figs. Their food was limited to milk, cheese, bread and fruits, and occasional beef, lamb, and goat meat.

The goats, the livestock of the ancient Hebrews, and the gazelle, the wild goatlike game of Palestine, were the destructive animals: They ate the young tree roots as well as branches and the grass roots, destroyed the forests, and turned the precious fertile land into desert by covering off the top soil.

The hot desert wind could easily turn green vegetation into brown wastes, or locusts could come to devour vegetation. A long dry spell or ceaseless local battles could easily wipe out one's fortune overnight; consequently, no one could remain rich for long and each man, poor or rich, always could claim himself as the equal of any other individual.

The Hebrews in Palestine continued the life of their ancestors, which was part of the Arabian desert world, by always seeking new green pastures. More often than not, a spell of drought during the hot and dry season drove them to scramble for greenery and water for cattle, and accentuated the need for constant inter-village and localized struggle among various peoples in Palestine. Living was precarious for them and the peoples in Palestine had to be ruthless and even scavengerish. Their religious and socio-economic systems and customs were moulded by their life experiences.

The writers narrate that God inscribed the Decalogue on two stone tablets with His finger: Each Hebrew should love and serve one and only God, love his parents, and should not commit, in thoughts and deeds, murder, adultery, stealing, and false testimony.

The Decalogue and the Laws of the Covenant are the oldest among many layers of the Law scattered throughout the Book of the Law. The Decalogue and the Laws of the Covenant are compilations of the ancient pre-exilic Hebrew customs. Some other law codes might have been drafted before the time of exile but were promulgated and enforced in the post-exilic Judea.

Before the Exile each family patriarch had absolute power over his family members. The codified law had to be binding upon family patriarchs first before such laws could reach down to individuals; conversely, the preexilic Hebrew society was based on the tribal and patriarchal family system and no codified laws could reach down to individuals.

The Laws of the Covenant, with specific provisions about fields, vineyards, and stacked and standing grain, was a compilation of the customs which were suitable for settled agricultural communities and which were adopted by the Hebrews after moving into Palestine. No one today, however, can say for sure if the Decalogue is older than the Laws of the Covenant. It is very probable that the Decalogue is the summary of the Laws of the Covenant. The Laws of the Covenant are simple enough by modern standards but were complicated to the ancient Hebrews.

All of the Ten Commandments except one are also spelled out in the Laws of the Covenant. That exception is the commandment against adultery: The Laws of the Covenant did not have any specific provision about adultery. Adultery in the ancient Hebrew society cannot be interpreted in a narrow sense as modern men understand, but the commandment against adultery should be considered in conjunction with social mores of polygamy and the ancient Hebrew patriarchal family system.

The patriarchal families played the vital role in seeing each member observe family or tribal customs. Each patriarchal family included as many as hundreds of marriage groups and families: The patriarch as the head of the family, his wives and concubines; married or unmarried children and their wives and concubines and their children; servants, slaves and strangers living with the family; the patriarch's brothers' families; and kin who would look up to the patriarch for guidance and protection.

Each family within a patriarchal family had a one- or two-room house, and families belonging to the same patriarchal family lived in one town or neighboring towns. The patriarchal family was more akin to a clan. A number of related patriarchal families or clans made up a tribe.

It was the patriarch who acted as the judge and disposed of intrafamily disputes including matters of life and death. Each family within the patriarchal family had to earn a living, and a creditor could seize the wife, child or slave of a debtor until the unpaid debt was satisfied. The mode of economic cooperation among family members of each patriarchal family varied, perhaps, from one family to another and depended on the changing fortune of each patriarchal family.

The renting of wives by their husbands was practiced, if not commonly, among many ancient peoples of the Middle East, including the Hebrews, especially when a traveling husband in a strange town did not have any choice but to offer his wife to a man of the town in exchange for protection.

As the Hebrews were engaged in ceaseless battles, women outnumbered men. A low status was assigned to women and a wife was the property of the husband. Wives were often bought and the women captured in the vanquished towns and villages were made wives and concubines of the victors.

A man could divorce his wife at will and did not have to prepare a bill of divorce or any other document. The divorce involved no ceremony or document just as the wedding involved no ceremony or document at all. Most marriages took place within the patriarchal family or the tribe, and one hesitated to marry a woman of even another Hebrew tribe. The betrothal, which specified the amount of payment for the bride, was important. As there was no dowry which the bride had to bring to the husband, the divorced wife had to move out empty-handed.

There were decisions for the patriarch to make in such cases as: the wife who had attempted to run away but got caught; the right of the son to inherit the properties, including wives and concubines, of his deceased father; the obligations of the kins to support the widows and orphans, and so on. Such decisions by the patriarch were made on the basis of good or evil, whether they pleased or offended God or the gods.

A man could have as many wives or concubines as he could afford. The number of wives or concubines a man had signified his social status as well as his wealth. One's wives were looked upon with some jealousy and disfavor by one's concubines; accordingly, one's concubines often connived to drive the wives out. Once a husband divorced a wife or wives, favored concubines became wives, and new concubines would plot again.

The distinction between the status of a wife and that of a concubine lay in the customary assumption that a husband was supposed to spend more time with his wife or wives than with his concubine or concubines; however, more often than not, a husband tended to spend more time with his concubine or concubines than with his wife or wives.

In any event, the fact that, in polygamy, a rich man could have as many wives and concubines as he could provide for meant that a poor man could not have any. This caused sexual frustration among many wives and concubines ignored by the husband and the poor men who could not afford to have wives or concubines.

Lax sexual morality and social disturbances went hand in hand together with the custom of polygamy. In the days of Judges the Benjaminites at the town of Gibeah seized a concubine of a certain traveling Levite and raped her to death. Hence, the enraged Levite "took a knife, and laying hold of his concubine he divided her, limb by limb, into twelve pieces, and sent her throughout all the territory of Israel."

(Judges 19:29.) In the ensuing civil war the tribe of Benjamin was nearly exterminated. (The writers came to codify stern measures of death against forbidden sexual conduct for the post-exilic Jews, but failed to remove the underlying social force, i.e. polygamy itself.)

There was no definite custom that either the adulterer or the adulteress should be stoned to death in public in pre-exilic Israel or Judah. A fight between the husband and the adulterer settled the matter at times; the adulterer paid the husband for damage to the property, i.e. wife; or the husband of the adulteress could divorce her or reduce her to the status of a concubine. The Pre-exilic Hebrews did not have any custom of mutilating or branding an adulterer or adulteress.

Offspring of concubines were not labelled as bastards. In fact there were no distinctions between legitimate and illegitimate children.

Prohibition of incest was limited to one's mother, sister, or daughter; otherwise, one could marry one's half-sister, step-mother, daughter-in-law, so on. In all these cases there were no definite customs. It was for the patriarch to listen to family members and decide if there were violation of any family or tribal custom after the facts. Customs and customary evaluations came after the facts, not before.

Each patriarch would watch carefully how other patriarchs of the blessed families handled the cases similar to what he had to decide on, because some rash act might invite the wrath of God or the gods. Male members of each patriarchal family would observe the decisions of the patriarch. If a patriarch turned despotic or indecisive, male members would attribute such despotism or indecisiveness of the patriarch to bad spirits and a new patriarch would emerge.

Male leadership in each family was considered essential to the nomadic life. A woman without a son was considered as cursed by God or gods. A brother had to marry the widow of his brother who died without a male heir. When Tamar, the daughter-in-law of Judah, failed to conceive a son by the brother of her late husband, she disguised herself and played a harlot to Judah, and conceived a son. When Judah later learned that it was Tamar whom he had made love to, Judah judged Tamar to be righteous in view of Tamar's devotion to the family of her late husband. (Genesis 38.)

It was important for any Hebrew male to memorize the list of the male ancestors which determined his social station, his individual identity, and his share in the patriarchal family and the tribal life.

All the disputes involving two or more patriarchal families which the patriarchs could not dispose of were initially referred to the tribal chief. In the days of Judges, Deborah, a prophetess, used to sit under a palm tree in Ephraim and judged even intertribal matters. Her opinion was carried out not because she had the power to enforce it but because she commanded the respect of the tribal chiefs.

The Hebrew customs, like other ancient customs, were merely to maintain peace and order. If peace was broken the patriarch's and tribal chief's first objective was to contain disorder and prevent disorder from spreading. Once peace was broken even the immediate family of the injured was not allowed to take matters into its own hands, so that further chain of retribution might not take place. The custom of retaliation which prevailed in the pre-exilic Hebrew society did not allow kinsmen to avenge eye for eye or tooth for tooth, except when men struggled together and an injury to a pregnant woman followed. (Exodus 21:22-25.)

If a fight broke out and a man was injured but later recovered, the other party to the fight had to pay for the time loss of the injured party. If a master had beaten a slave and caused the loss of an eye or any part of a limb, the injured slave was to be set free. The community, i.e., the gods or God, sanctioned physical coercion in terms of fighting or beating to the extent that such self-help did not result in severe injuries.

This form of self-help was sanctioned by the tribal community. The fighting was to take place fairly, and the kin of the injured were not to vent vengeance because of an injury caused in a fair fight.

Might made right when such self-help was sanctioned, but might was restrained in a number of ways: The weak ones might band together to fight against the known bully, or the patriarch might intervene, chastise the bully, or banish him.

When severe injuries or death followed any fighting, acts of redress, which were normally regarded as rightful and moral, went beyond the limit the tribal community sanctioned, and the patriarch or the tribal chief intervened for the violation of the customs.

It cannot be overemphasized how remarkable the Laws of the Covenant are in many ways: The death penalty is limited to premeditated murder, kidnapping, cursing or striking one's own parents, bestiality, worship of false gods, and sorcery; the principle of restitution prevails in all other cases; and there are no provisions for trial by ordeals.

In the days of Kings, Saul left the judicial matters to the patriarchs and the tribal chiefs. King David heard the cases, and King Solomon was praised for his judicial wisdom. The tribal chiefs, however, never let the royal power of the king become absolute, even during the reign of Kings David and Solomon: The Hebrew tribal chiefs forced the king to rule on the basis of customs. The relationship between the king and the tribal chiefs laid the basis for the rule that king was subject to customs rather than above or outside them. The king himself was obliged to obey the customs just as other Hebrews were, and the king was to respect rights which customs guaranteed to the patriarchs and the tribal chiefs. Contests between the royal family on one hand and the tribal chiefs and the patriarchs on the other largely prescribed the limit of royal power.

Both Kings David and Solomon recognized the importance

of judicial opinions as affecting not only individuals and their patriarchal families involved but also the king-tribal relationship as well, and seldom appointed deputies to render decisions on judicial matters. Absalom, a son of King David, coveted the judicial power seditiously in order to weaken the authority of King David. Absalom would say to one who had a dispute to bring before the king for judgment, "See your claims are good and right; but there is no man deputed by the king to hear you." "Oh, that [if] I were made judge in the land! Then every man with a suit or cause might come to me, and I would give him justice." He flattered those who came to pay respect to him, and "stole the hearts of the men of Israel." (2 Samuel 15:1-6.)

The judicial roles of the patriarchs and the tribal chiefs and their relations with the central power of the king prevented a legal profession and an organized system of secular courts from developing in Israel and Judah until the time of Babylonian exile. A mode of settling controversies in most matters was for the patriarchs, the tribal chiefs or the king to find a settlement agreeable and acceptable to the parties, their families and their tribes involved. Only in the last resort did they render a decision to be enforced.

While the king was subject to the customs, he, of course, had broader rights to adopt and foster measures for the well-being of the Hebrews, just as the tribal chiefs and the patriarchs had their respective rights which accompanied their traditional functions. Such rights of the king, the tribal chiefs and the patriarchs, however, did not contradict or nullify the notion of the equality of every Hebrew before the customs, which insured each Hebrew the social station to which he was entitled.

From the viewpoint of actual influence the Levite priestly family never gained a position of primacy in the pre-exilic Palestine. The ancient Hebrew priests and the Temple played no role in the judicial matters despite the fact that the

Hebrew customs, religion, and morals were all blended together, and God was the ultimate judge and enforcer.

The ancient Hebrew priests and Temple were not depositories or administrators of Hebrew customs. The writer of Chronicles stated that King Jehosh'aphat of Judah appointed judges to hear local cases and a court of appeal, made up of some Levites and priests as well as heads of families, to hear disputed cases, but such a measure was not carried through (2 Chronicles 19).

Even in religious matters the Levite priests remained rather impotent throughout the pre-exilic period. Only a few priests were hired hands of the king and they could never reach out to the average Hebrews. A reader of the Bible may find it puzzling why that was the case.

In the day of Judges the Levites were hired to serve as priests to the household god or to the tribal god. The graven image and the molten image represented the household god or the tribal god (Judges 17-18). King Saul sought the guidance of a witch. King David did not hesitate to appoint his numerous sons priests although they were not Levites, i. e. descendants of Aaron, members of the priestly family.

When King Solomon built the Temple it was a small chapel in size, measuring about 90 feet long, 30 feet wide, and 45 feet high. (This small scale of the Temple was an incredible contrast to each magnificent but useless Egyptian pyramid which required the slavery of millions for the afterlife of a single soul, or the massive temple towers of Babylon which were as tall as 300 feet.)

King Solomon also built high places for Baals and made offerings. When the divided kingdoms of Israel and Judah followed Solomon's death, most unforgivable was the fact that Jeroboam, the first king of the Northern Kingdom of Israel, and his sons deported all the Levites out of Israel and did not allow the Levites to serve as priests of the Lord in Israel (2 Chronicles 11:13f.). Perhaps for this reason the priestly writer of Chronicles refused to record the history of the Northern Kingdom of Israel.

As only one Temple was needed for the one and only God, it necessarily limited the number of the priests and priestly assistants serving and attending the Temple, whereas innumerable priests and priestesses came to serve the many high places for Baals. Just as prophets were outnumbered by false prophets the priests for the Temple were outnumbered by the priests and priestesses serving Baals. It was the unique feature of one Temple for the one and only God which prevented the priestly power from growing in the pre-exilic Judah.

Kings were considered devout and reverent if they recognized the position of God as equal to those of Baals, maintained the Temple, and treated its priests as well as the high places for Baals and their priests and priestesses. There were more impious and unrighteous kings who ignored the Temple and its priests, or assigned to God a status inferior to Baals. Even the pious kings did not dare to remove the high places. Josiah, the King of Judah (640-609 B.C.), was the only one who attempted to carry out a thoroughgoing religious reform by purging the high places, but he died prematurely in the senseless battle against the Egyptian Pharaoh Necho.

The tide was against the Levite priests and the Temple: God as the national warrior deity was not appealing to the pre-exilic Hebrews when they were experiencing defeats and sufferings; and the perception of the moral God was not appealing to the pre-exilic Hebrews because intellectual and moral scruples did not concern them, engaged as they were in ceaseless battles. The pre-exilic Hebrew customs, therefore, carried with them a totally secular tone, because of their secular judicial system and the impotent Levite priestly family. In the minds of the pre-exilic Hebrews God as the ultimate moral Judge was perceived rather vaguely, just as little gods were so regarded.

The Decalogue does not prescribe punitive sanctions, and

the Laws of the Covenant prescribe the minimum of punishments. An individual act was, after the facts, examined by the Patriarch or tribal chief. If the degree of coercion and violence as a measure of self-help met the patriarch's or tribal chief's approval there was no violation of customs.

The customs were effective because the Hebrews perceived such customs as beneficial to them, and because the Hebrews thought such customs as pleasing to God or the gods.

The Laws of the Covenant and the Decalogue did not regulate the atavistic in men. Sexuality, other innate urges of men, and even men's aggressiveness toward others were left to a great extent unregulated. The pre-exilic Hebrew society left many areas of personal life and interpersonal relationships to individual moral choice and these were, after the facts, subject to customary evaluations.

The pre-exilic Hebrews lived by an intricate set of customary understandings, not highly developed and detailed man-made laws. The pre-exilic Hebrews observed the customs of the family or the tribe but would not yield to an organized social discipline or observe the man-made laws which a developed and complex society demands of its members. Both Israel and Judah were neither well-developed and complex societies nor well-organized and unified nations. King Solomon's attempt to do away with the tribal boundaries and to organize backfired and created a permanent division of Israel and Judah.

The pre-exilic Hebrew customs lacked detailed and precise rules and left administration of justice largely to self-help. Such a system of rough justice served the pre-exilic Hebrews well. The pre-exilic Hebrews were ready to adjust or readjust to new situations by commonsense and a vague sense of fairness and the verdicts of God or the gods.

A patriarch by nature was least susceptible to bribes, corruption, and any other personal gains not only because the interests of each patriarch were completely identical with those of his family, but also because he had the spiritual obligation to please and not offend God or the gods and bring blessings to his family.

It was a spontaneous freedom to think, feel, move about and act that the pre-exilic Hebrews cherished. The minimum penalties of the customs, the secular but unorganized judicial system, the lack of a unified religious system, and the tribal clannishness contributed to the emotional security of a spontaneous freedom.

An uninhibited autonomy and the moral choices of the pre-exilic Hebrews did not necessarily tilt toward proper conduct. They were supposed to free Hebrew slaves, male and female, under the customs, but they kept renewing the period of slavery. The strong rarely let go of chances to plunder weak strangers by treachery, or by sheer brutality to justify one or another pretext of theirs. Simeon and Levi, the sons of Jacob, killed all the males and plundered the city of Shechem under the hazy pretext that the son of the Shechem prince either made love to Dinah, Jacob's daughter, or raped Dinah or was seduced by Dinah (Genesis 34).

The Laws of the Covenant state: "You shall not wrong a stranger or oppress him." (Exodus 22:21.) Of course one had to exercise moral scrutiny in determining if a certain trader or peddler was "a stranger" or "a spy."

Amos, the Hebrew prophet, in the 8th century B.C. challenged sharp business practices and the lawlessness of the rich Hebrew merchants who used false balances in weighing silver and grains and dealt deceitfully with the poor (Amos 8:4-6).

The Laws of the Covenant carried over the nomadic concept of protecting the weak as a moral imperative to the settled life in Palestine. "You shall not afflict any widow or orphan. If you do afflict them, and they cry out to me [God], I will surely hear their cry; my wrath will burn, and I will kill you with the sword, and your wives shall become widows and your children fatherless." (Exodus 22:22-24.) Assyrian and Babylonian laws and Egyptian religion also mandated the protection of widows and orphans, and this moral and religious tone of the Laws of the Covenant was not unique.

The Laws of the Covenant stipulate: "If you lend money to any of my [God's] people with you who is poor, you shall not exact interest from him." (Exodus 22:25.) Farmers and cattle-raisers lived near the subsistence level and they often needed something to carry them over from one harvest season to next. Often the farmers found that the grain to feed the families was gone two or three months before the harvest season.

In many parts of the world a farmer used to borrow a bushel of wheat or corn from a rich man and promise to pay back one bushel plus one third of one bushel as interest for that hard period of a few months. A bad harvest was a curse to marginal farmers but a blessing to money lenders: Thus, the rich could buy up things for hoarding and later hold the poor to ransom. The amount of hoarding increased as years went by and more and more crops were collected and set aside for storing and lending. Eventually there were no crops left for the farmers to consume even during the harvest season. The vicious cycle forced farmers to sell land, children, and themselves into slavery for the debts.

It was not possible for the wandering nomads to store grain; therefore, interest charges had significant socio-economic implications by enriching the rich in settled agricultural societies where hoarding could be carried out easily. Some of the pre-exilic Hebrews in agricultural societies of Palestine also were getting richer and the rest impoverished. The Prophet Isaiah defiantly described the discrepancy:

> Woe to those who join house to house, who add field to field, until there is no more room, and you are made to dwell alone in the midst of the land.
>
> The Lord of hosts has sworn in my hearing: "Surely many houses shall be desolate, large and beautiful houses, without inhabitant. For ten acres of vineyard

shall yield but one bath, and a homer of seed shall yield but an ephah."

(Isaiah 5:8-10.)

In the pre-exilic period even the First Commandment against worship of false gods was not observed by the Hebrews. There is no single period, in the pre-exilic Hebrew history, when that commandment was observed except the Mosaic period; accordingly, the pre-exilic Hebrews not only tolerated little gods but also actively embraced local Baals.

Both the Decalogue and the Laws of the Covenant, however, were significant because the Hebrews thought of their customs as belonging to the Hebrews as a people as if the customs were their common possession. Disunited politically and religiously as the Hebrew tribes were, the customs, originated in religion, symbolized the common characteristics by which the Hebrews as a people were held together.

The customary mutual help and protection was extended to non-Hebrews living in Palestine because, the First Commandment not being observed by the Hebrews, there were not many customary provisions which had to be applied exclusively to the Hebrews.

The fact that the ancient Hebrew customs originated in religion applied also to other peoples of the Middle East. The ancient peoples pondered what were those human activities pleasing or displeasing to gods or God. They identified the customs as an enumeration of such activities pleasing to gods or God.

The ancient Hebrew customs, like the customs of other peoples in the ancient Middle East, were not prescribed or enacted by a group of legal experts or a king. Such customs were observed, not because the Hebrews were afraid of the enforcing public agency, but because such customs had been repeatedly observed by their ancestors and contemporaries and had been identified as the norm of conducts acceptable to the Hebrew community and to the gods or God.

Customs, good or bad, were based on the life experiences and consensus of the people in the community and were considered vaguely and subconsciously indispensable to the well-being of each individual, the family, the tribe and the community. In most instances disobedience to such customs was considered a silly act which invited social ridicule, contempt, scorn, or ostracism.

Once the Hebrews moved into Palestine the way of settled agricultural life itself stood in the way of the nomadic notion of egalitarianism. The changing way of life and social forces in the agricultural society of Palestine gradually forced the Hebrews to give up their nomadic traditions. In Jerusalem and Samaria, the capitals of Judah and Israel, the royal princes and princesses and the families related to them had the noble titles and lived in luxury. Merchants profited from the Caravan trades.

Jewels, such as gold bracelets for arms, nose rings, pendants, precious stones like diamonds and emeralds, ivory ornaments, fabrics and cosmetics were brought in by traders and were eagerly sought after by those who could pay. The more unstable and uncertain situations the Hebrews had to live in, the more jewels and luxury they sought after, as the jewels represented liquid assets which could be easily concealed and carried and meant the lifeline in times of war and escape.

Prophet Amos, a shepherd from a small town of Tekoa, had these words to say:

> Woe to those who lie upon beds of ivory,
> and stretch themselves upon their couches,
> and eat lambs from the flock,
> and calves from the midst of the stall;
> who sing idle songs to the sound of the harp,
> and like David invent for themselves instruments of
> music;

who drink wine in bowls, and anoint themselves
with the finest oils,
but are not grieved over the ruin of Joseph!
Therefore they shall now be the first of those to go
into exile,
and the revelry of those who stretch themselves shall
pass away.

(Amos 6:4-7.)

Jeremiah, at the time of Babylonian Exile, wrote:

Behold, the days are coming, says the Lord, when I will make a new covenant with the house of Israel and the house of Judah. . . . And *no longer shall each teach his neighbor and each his brother* saying, 'Know the Lord,' for they shall all know me, from the least of them to the greatest, says the Lord; for I will forgive their iniquity, and I will remember their sin no more.

(Jeremiah 31:31-34.)

The writers, in compiling their national saga, found themselves precisely looking for a second Exodus and a new covenant. Several hundred years separated the first and second Exodus. In the first instance Moses, inspired by the Godly vision, led the ill-disciplined Hebrews out of Egypt and had them make the Sinai covenant with God. In the second instance the Hebrew exiles in Babylonia believed that God would anoint a second Moses to lead the Hebrews out of Babylonia and bring them to the homeland where they, tainted with degenerate and undisciplined ways of living, would make a new covenant with God. In both instances the needs and desires of the Hebrews were identical.

The Hebrews made a full circle and arrived at the first and original starting point. Times and places of divine-human dramas in the first and second Exodus differed, but the nature of God, the qualities of leadership which were characteristics of God, the major actors–Moses and Ezra, the nomadic tradition as the background setting, the underlying religious aspirations, and the rest of the scenario were identical in both instances.

Moses' historical existence, the changing perceptions of God, the exact number of the Hebrews who had come out of Egypt and other numerous questionable particulars of the first Exodus matter very little, in view of the second and historical Exodus. The writers bared all the unfavorable and ugly aspects of the religious lives of their ancestors.

The national saga, written in the critical viewpoint of the writers, demonstrated the absolute need to overturn the customary values and structure of the traditional Hebrew society and pointed out the new direction which the post-exilic Jews should take after the second Exodus. A perpetual nostalgia about the uniqueness of the ancient Hebrew religious beliefs that harked back to the days of Moses was not a mere sentiment of the writers but that new direction for the post-exilic Jews. The post-exilic Jewish religious outlook and life is in sharp contrast to that of the pre-exilic Hebrews.

CHAPTER III

Judaism

SECOND EXODUS

It appeared to be a wishful illusion for the Hebrews in Babylon to think of the collapse of the Babylonian Empire. The city of Babylon with its double walls was impregnable. The Babylonian theocracy, however, created the problems of maintaining numerous temple buildings and supporting priests, priestesses, temple assistants, and no amount of revenue was enough. The army was demoralized, and the priest-princes were bitterly engaged in plots, intrigue and power struggles to succeed the priest-king, and the well-organized government machinery was rendered inefficient and unstable.

The city of Babylon was taken without resistance by a Persian general and his army one night in 538 B.C. when a dissatisfied Babylonian monk opened a gate to the city for the onrushing Persian army, ending the political independence of the great ancient Mesopotamian empires for ever.

Cyrus, the Persian King and the greatest conquerer in the history of the ancient Orient, had established an imperial policy on the vanquished peoples and territories, and that policy was an about-face of the policy of the Assyrian and Babylonian empires. Cyrus deferred to local traditions everywhere, and placed himself on the throne of each territory instead of inept native dynasties. He made use of the existing local institutions as his own, appointed the native leaders as his governors (satraps) and administrators, and adopted local gods as his own.

The Hebrew leaders could not hope for any better royal policy, for the Persian imperial policy guaranteed the Hebrew leaders a free hand to implement their future plans for the religious and civic independence and the welfare of the Hebrews. The Hebrews were in no position to seek political independence; furthermore, they saw with their own eyes the ebb and flow of the empires and the political independence and the mighty military powers of giant empires coming and going. A collapse of these empires eventually carried the cultural and civic life and even the identities of the peoples of the ancient Orient to oblivion.

An edict was issued in the name of Cyrus, the King of Persia: The Hebrews became free to return home. The decision for the Hebrews on whether to go home or stay in Babylonia was a different matter in spite of their longing for the homeland. The Hebrews from Israel had been living in Babylon and other Mesopotamian cities for nearly two hundred years, and perhaps nearly all of them considered themselves Mesopotamian natives rather than Hebrew exiles. The Hebrews from Judah, however, who had been living in Babylonia for about fifty years, considered themselves the exiles.

No matter how each Hebrew in Babylonia might have felt, he had to think twice about the foot travel which would normally take about four months for the whole family, young and old, from Babylon to Palestine. The journey without an armed escort was not safe because of ambushes by highway robbers. Most of the Hebrews decided to live in Babylon for the time being as they were rooted there as businessmen, cattle owners, and farmers, and were not ready to trade in a comfortable living in Babylonia for an unknown life in the homeland.

Initially a small group of the Hebrews led by Zerubabel, a prince of the house of David, returned to Jerusalem, and found Jerusalem in utter waste and desolation, caused by the devastating war, which had resulted in their deportation in the first place.

Some Hebrews also came back to Judah from Egypt. These Hebrews, coming home from Babylonia and Egypt, settled down exclusively in Judah, and they came to be known as Jews and the area of Judah as Judea.

It was more than fifteen years after the first group of the Jews came home that the Jews began rebuilding the Temple, and completed the work in 516 B.C. Crop failures, droughts, and localized squabbles with the Ammonites, the Edomites and neighboring Arab tribes added further misery to the bare existence of the returned Jews.

Although the Persian King appointed Shesh-bazar, a prince of the house of David, Governor of Judea, and could not care less about the internal affairs of Judea as long as Judea remained a peaceful district of a province within the Persian Empire, the King needed revenue badly. The Persians and the Greeks became engaged in a bitter but inconclusive struggle for the supremacy of the West during the first half of the fifth century B.C.

The Egyptians had taken advantage of the situation and rebelled against the Persians, who marched back and forth through Palestine to quell the rebels in Egypt; and the Jews, living in the middle of the traffic, had to pay for the Persian adventures in the form of heavy taxes and a voluntary or involuntary induction of the Jewish youth into the Persian army.

The life was difficult for all. The corrupt priests beguiled or terrified the gullible multitudes to exact the offerings. The wealthy and strong foreclosed on mortgages and reduced the poor families to slavery. A prophet of this post-exilic period described the lot of an average Jew: "He who earns wages earns wages to put them into a bag with holes." (Haggai 1:6.)

A glorious future for the post-exilic Jews, promised by God, appeared quite remote after the post-exilic life of about one hundred years. Then came to Jerusalem the important figures and events to shape and complete the foundation of Judaism.

EZRA

Two groups of the Jewish exiles returned to Jerusalem toward the end of the fifth century or early fourth century B.C. One group was led by Ezra, a zealous Levite priest and scribe, and another group by Nehemiah.

Ezra envisioned a mission of utmost importance. He was an eccentric priest-lawyer. Any drastic change, creativeness or imaginativeness run counter to the professional nature of lawyers and priests who prefer the status quo or gradual steps, but Ezra was bent on the mission to accomplish drastic change, which was to overturn the traditional Hebrew society, to remake the new Jewish society in the post-exilic Judea, and to lay and complete the foundation of Judaism.

Eventually Ezra convinced the Persian royal court that his mission would be favorable to the Persian desire to keep subject peoples, including the Jews, in line. The mission was somehow an obscure one to the Persian royal court, but Ezra secured a copy of the letter written in the name of the Persian King, who instructed Ezra, "to make inquiries about Judah and Jerusalem *according to the law of your God, which is in your hand,* . . . appoint magistrates and judges who may judge all the province beyond the River [i.e. Palestine], all such as know the laws of your God; and those who do not know them, you shall teach. Whoever will not obey *the law of your*

God and the law of the king, let judgment be strictly executed upon him, whether for death or for banishment or for confiscation of his goods or for imprisonment." (Ezra 7:14-26.)

When Ezra arrived in Jerusalem his claim of the backing of the Persian King on his mission did not impress the local Jewish officials and the Jews in Jerusalem because he came without any armed escort of soldiers and horsemen, which were supposed to accompany any dignitary. Ezra's mission was clear but he did not have the real power or influence to implement and enforce policies. It is not clear if Ezra returned to Jerusalem prior to Nehemiah's return, or how long Ezra and Nehemiah worked together.

Nehemiah, who had risen to the position of cup-bearer to the Persian King, was appointed Governor of Judea and came to Jerusalem with a military escort. He immediately rebuilt the walls of Jerusalem for protection against the neighboring enemies.

Nehemiah, Governor of Judea, discovered in Ezra a great priestly lawyer, and Ezra perhaps found in Nehemiah a man of action willing and powerful enough to implement specific reform measures according to the Law. They established their leadership through their moral integrity and inspiration rather than through a show of force or power. They sought no advantage of their own but lived a simple life, without the superfluities and luxuries of Babylonian and Persian life, and that at the least expense of the fellow Jews.

It was the belief of the Jews that their exile came about inevitably because they and their ancestors kept violating the Law, the will of God, and that God was merely giving a lesson to His chosen people by banishing them to Babylonia. Therefore, the first goal of Ezra and the post-exilic Jewish leaders was to define what that Law was and to obey that Law. Ezra had the copy of the Book of the Law or the core of it carefully handwritten and edited by priests and scribes.

The canonizing of the Book of the Law (i.e. the Torah or

Pentateuch) under the auspices of Ezra in Jerusalem was a moving moment and "all the people wept when they heard of the words of the law." On this day of national destiny Governor Nehemiah said to them, "Go your way, eat the fat and drink sweet wine and send portions to him for whom nothing is prepared, for this day is holy to our Lord, and do not be grieved, for the joy of the Lord is your strength." (Nehemiah 8:10.)

Thus, in canonizing the Book of the Law, the first written covenant in the history of the Jews was drawn up and signed by Governor Nehemiah, 22 Levite priests, 17 Levites, and 44 chiefs of the people. Anyone breaking this covenant was to be cursed.

The new covenant mandated the Jews to uphold all the legal requirements on proper individual behavior toward their fellow Jews as well as marriage, sabbath, tithes, offerings, and the proper upkeep of the Temple, priests and Levites (Nehemiah 9:38-10:39). It was the pledge of the priests, Levites and the patriarchs to uphold sweeping religious reforms and the pledge was made to God and His anointed representative, Ezra, who did not have to set his seal.

On the day following the canonizing of the Book of the Law the patriarchs, with the priests and the Levites, came together to Ezra to study the words of the Law (Nehemiah 8:13).

It will never be known whether or not the patriarchs realized, in making the new covenant, that they were signing away the traditional rights and privileges of patriarchs. Whether Ezra intended it or not, the first step to take judicial power away from the patriarchs was being taken. The Law, unlike the pre-exilic customs, was too complicated for the patriarchs to understand without the help of an expert, i.e. either a Levite priest or scribe. The patriarchs perhaps did not grasp what was happening.

For the first time in the Hebrew history the Jewish society

as an amalgamation of patriarchal families and tribes was being dismantled, and was to be transformed into a society guided solely by the Levite priests and scribes. The canonizing of the Book of the Law marked a reconstruction of the Jewish society and an organization of the Jews by a tight network of a judge over every ten Jews.

Ezra reconstructed the Jewish society on the basis of Judaism. Never was any man so great a stimulus to his contemporary Jews and later Jewish generations: He was indeed a second Moses, if not the historical Moses. Ezra is the most important and controversial figure in the Jewish history. Little is known, however, about his later life and even where and when he died. The generation of Jews to this date in Palestine and elsewhere have followed the whole religious tenor of Ezra manifested in Judaism.

Judaism, thus, came to be defined as an absolute obedience to the Law, the will of God, or an absolute spiritualization of objective standards of Jewish conduct: the absolute faith in one and only God has no meanings apart from the strict adherence to the Law. So wrote the writers proudly: "And what great nation is there, that has statutes and ordinances so righteous as all this law which I [Moses] set before you this day?" (Deuteronomy 4:8.) If one wanted to know the will of God all he had to do was ask a priest or a scribe, who would look it up in the Book of the Law. The writers did not recognize any other way for anyone to communicate with God and find out His will or nature.

The Law contains both religious and civil as well as criminal laws mixed together; it was inconceivable to divide the Will of God into religious and secular laws. The legend, national saga, and even myth in the Book of the Law were designed to spiritualize objective standards of Jewish conduct as the will of God. The national saga was meant to be merely an introduction or complement to the legal codes in the Book of the Law.

In the book of Genesis the writers stress that the closer the people are related in kinship the more rivalry and jealousy prevail among them. A rivalry between the closer kin can become much more bitter and intense than that between strangers. Such were the stories of Cain and Abel, Jacob and Esau, Jacob and Laban, and Joseph and his brothers. The writers conclude the book of Genesis with a moving account of Joseph generously forgiving and reconciling with his brothers, and the deep sense of love guiding the destiny of Jacob, Joseph and his brothers.

WATERTIGHT LAW

The greatness and weakness of Ezra lay in his total passion and zeal for a total reform. As shall be noted in later chapters the religious task he laid down upon the post-exilic Jews was the rigid, idealistic, and extensive one to be humane and self-enforcing. Yet he, standing on a towering rock, could point out to the Jews of every generation the clear future as a people in the distance.

The reconstructive vision of Ezra that ennobled him lay not in the merits and demerits of the Law drafted and codified but in the fact that he was totally immersed in love of his fellow Jews and kept marking the road map to the destination of his people. For his unreserved love of the fellow Jews Ezra, obstinate and self-righteous, could inspire and sway the Jews to share his Godly vision. It was simply a monumental task for Ezra or any one to dismantle the tribal and partriarchal Hebrew society and reconstruct a cohesive religious society guided solely by the Levite priests and scribes.

Each generation of the writers was faithful to the letters of Law written previously, for the Law represented the will of God, and could not be abolished even in part or amended. If, in the post-exilic Judea, anyone tried to entice another to false gods, he or she was not to be pitied but to be put to death with stones regardless of whether he or she was one's own brother, son, daughter, or wife or friend. If the parents tried to entice the children to false gods, the children could *not* put the parents to death. Such an exception was recognized because the earlier Laws of the Covenant stated: "Whoever curses his father or his mother shall be put to death" (Exodus 21:17), and the Decalogue also commanded each Hebrew to honor his father and mother.

The writers believed they did not have authority to make new laws but they were merely filling up the loopholes found in the earlier Decalogue and the Laws of the Covenant so that the watertight Law would become the true guide of the post-exilic Jews. No one had the authority to abolish any provision of earlier customary laws and allow the later substitutes to supersede the old. Such was the logic behind seemingly consistent old and new layers of laws, which in reality were totally contradictory to one another.

The Decalogue and the Laws of the Covenant were compilations of customs, and other laws in the Book of the Law were a genuine codification. The Decalogue and the Laws of the Covenant commanded the Jews not to engage in certain activities but did not prescribe penalties if one violated such commandments: The Decalogue and the Laws of the Covenant did not stipulate penalties for blasphemy, working on the sabbath day, adultery, reviling or cursing a ruler; but the post-exilic codified laws imposed death penalties for those offenses. The spirit of the old customary laws commanding "please do not" could not be the same as that of the new codes stating, "You shall be put to death if you do."

The Decalogue and the Laws of the Covenant did not stipulate retaliation of eye for eye and tooth for tooth for making a false accusation or causing bodily injuries to others in fights, but later codes specified penalties of retaliation to those offenses. There were no punishments prescribed for charging interest to fellow Jews on the money loaned or taking a bribe in the post-exilic Judea, as there was in the pre-exilic Judah.

In the post-exilic Judea a newly married woman was put to death if she failed to prove her virginity, and the hand of a wife was cut off if she attempted to help her husband, engaged in a fight, by grabbing the private parts of the other party to the fight. In the post-exilic Judea, if a betrothed woman had an affair with a man in a city or town, both were put to death, and if it took place in an open country only the man was put to death. If the woman was a virgin, not betrothed, the accused rapist had to marry her, as was the case under the earlier Laws of the Covenant.

The penalties imposed for various offenses in the post-exilic Judea were much more regressive than they were in the pre-exilic Israel and Judah. The writers justified such drastic changes by citing specific cases in which Moses put to death a man who had blasphemed and another man who had gathered sticks on the sabbath day.

The writers were not merely interpreting or filling up the loopholes found in the earlier customs, but, in reality, they were enacting new laws to achieve the new goal for the post-exilic life solely motivated by religion and guided solely by the Levite priests and scribes. The writers invariably had misgivings about the religious life of their ancestors, and the ill-disciplined life of the pre-exilic Hebrew society. They were bent on planning for a perfect and orderly Jewish society based on a strict adherence of every Jew to the watertight Law.

The pre-exilic customary laws left the observance of such customs largely to private judgment on moral choices and individual freedom of action, and relied heavily on the forms of coercion by persuasion, social pressure, and even ridicule rather than death penalties or banishments. Such customary laws did not require a centralized and well-organized executing public agency, and did not see the need or causes for change, and especially too rapid and drastic changes.

On the other hand, the Law, unlike the earlier customs, assumed the infinite ability of men to choose a course of action, reshape their future, and make decisions without being subject to restraints and limitations imposed by little gods. Such was the belief of the writers when they wrote:

> Then God said, "Let us make man in our image, after our likeness, and let them have dominion over the fish of the sea, and over the birds of the air, and over the cattle, and over all the earth, and over every creeping thing that creeps upon the earth."
>
> (Genesis 1:26.)

It is men, not little spirits, who have dominion over locusts, floods, droughts, pestilence and everything on the earth and who have to harness the forces of nature. The Jews are not to endure their miserable fate but to reshape their future. God left the material world for men to subdue, and that left the moral world in question. A Jewish survival depended on co-operation, discipline, resolute determination, and perseverance. It was the moral relationship of the Jews to the moral God which the writers came to be solely concerned with.

God, the sole cause of all effects to follow, causes a man to think and feel as he does. If each Jew let his understanding, purpose, and determination flow from that sole principle, and lived in absolute obedience to the Law, God would not deny a glorious future and the realization of a perfect society for the Jews. The writers did not recognize any limitation beyond which the Law could not channel and regulate human passions and desires. They did not recognize any bounds beyond which they could not guide and control the future of the Jews and even the external circumstances in which big empires always seemed to push the destiny of the Jews around. The belief of the writers in this regard was strongly reflected in dietary and sanitary laws.

The laws in regard to diet, hygiene and sanitation by way of quarantine and isolation reflect the belief that men will establish dominion over everything on the earth. In the ancient time when the source of leperous and other infections and the contagious nature of some diseases were little known, the writers did not attribute them to the malicious works of little spirits or to fate. The priest-physicians were to diagnose various physical symptoms to see if any proved to be benign or malignant, acute or chronic. Some of the details of the dietary and sanitary laws proved to be meaningless and others command scientific merit even by modern standards.

If a woman delivered a boy she was unclean for seven days, should not touch any hallowed thing, enter the sanctuary or have sex for thirty-three days following the initial seven days. If a woman delivered a baby girl the corresponding periods were fourteen days and sixty-six days respectively (Leviticus 12:1-5). Detailed procedures of purification following child birth may be holy, but this mathematical equation of life was so dry and wooden and so removed from actual life that it could not be self-enforcing generation after generation.

In the post-exilic Judea one had to buy back the first son by paying the priest several shekels of silver. This was no small amount to average Jews even in times of prosperity. Many similar provisions in the Law were highly idealistic and were easier to conceive than to implement or enforce. They were likely to produce results quite contrary to the intent and purpose of the writers.

The post-exilic Jews might have learned much of their medical knowledge from the Babylonians and even from the Greeks. Significant was the fact that the dietary and sanitary laws were made an integral part of the post-exilic beliefs and life in their relationship with God, and such medical knowledge was not to benefit just a few who could afford it but to actively promote the whole nation's and every Jew's health and well-being.

The Book of the Law was unique in the sense that it was not designed merely to maintain the status quo of peace and order in the society but also to actively plan and promote the social welfare, satisfy the wants, desires and needs of the Jews, and mold the moral perfection of the Jews.

The ritual, worship and sacrificial laws were the external symbols reminding the Jews of the need for moral perfection and were important to the writers who were members of the Levite family. The ritual and sacrificial religion in the post-exilic Judea recovered from the critical attack of the prophets, who invariably had portrayed God as the moral Being whose concern was righteousness of the Hebrews in adhering to His Law, not the temple feasts, solemn assemblies, various offerings, songs, and harps.

The writers felt that the exact conduct required in the rigid ritual, worship and sacrificial laws would mold the Jews to conduct precisely and exactly in all aspects of their lives as required by the Law, and would necessarily bind the Jews, from the High Priest to the average Jews, into a viable collective will. The writers, like the prophets, perceived God as the moral Being who was intangible and formless and would not require feasts and offerings, and so on. In this respect too, the writers did not discard any of the old ritual and sacrificial customs. The writers could add to or elaborate the old customs but did not feel they had any authority to abolish or nullify any portion of the old laws.

There are many layers of ritual and sacrificial laws in the book of Leviticus, and each layer of laws was written by a different generation of priests. No Jew was allowed to charge interest to fellow Jews but later the Temple became the only authorized bank, allowed to take the mortgage of persons, animals, houses or land, and charge the interest of twenty percent under the Levitical laws. A Jew, owing so much debt to the Temple, became a Temple slave but became free if he paid the Temple the money owed plus twenty percent over a number of years. If one built a house with money borrowed from the Temple he had to pay the Temple the money owed plus twenty percent. The interest of twenty percent is not an annual rate but the total amount charged over a number of years depending on the ability of the debtor to pay and could work out to the maximum benefit to the debtors.

In the post-exilic Judea, if a person turned to mediums and wizards he would be banished under the Levitical laws but was to be put to death under the Deuteronomical laws. Magicians and sorcerers were put to death under both Levitical and Deuteronomical laws. It was the priestly function to try a wife, suspected of adultery, by ordeal (Numbers 5:11-31). This was the only case of trial by ordeal specified in the Law, and it was a mild form of tribulation by forcing the suspected adulteress to drink "the water of bitterness," which perhaps was intended to induce miscarriage.

The priests were not to share in the inheritance of the land and were not to own the land but could possess the fields of the common land. Eventually the Levite priests came to hold all the choice land in Judea. In the post-exilic Judea there was no boundary between public matters and private affairs because one's disobedience to the Law invariably affected the lives of all Jews. All aspects of one's life were subject to the Law. If any priest approached the holy things while he was unclean through contact with the dead or one who masturbated or had nocturnal emissions or other unclean things, he was to be cut off from the priestly functions. A priest was not supposed to attend his wife's funeral, although he might attend funerals for his parents, his son, his daughter who might be either virgin or not, his brother or his virgin sister. If a man made love to a woman while she was menstruating both were to be banished.

Oppressive and reactionary though the examples cited may sound today, the writers believed such laws demanding moral perfection of the Jews were closer to the will of God in their jealous belief that the Law of God in its details had to be strictly observed, and refused any halfway measures or compromises.

Whether or not these "perfect" standards the ancient Jews subscribed to were oppressive or reactionary by today's standards is not important as a religious issue. Significant is the fact that the post-exilic Jews strove for those standards which they believed to be impeccable and perfect spiritually. It was the daring ambition of the writers to overturn the traditional Hebrew society and its easygoing customary values, to do away with little spirits, harness forces of the nature, and bring about an ideal and orderly Jewish society in which the needs and desires of the Jews were to be satisfied in the absence of political independence.

CHOSEN AND EXCLUSIVE

To break any specific provision of the Law was a "sin." It was more than a civil damage or a crime against any individual or the society to be disobedient to the will of God. The writers depict God excluding from his favor the unrighteous: Ham and his descendants were rejected from His favor when Ham saw his father Noah naked; Lot and his descendants became excluded when Lot had incestuous unions with his two daughters; and the stories go on down the line in the national saga.

Judaic exclusivism, proclaimed in the post-exilic Judea, became reflected in many ways. One of the reforms initiated by Ezra and Nehemiah was the proclamation to forbid mixed marriages of the Jewish men with foreign wives, and the stakes were personal to each family. If married, the Jewish men were asked to divorce foreign wives and put away the children of such mixed marriages.

Ezra was not a skeptic but an unshakable idealist who did not hesitate, out of his angry love of fellow Jews, to denounce his imperfect fellow Jews. He saw the straight future ahead for the Jews, and was free of doubt in making a choice between a destiny or the accompanying personal sufferings. He was enraged and saddened to learn about mixed marriages going on: "While Ezra prayed and made confession, weeping and casting himself down before the house of God, a great assembly of men, women and children gathered to him out of Israel; for the people wept bitterly" (Ezra 10:1). Many sons of the priests and Levites and even a son of the High Priest had married foreign wives.

Traditionally such a proclamation would not matter to the Jewish men who could easily reduce foreign wives to the level of concubines, and there were no distinctions between legitimate and illegitimate children in the pre-exilic Hebrew society. But a provision was meticulously incorporated into the Law: "No bastard shall enter the assembly of the Lord; even to the tenth generation, none of his descendants shall enter the Assembly of the Lord" (Deuteronomy 23:2). Here, "bastard" is not a child born out of wedlock but a child born out of the union between a Jewish father and a non-Jewish mother. Then, one was either born into Judaism or was denied any possibility for conversion to become a pure Jew.

It should be noted that the tribe of Judah did not or could not object to the proclamation in spite of the fact that their ancestors, including Kings David and Solomon, were descendants of such a mixed marriage (Genesis 38:2-4).

The proclamation, considered as indispensable to religious purity and survival and preservation of the post-exilic Jews as a people, was a reaction against the degenerate religious life of the pre-exilic Hebrew ancestors. The books of Kings and Chronicles suggest that many little gods were introduced into Palestine by foreign wives and concubines who prevailed upon the kings to build high places and hire priests and priestesses for such high places while ignoring the Temple and its priests.

Greater was the impact of the Proclamation on the Samaritans, the overwhelming majority of the Hebrews, excluded from God's chosen community: The Jewish minority was rejecting the majority of the Hebrews. The Samaritans, the poor Hebrews of the Northern Kingdom of Israel, allowed to remain in Israel by the Assyrians, had been intermarrying with other peoples who had moved there after the fall of Samaria in 722 B.C. Such mixed marriages were forced upon them because of external circumstances beyond their control. These Samaritans worshipped God and believed in the Law of Moses just as the Jews did.

The differences between the Jews and the Samaritans lay in the fact that the Jews had been intermarrying with the Canaanite natives in Palestine and the Samaritans had been intermarrying with the non-Canaanite peoples, brought in from outside of Palestine during the Assyrian rule. Furthermore, the Proclamation simply could not be implemented and enforced in Samaria because such mixed marriages had been going on for nearly three hundred years.

The post-exilic Jews rejected the offer of the Samaritans to help in rebuilding the Temple in Jerusalem and prohibited the Samaritans from the Temple worship, thus forcing the Samaritans to build their own Samaritan temple on Mt. Gerizim and sealing the division permanently. Ten northern Hebrew tribes were forever "cut off" from God's chosen community. For practical purposes Judaic exclusivism in the post-exilic Judea ended clannish tribal distinctions which used to mar the essential unity and discipline of the pre-exilic Hebrews as one people.

Whether such a policy of exclusion and the Jewish hatred and disdain for the Samaritans sprang more from historical and other considerations than from religious reasons is debatable. The Levite priesthood in the Kingdom of Judah and the non-Levite priesthood in the Kingdom of Israel gave a religious connotation to the post-exilic conflict between the Jews and the Samaritans.

It is a matter of conjecture how much the lofty and self-seeking considerations of the Levite family to monopolize priesthood played against higher motives to unite and discipline the post-exilic Jews according to the Law. One thing certain, however, was that the Levite family was not ready to share priesthood with the non-Levite priests from Samaria and found no cost too high to pay for a strict adherence to the Law.

The measure of exclusion was equally applicable to the Jews. Any Jew who ate the fat of an animal offered to God, or drank blood of a fowl or an animal in his house was to be banished from among his people. Anyone who killed an ox or a lamb or a goat but did not offer to the Lord was to be also banished. A number of minor offenses were placed under the penalty of "cut off," banishment.

The pre-exilic customs had no penalty of "cut off" for any offense. In the Middle East of the post-exilic period, where one could earn a livelihood and get protective mutual help solely because of his membership by birth in a tribe, it is not difficult to conjecture what that penalty of "cut off" meant to those excluded from their tribes. No Jew would talk to the excluded, or help the excluded in any way or even come near him. Once excluded one is no longer a Jew or a person.

The necessary corollary of exclusivism was ethnocentrism or the concept of the chosen people. The concept is not unique to the Jews. Nearly all the ancient Middle Eastern tribal nations had a national god for each nation. Each national god was to favor specifically that tribal nation and people.

Nevertheless, remarkable was the fact that the concept of the chosen people survived the crushing defeats in wars and humiliation in exile. Other ancient Middle Eastern peoples exalted their national god in victory and demoted the status of their god in defeat or replaced the national god with another ascending local god. God, however, was exalted in crushing defeats and humiliation, and came to be perceived for the first time in the history of Jews clearly as the perfect moral Being.

In the post-exilic Judea the tribe of Levi emerged as the chosen or elite of the chosen people. The writers, who were the Levite priests and scribes, used to share the civic leadership in Babylonia. Were they narrowly self-seeking to establish the Levite theocracy in the post-exilic Judea? Whatever the answer might be, in rude fact they were not ready to turn over political, civic or any other leadership to the Davidic family, who were descendants of the mixed marriages, or to restore the primacy of the Davidic family in the post-exilic Judea, much less to reestablish the Davidic line as the royal house.

The writers stated:

> When you come to the land which the Lord your God gives you, you possess it and dwell in it, and they say, 'I will set a king over me, like all the nations that are around me'; you may indeed set as king over you him whom the lord your God will choose. One from among your brethren you shall set as king over you; you may not put a foreigner over you, who is not your brother. Only he must not multiply horses for himself or cause the people to return to Egypt in order to multiply horses, since the Lord has said to you, 'You shall never return that way again.' And he shall not multiply wives for himself, lest his heart turn away; nor shall he greatly multiply for himself silver and gold.
>
> (Deuteronomy 17:14-17.)

The statement on the monarchical system is the briefest possible as a matter of rebuke to the past Hebrew kings rather than a future concern.

The writers envisioned that the priestly family of Levi should ideally be the depositories and administrators of the

Will of God. Of the chosen race the Levites became God's most favored. Kohath, a son of Levi, had four sons. Amram, a son of Kohath, "took to wife Jochebed his father's sister and she bore him Aaron and Moses." (Exodus 6:20.) Priesthood was reserved for Aaron and his descendants. Moses married foreign women, and his descendants ceased to be favored.

Of the Levites, the Kohathites became favored next to the descendants of Aaron, and the rest of Levites were slightly more favored than other non-Levite Jews.

For the first time in the history of the Hebrews the Levite priests and scribes emerged as the leaders of the Jews. When Ezra and Governor Nehemiah invoked the Great Synagogue or the Great Assembly to canonize the Book of the Law, about half of more than eighty leaders were the Levite priests and scribes.

An organizational network also emerged to insure a highly disciplined post-exilic life among all the Jews. The mandate of a tight regimentation was also attributed to Moses himself. The writers portray Jethro, Moses' father-in-law, suggesting that Moses, burdened with duties, delegate the judicial duties:

> Moreover choose able men from all the people, such as fear God, men who are trustworthy and who hate a bribe; and place such men over the people as rulers of thousands, of hundreds, of fifties, and of tens. And let them judge the people at all times; every great matter they shall bring to you [Moses], but any small matter they shall decide themselves; so it will be easier for you, and they will bear the burden with you.
>
> (Exodus 18:21-22.)

Needless to say, this organizational system was utilized by the Hebrew kings for their army but was never a framework of a judicial system placing one judge over every ten Hebrews in the pre-exilic Hebrew society.

In the villages and towns of Judea sprang up synagogues where priests and scribes conducted prayer meetings and taught the multitudes of the Jews about the Law. Such synagogues became centers of the Jewish religious and civic autonomy. Any cooperative work such as tilling one's field, building one's house, helping the needy, and other works were arranged at the synagogue one belonged to. Scribes and priests began replacing the patriarchs as knowledgeable arbitrators who persuaded the disputing parties to resolve the differences according to the Law.

The Book of the Law was more a tool of religious education in the period of Ezra and Nehemiah. Aside from the religious, social and educational functions performed, synagogues had an intrinsic value as a constant reminder to the Jews of every generation of the years of the Hebrew exile in Babylonia. The daily life of each Jew centered around his synagogue. "Death" and "cut off" penalties, stipulated in the Law, were reminders in the strongest possible terms to the Jews how seriously the Law had to be taken.

In order to remind the Jews of their duties to adhere to the Law Governor Nehemiah grumbled and complained that the Jewish nobles and officials were charging interest to fellow Jews and were amassing land while he was trying to keep his government expenses to the bare minimum without using up even his food allowance of Governor, and his servants labored to share the burden of rebuilding the wall of Jerusalem so that the burdens upon the people might not be heavy. Similarly Ezra appealed to the people for a strict adherence to the Law by grumbling and complaining. Such quality of leadership was also attributed to Moses and even to God.

The Spirit of the Law was quite different from its letter in the sense that one who committed a sin deserving death or banishment but atoned and was saved felt that he was mercifully given a new life as a Jew, and was all the more grateful to God. Even the average non-Levite Jews believed themselves part of a unique relationship superior to the Samaritans and other peoples. Rebellious non-conformists were brought in line under the threat of death and cut-off. The only choice for the Jews was to obey the Law and be a part of God's chosen community, or to be excluded.

Each synagogue in this period was concerned with the health, need and security of each member. The penalties of death and banishment seemed to the Jews a reminder of sins committed by the Samaritans and the shortcomings of their ancestors rather than constant guilt trips imposed upon them, and produced the opposite effect of encouraging the Jews to pridefully participate in the glorious future potentiality of the chosen community and regain self-respect as the pure Jews. In short, the penalties of death and cut-off in the Book of the Law as an educational tool worked more as flattery than as threats.

LEVITE ELITISM

Another corollary of Judaic Exclusivism was the Levite elitism shrouded in the aura of sanctity and secrecy.

The Jews, for the first time, came to have a truly centralized priesthood, and the priests and scribes gained the primacy and prestige as they were leaders of the Temple and synagogues in the post-exilic Judea. The writers portrayed God as commanding the Jews that "you shall be to me a kingdom of priests and a holy nation." (Exodus 19:6.) The Prophet and priest Ezekiel in Babylon preached: "They [the Levite priests] shall teach my [God's] people the difference between the holy and the common, and show them how to distinguish between the unclean and the clean. In a controversy they shall act as judges, and they shall judge it according to my [God's] judgments." (Ezekiel 44:23f.)

The Levite members had many more leadership positions open to them in the synagogues springing up in the post-exilic period than in the pre-exilic days when only one Temple for one God necessarily limited the number of positions for Levite priests and temple assistants. In the post-exilic Judea, in order to oversee the Temple and synagogues which were local administrative and judicial offices as well, the hereditary office of the High Priest became strengthened.

What the writers envisioned came to be realized: that is, a theocracy, a Government by God, who is the sole sovereign and whose will is the Law. Although the nominal overlordship belonged to the Persian King and his appointed satrap in Judea, actual leadership of the Jews came gradually into the hands of the Levite priests and scribes with the High Priest at the top of religious and civic autonomy. The High Priest was to have no army or chariots, but it did not matter because the priests and scribes kept inspiring and swaying the Jews to share the glorious future God had in store for the righteous Jews rather than enforcing the Law; accordingly, the Jews became a people solely motivated by religion. The High Priest functioned as if he were the priest-king of the Jews, representing the Jews to other nations.

The High Priest and priests were subject to the Law. The Law is better than personal caprice, and besides the Law is the will of God. The writers portrayed all the heroes of the Biblical dramas, Moses and Kings David and Solomon, without flattery. Of course their personal shortcomings and their disregard of the Law came about when the Law was not fully spelled out in writing. The assumption was that all men and all human institutions are fallible but holy institutions of the Law and the Levite theocracy cannot fail.

The Law, codified in minute details, pointed to the health and welfare of the Jews, and would leave no room for the High Priest and priests to disregard the Law as the past Hebrew kings did. The writers foresaw that the watertight

Law was all that the Jews needed to guide their lives: The Law specified what was right and proper and what was wrong. None of the Jews could possibly disagree on what was right or what was wrong, which the Law stipulated. In short there could not be conflict between classes, between the tribes or between the priestly family and the non-priestly families, as would happen under man-made laws. The priests as well as non-priests were answerable to God under the Law.

The writers were under an illusion as far as their assumptions were concerned. Firstly, they thought they were merely interpreting and filling up the loopholes found in the pre-exilic Hebrew customs. In the process they were making new laws.

Secondly, there is no law which does not require interpretation. An interpretation invites further interpretation and such is the nature of every law, divine or human.

Thirdly, the law and a theocracy or the centralized priesthood may be holy; nonetheless, they are human institutions, and become operationally only as good as the people who administer them. All men are fallible, and all institutions, divine or human, administered by fallible men, are equally fallible: Decay besets all institutions and the Law and the Levite theocracy are no exceptions.

The writers were a unique breed of people, whose spiritual perspective was firmly set on love of the fellow Jews. They were ready to trade their secure life in Babylon for a hazardous trip to home and an uncertain life in Judea. For them it was inconceivable for any class or tribe or family or occupational group to make an interpretation of the holy Law to the advantage of one group. Each Jew had a life only because he participated in the present and future destiny of God's chosen community, and is united to his fellow Jews by the holy blood tie and by the Law of God: Indeed, the pure Jewishness is where a Jew's life begins and where his life ends; and the pure Jewishness is the only thing worth living for. The writers did not see why any Jew would dare to tamper with such perfect Law.

The writers were not fanatical nationalists who were blind about everything but the good of the Jews as a whole. On the contrary they fully recognized the inevitable conflict of interests between the individual good and the good of the whole. Exempt from military service even in times of national crisis was the man who built a new house but did not dedicate it, the man who betrothed a wife but did not live as a husband and wife, and the fainthearted. The writers accentuated the well-being of individual Jews as well as collective purposes.

The writers, like Ezra and Ezekiel, were forceful and willful leaders who had no doubts whatever that the Law, which was in fact their planning and legislation, would bring about a faultless harmony among the Jews. The willfulness, forcefulness and righteousness of God and Moses, as portrayed in the Old Testament, represented the urge and the desire of the writers to model themselves upon such a perfect quality of leadership. They were superimposing their idealized quality of leadership upon that of God and Moses. The Law, which the writers planned, edited and codified, was sealed under authority and credulity of Moses.

The writers did not see any necessity for further interpretations of the Law or amendments. They did not see any need for any criticism or dissension. The writers who had owed their spiritual perspective to the prophets saw no further use for prophets in the post-exilic Judea: A future prophet is "a dreamer of dreams" who ought to be put to death and is "an evil" to be purged. (Deuteronomy 13:1-5.) God promised to raise up in the post-exilic Judea just one more prophet, who was like Moses (Deuteronomy 18:15-22), and that one more prophet was perhaps none other than Ezra himself.

The earnest desire and the absolute dedication of the writers to build a perfect future for the Jews necessarily involved impatience of the writers with those Jews who would not uphold the Law wholeheartedly. Ezra was respected and feared, but perhaps he was not held dearly by his contemporary Jews. The Prophet Jeremiah denounced "the false pen of scribes." (Jeremiah 8:8.)

The writers were extremely jealous and demanded that Jews of all succeeding generations accept the Law as written, and without further interpretations or amendments. The writers cited Moses as saying: "You shall not add to the word which I [Moses] command you, nor take from it; that you may keep the commandments of the Lord your God which I [Moses] command you." (Deuteronomy 4:2.)

The writers who had made all the moral choices, in codifying the Law, precluded every Jew from making further choices. In other words the writers exercised free will but left little room for average Jews to exercise any free will. There are no moral choices or ethical standards apart from or outside of the Law. In the pre-exilic days the customs based on consensus of the people left a wide area of activities in which each pre-exilic Hebrew could make moral choices and determine what was his own good and the good of the Hebrews.

The writers set aside the rule of consensus which had prevailed in the pre-exilic Hebrew society and majority rule as detrimental to the good of the Jews as in the days of Moses. At one point Moses planned to move into the promised land of Canaan. God instructed Moses to send out twelve spies to explore the land of Canaan. Ten pessimistic spies reported back to Moses with the tales of giants and strong enemies. Moses listened to faithless and pessimistic spies rather than to God. Within sight of the destination, the promised land, the ancient Hebrews were about to rebel against Moses; consequently, the ancient Hebrews encountered staggering defeats at the hands of the Amelekites, and the goal of moving into Canaan was further postponed.

The writers clearly perceived the moral problems involved in the life of their ancestors under the pre-exilic customs based on consensus. There was the difficult problem of determining what was right or wrong and just or unjust. Should a man help a fugitive slave or slave girl hide or return the slave to the harsh owner for flogging and mistreatment, or sell the fugitive slave to one who would be more generous and get paid as well? If a concubine ran away and was later caught should the master or husband cut off her ears? If each Jew was allowed to determine right or wrong for himself and just or unjust, his choices might be more bungling than being right or just.

There was further difficulty: whether right or wrong should be determined in the light of one's own pleasure, happiness, survival or any other criteria. What was right in a hardy nomadic life might not be right in a settled agricultural village life. In a settled agricultural life the eldest son succeeded the father who passed away; however, in a hardy nomadic life the most decisive of the sons demanded that the dying father bless him as the successor.

The writers talked about the nature and will of God in two totally contradictory ways: the way their ancestors and the multitudes of the post-exilic Jews observed the attributes of God and the way the writers themselves perceived them. The writers were not inventing the religious concepts but were recounting the attributes of God in the way the average Jews used to believe. A reader of the Bible may readily find how well the writers were aware of this contradiction and made the very best use of it.

The writers stuck to the propositions that objective standards of Jewish conduct should not be left to chance or individual judgments as in the pre-exilic Hebrew society, that the details of the Law had to be spelled out in full, and that no Jew, not even knowledgeable Jews, should be allowed to determine right or wrong; moreover, the writers incorporated the perception of their ancestors and the multitudes of the post-exilic Jews that whatever activities were pleasing to God or the gods were right and just.

It was, however, one thing to say, "Listen to God," and one would know the Law, the will of God, and it was another matter how one could listen to and know the will of God. Even the post-exilic average Jews raised the same millennium-old question of how one could communicate with God and find out his will as Moses did.

The only thing the writers believed was the Law as the core of Judaism, and they had nothing to do with the supernatural. The writers knew God as the formless sole cause and the source of moral righteousness, but at the same time reinforced the totally contradictory ancient perception of God as a monstrously stern uncle who, like little gods, kept inflicting upon the unrighteous terrible punishments and even acted freakish from time to time.

The writers, like prophets, perceived that rituals and offerings would not please God but the writers, unlike prophets, stipulated elaborate laws on priestly functions and conduct, and the strict rules of Temple worship and offerings to keep reminding the multitudes of the Jews of the divine mandate to obey the Law.

The writers threw an aura of sanctity and secrecy over the gulf between two contradictory perceptions of God. They were meticulously careful to include specific laws on the Temple structure. The High Priest was permitted to enter the Holy of Holies, i.e. the innermost court of the Temple, only once a year, on the Day of Atonement (or Yom Kippur). No man, not even priests, was allowed to remain inside the Temple when the High Priest "entered to make atonement in the holy place until he comes out and had made atonement for himself and his house and for all the Assembly of Israel." (Leviticus 16:17.)

The Kohathites, who were God's favored next to Aaron

and his descendants, were to carry on their shoulders but were not to "touch the holy things, lest they die," and were not allowed to "look upon the holy things even for a moment, lest they die." (Numbers 4:15, 20.) Any human curiosity seeking to take a glimpse of the animated God by breaching the aura of sanctity and secrecy was subject to death which the wrathful God personally inflicted.

So the writers narrated:

> Thus the Lord used to speak to Moses face to face as a man speaks to his friend [but the Lord said to Moses], "You cannot see my face: for man shall not see me and live."
>
> [God further said to Moses:]
> Behold, there is a place by me where you shall stand upon the rock; and while my glory passes by I will put you in a cleft of the rock, and I will cover you with my hand until I have passed by; then I will take away my hand, you shall see my back; but my face shall not be seen."
>
> (Exodus 33:11, 20-23)

Such were the Old Testament stories in which God did not allow even the priests and people to come near Mt. Sinai when God gave Moses the Decalogue there. The reason for such an aura of sanctity and secrecy was clearly not meant to deceive the average Jews but to let the average Jews perceive God and His Law as the average Jews understood. The writers realized that there was hardly a meeting of minds between them and the average Jews in understanding religion and the Law of God: The truth would perplex, confuse, and throw the multitudes, who would not know how to deal with the intricate perceptions of the writers. Whatever other reasons there might have been, the aura of sanctity and secrecy strengthened the Levite members as the vanguard of the Law.

The Levite members as the vanguard of God's Law served the post-exilic Jewish society well. The moral integrity of Ezra and Nehemiah insured their effectiveness in implementing the new Jewish order they had envisioned. The restoration of city walls to guard the Jews against neighboring enemies, the cancellation of debts owed by the poor Jews, a prohibition of the interest charges which tended to enslave the impoverished Jews, a strict observance of the Sabbath, the Temple worship services, a dismantling of the tribal and patriarchal family system, prayer meetings and educational sessions at synagogues enhanced the self-respect of the post-exilic Jews and turned the Jews into a cohesive religious people, aware of their unity, destiny, and common values.

The initial zeal, spirit, and enthusiasm of reform permeated through the post-exilic Jewish life, established a new Jewish society, and turned the loss of political independence into a civic and religious autonomy. In this sense the Law, far from being ideally drafted and codified, was administered in the way quite beneficial to the welfare of the Jews.

The Book of the Law is highly ethical and spiritual but that is not its uniqueness; the unparalleled originality and uniqueness of the Book of the Law, however, lie in the Spirit of the Law, which the writers kept underscoring.

CHAPTER IV

Judaic Practices Under Changing Circumstances

JUDAISM UNDER GREEK RULE

The Jews enjoyed a relatively peaceful life as a cohesive religious people for about seventy years after the inception of post-exilic religious reform until 332 B.C., when Alexander the Great crushed the Persian Empire and became the new master of Judea as well. His death followed shortly; consequently, his Macedonian generals struggled for bigger shares of the spoils, and eventually divided the vast empire among themselves.

Ptolemy established a Greek dynasty in Egypt and Seleucus another Greek dynasty in Syria, Mesopotamia and Persia. Judea again became a buffer state, and came initially under the rule of Ptolemy, who considered Judea a part of Egypt, but later came under the rule of the Seleucid king, who considered Judea a part of Syria.

The Jews were used to the change of overlords and it did not matter to them whether the armies of Ptolemy or Seleucus took control of Judea. Although the Ptolemy dynasty, unlike Persians, preferred the Macedonian Greeks to administer its domains of Egypt and Judea, the Greeks did not disturb the civic and religious autonomy of the Jews.

The Jews were allowed to move around freely. Many Jews moved to Alexandria and Memphis in Egypt and Antioch in Syria and were granted full Greek citizenship. Alexandria became the most prosperous metropolis, the commercial port city linking Greece and Egypt, and the religious and cultural center in the known Greek world. The growth of opportunities for commerce by land and sea brought innumerable Jews to major port cities on the shores of the Mediterranean Sea, the Greek Islands and the Black Sea. Gradual intermingling of various peoples in major cities of the Greek domains in Europe, Egypt, Syria, Mesopotamia, India and Africa, weakened the intimate tie one felt about his city-state or tribal nation.

The Greeks showed little prejudice against any people within the domains. The Greeks themselves were never one people but made up of one hundred or more local tribes or clans and city-states, each strongly independent. The Athenian Greeks would tolerate Jews readily as they would the Macedonian or Spartan Greeks and so on. The Greeks had so many dialects that Attic Greek was the secondary language to most Greeks just as it was to the Jews. At the same time the Greeks dealt with the Jews or Egyptians at arm's length, did not care to learn the native languages or intermarry with the Jews or the Egyptians. The standoffish attitude of the Greeks minimized the friction between the Jews and the Greeks.

In order to engage in prosperous commerce one had to learn Attic Greek. With Attic Greek one could communicate in all major cities in the known world. Being able to speak Attic Greek represented one's status as a man of wealth and commerce or knowledge. Inevitably too the Jews came to take Greek names, read Greek literature, and adopt Greek architecture, dress fashions, and even sports. The House of

Tobias became the most wealthy Jewish family by engaging in the monopolized export business of supplying the Greeks in Egypt with olive oil, honey, dates and figs. The Tobiases mingled with the Greek royal family members, officials and trading partners in Egypt and favored Hellenization of the Jews.

The young Jews were eager to adopt everything Greek. Naked Jewish, Greek and other gymnasts played Greek sports together in a stadium, and the Jewish gymnasts were willing to go through the painful surgical process of removing the marks of circumcision.

The Greek religion itself did not pose a threat to Judaism. The Greeks, like the Egyptians, the Assyrians and the Babylonians, believed in numerous divinities having human forms and feelings. Each of the little Greek gods controlled his domain of nature: Zeus was the chief of gods and men, his wife Hera, the queen of heaven, and so on. Little spirits were everywhere, in one's house, kitchen, and every room. Every man was the priest for his household gods.

The Greeks did not have the priestly class as such, and the Greek religion lacked a canon. Therefore, a Greek could readily create or invent a god by stretch of fancy, poetic imagination or philosophical notion: The god of wine was worshipped in a ritual of intoxication; the god of purity in the ascetic fashion by abstaining from sex and meat eating; and so on. The Greek rulers in Egypt pleasantly discovered that the Egyptian subjects considered them as gods and believed in bodily resurrection and the afterlife of the Greek rulers in Egypt.

The Greeks, who had lacked religious canons, had no reason to reject the Egyptian religious concepts so beneficial to the rulers. The mystic Egyptian religious notions began reshaping Greek religious beliefs. The Egyptians considered the Greek rulers "gods" even while living. The Greeks began identifying Aman-Ra, the chief Egyptian deity of the sun, with Zeus, the chief Greek deity, and considering great statesmen and philosophers "gods" while living. Everyone became a little god after death. Some became maleficent spirits who, like the ghosts of modern soap operas, acted mean to living relatives for a poor funeral service, offerings, or other reasons.

In general the Greek intellectuals were religious skeptics. The Greek leaning toward philosophical speculation came about because of their skeptical attitude toward religion. Although the Levite priests and scribes of this period lacked the initial zeal and enthusiasm of the post-exilic religious reform, there were no reasons for them to be attracted to the Greek little gods, which appeared to them ancient and primitive.

Many of the Levite priests and scribes, however, came heavily under the influence of Greek philosophy. High Priest Onias III was a moderate, who did not object to Hellenization as such. Furthermore, his family members were intermarrying with the Tobias family. The Egyptians, the Assyrians, the Babylonians or the Persians did not have anything like Greek philosophy which could challenge the Jewish beliefs. With the zeal and enthusiasm of the Levitical vanguard evaporating, the Law itself had to stand on its own merits and was to take on the challenge from Greek philosophy.

Of all little gods Greek philosophy was the mightiest of them all. The founders of both Judaism and various Greek philosophical schools shared the understanding of natural phenomena in a fundamentally similar way; indeed Judaism was more legal, with its philosophical and educational principles by rejecting animated gods and primitive religious beliefs, than religious beliefs in an animated God or gods or their attributes. The writers warned the Jews: "And beware lest you lift up your eyes to heaven, and when you see the sun and the moon and the stars, all the host of heaven, you be drawn away and worship them, things which the Lord your God had alloted to all the peoples under the whole heaven." (Deuteronomy 4:19).

The Greeks too came to observe certain regularity in ever-changing natural phenomena: The sun and stars were not gods but balls of fire; elements of air, water and heat, not little gods, cause changes in natural phenomena; and so on. In essence both the Jews and the Greeks were no longer attributing ever-occurring change in natural phenomena to little spirits or demons: in the parlance of today's language, both the Jews and the Greeks came to be scientifically oriented almost at the same period in history. But their similarities end there.

The Greeks boldly attempted explanations of natural processes and events by collecting scientific data and applying the precise scientific method. On the other hand, the writers, realizing how little they knew, left the scientific exploration of natural phenomena to later Jewish generations, and incorporated into the Levitical laws of sanitation and diet what they knew at the time.

The Greeks observed the material world, and raised the question of the irreducible component of matter, atoms. They kept conceptualizing their scientific findings, either false or true, and applied the precise method to find out even the ultimate values of one's life and one's ideal relation to the Greek city-state. The Greeks believed that rational and scientific inquiry into such ultimate values was the realm of wisdom or knowledge, and came to identify knowledge as the highest virtue of man.

In order to acquire knowledge about the ultimate meaning of life some Greek philosophers urged their followers to refrain from sensual pleasures, but others advocated that the ultimate value of life is to achieve the maximum amount of sensual pleasure and avoid pain and anxiety.

Some Greeks thought knowledge was innate in the soul of each man and all one had to do was to think and find out what knowledge was, but others thought one could find knowledge by generalizing experience.

Some Greeks thought all men were unequal by nature:

true ideas could be acquired by one or a selective few, like the philosopher-king, who had to rule the multitudes who strive only for sensual pleasures. However, others thought reason was a law for all men, not just one philosopher-king or the wise few.

Some Greeks thought that each individual had to make decisions for himself and that there were no such things as an objective knowledge of the ultimate values; therefore, one had to become indifferent to family, marriage, law, citizenship, state, social classes and all social institutions as artificial and useless. Some Greeks thought law was an instrument of the powerful to rule the weak, but others thought morality was a gimmick of the weak to place limitations on the strong.

Some Greeks thought man was the measure of all things and others thought material or money was the measure of all things.

Some Greeks thought every idea dichotomizing extreme black and white was nothing more than a half-truth and proposed the golden rule of the middle of the road.

Some Greeks believed in the need for a universal brotherhood of men as it became clear that the Greeks, consisting of over one hundred tribes, clans and city states, had to learn to live together somehow and intermingling of various peoples in every city necessitated that need. But to state the need of the people is one thing, and the willingness or proper conduct is another.

Some Greeks finally gave up on the puzzling questions of the ultimate values, and found solace in the belief that one should not try to know or judge. Greeks discussed the class division and struggle between the haves and the have-nots, the merits and demerits of intellectual aristocracy, communism for the aristocrats, the need for state religion to frighten men away from jealousy, acquisitiveness and erotic nature, the Greek ideas of heaven, hell and purgatory, and the need for breeding of pedigreed men, and so on.

In general the Greek approach to the ultimate values of life was the love of knowledge for the sake of reasoning and speculative contemplation, and even the idea of universal brotherhood lacked specific contexts aside from reason, fancy, and logic. Their moral and ethical values were highly logical, reasonable, and rhetorical but not necessarily realistic. Each Greek philosophical school presented the argument in the most rational and logical consistency; ironically too, each philosophical school arrived at ultimate values quite different from, if not diametically opposed to, one another.

It is not difficult to visualize what a sharp contrast the Greek philosophy of extreme diversity presented to the aristocratic Levite priests and scribes of single-minded devotion. To begin with, the Law did not represent love of knowledge but fragmentary knowledge of love of the fellow Jews, proper Jewish conduct, righteousness, prejudices, and even hate with specific meanings found in the religious interpretation of the history and customs of the pre-exilic Hebrews.

In the Book of the Law the writers listed specific provisions pertaining to specific conduct reflecting love of the fellow Jews, love of the Jewish society and homeland, but also the rights of individuals which could not be yielded to the good of the whole even in crisis, a relative equality of wealth but not necessarily equality as such, equal application of the Law to all men but with certain biases against foreigners, and so on. The writers, unlike the Greek philosophers, were not trapped into the fallacy of applying a scientific approach to define the Jewish destiny, to define the ultimate values of life or to fit the ultimate values into systematic theories.

The Law had two dimensions: The letter and the Spirit. The letter of the Law, listing innumerable specific righteous actions, were far from being rational, but were logically inconsistent and even freakish, as mentioned in the preceding chapters, and will be again discussed in the ensuing chapters. For now it suffices to state that the letters of the Law went far beyond the limited visions and needs of the post-exilic Jews living in a relatively simple society.

The letter of the Law prescribed in detail what should be, rather than what were, the needs and desires of the post-exilic Jews. The Law, a pervasive religious medium, set the rules of precise conduct and regulated every aspect of individual relationship with fellow Jews, the Jewish society and the Temple.

The Law was man-made but not even well systematized, as one layer of the Law logically contradicted another layer and yet the Law was designed to plan a well-ordered Jewish society. Nonetheless, the well-ordered society is not necessarily a happy and harmoneous society: It is the characteristic of the dehumanization process to reduce all human relationships to precise legal relationships and exact conduct. The Law leaves no room for individuals to make choices, moral or otherwise.

Abuses by legal experts can creep into any law; likewise, the Law leaves the door wide open to potential abuses. It is one thing to state that the Law is divine and must be obeyed and another matter to say that only the Levite priests and scribes know the Law better, and accordingly must administer the Law, because the Law can be abused more by those who know and administer it than by those who do not know.

Furthermore, the laxity of morality on the part of the leaders matters because not only the livelihood and well-being but also the morality of the multitudes are largely dictated by what the leaders uphold or disregard: the leaders can uphold or set aside rights which the Law guaranteed to the multitudes. In the post-exilic Judea there were no longer tribal chiefs and patriarchs who collectively could pose as a pressure group which the High Priest had to reckon with.

Since the law demanded unquestioning submission there was no room left for prophets to rise and stand against the High Priest, who was anointed of God.

The multitudes of Jews envied the free-wheeling way of Greek thinking and their uninhibited spontaneous freedom. The Greeks never developed a system of law although they demonstrated their ingenuity in politics, philosophy, literature, sculpture, painting, and architecture. The Greek system of justice was carried out just like democratic politics, when the jury of 1001 or 501 men listened to the speeches delivered by the parties involved in a case in a market place or other large square and cast ballots to render a decision. This kind of popular jury system was very much susceptible to caprice and a mob rule, and there were no professional judges or jurists. Each Greek, however, had ample room to make moral choices according to his own philosophical standard.

Compared with the Greeks the Jewish multitudes were living in a divine but regimented society. The Jews of this period believed specific conduct stipulated in the Law was absolute truth, and no Jew could base right or wrong on his own personal standard. Such concepts of absolute and objective truths and righteousness were strange to the Greeks.

For the Greeks there was nothing they could not doubt or question and engage in a subtle argument, whereas the Jews had to accept the letters of the Law as ultimate truths with no room for anyone to dispute or take with a grain of salt. The Greek and Jewish beliefs simply could not be adjusted to each other and reconciled because each belief stemmed from a viewpoint opposite to each other. It was a puzzling state of affairs for most Levite members and the Jewish multitudes. They did not realize where the differences between the Judaic way and the Greek way of thinking lay.

The clear distinction of the Jewish way lay in the original and unique Spirit of the Law. Whatever shortcomings the letters of the Law might contain, the Spirit of the Law was unique in the sense that it was to promote the pure Jewishness, a civic and religious autonomy and solidarity of the Jews as one people in the absence of political independence, restoration of the self-esteem of the Jews in defeats and humiliation, promotion of racial purity and purity of Jewish religion, moral fervor for social righteousness, longing for the homeland and the nomadic traditions and other aspects of national and social consciousness to preserve the Jews as a perpetual group. This Spirit was deeply embedded in the letters of the Law. Today, only retrospectively, it has become gradually clear that what was unique was that Spirit of the Law, the one and only God, which could not be systematized or reasoned away.

The letters of the law were rigid and excessive as the fervent zeal and ideals of the writers for religious reform wanted to make sure the succeeding generations of the Jews stayed right on the course to the envisioned destiny.

In general every ideal and zeal become mellowed down as generations change, and the initial rigid letter of the Law served to help the later generations of Jews see clearly the general sense of new direction where they should be heading. Whatever inferences we may make as to the practical merits of the letter of the Law, the Spirit of the Law was distinct, dynamic, unique, and powerful in guiding the Jews in times of crisis.

Nevertheless, rigidity and other weakness in the letter of the Law drove the multitudes of Jews and even many Levite members to the wholesale adoption of whatever was Greek, and they were called Hellenists. Uncompromisingly opposed to Hellenists were "pious persons" who were called Hasidim or Chassidim. These were the diehard older generations of the Jews who were bent on upholding the letter of the Law in exact detail at any cost, even death.

The Jews in the synagogues and the old and young in the same family were sharply divided and each group did not see room to give in or compromise. With unity as an important Judaic goal all the unorthodox ways of thinking or behaving were considered poisonous. Each believed he was more pious than others and labeled others either unrighteous fools or impious hypocrites. Nearly all dispersed Jews, living outside of Judea, nearly all the young male and female Jews, and even numerous Levite members including many priests, were

Hellenists, who were gaining strength as years went by and generations changed. Hasidim and the Law as the core of Judaism seemed destined to doom as a change in a few more generations of Jews was inevitably to come.

The Greeks did not have to do anything because Hasidim and Judaism were on the verge of extinction, but a notable Greek came to the aid of Hasidim and Judaism.

In 175 B.C. when Antiochus IV, also known as the mad man, became the new Greek King of Syria and came to rule Judea as a part of Syria, he discharged Onias III as High Priest and appointed Onias' brother, Jason, as the High Priest after Jason had pledged his utmost effort to Hellenize all the Jews. Jason was replaced as the High Priest by Menelaus who had outbribed and outpromised to Antiochus. Although Menelaus was a leader of radical Hellenists he was not even a Levite but a Benjaminite, and even moderate Hellenists could not accept him as High Priest under the Law.

The Greek perception of many gods necessarily entailed religious toleration of other gods. It could not possibly matter for any Greek to add God to the Greek pantheon. Politically, however, Antiochus had many enemies: the rising Romans, Ptolemies in Egypt, and Pergamum (today's western Turkey). Somehow he concluded that a Hellenized Judea would help him in safeguarding his domains against his enemies, but he did not realize what he was getting into when he decided to side with the Hellenistic Jews.

Antiochus was unwittingly being caught up in a religious struggle among divergent Jewish religious groups. Some Jews favored Hellenization but also the Greek dynasty in Egypt over that of Syria. Other Hellenistic Jews favored the Greek dynasty in Syria over that of Egypt. Some Jews preferred a moderate effort to Hellenize and others impatiently wished to Hellenize the Jews immediately. The situation was perhaps too complicated for a non-Jewish mind to grasp.

Once caught in a Jewish religius struggle Antiochus compounded his mistakes by supporting the Hellenists even more. In 168 B.C. Antiochus proclaimed that Judaism was illegal and decreed altars to Zeus, the chief deity of Greek gods, be set up in the Temple in Jerusalem and towns and villages, and had pigs sacrificed at the altars. He ordered the Jews to eat pork or face death, and Antiochus' mercenaries "took their pleasure with prostitutes and had intercourse with women in the sacred enclosures." (2 Maccabees 6:5.)

Mattathias Maccabeus, a Hasidic priest, refused to comply with Antiochus' demands and killed a pro-Antiochus Jew. In 167 B.C. the Hasidic Jews, under the leadership of Mattathias and his five sons, fled to the hills to launch a guerrilla war against Antiochus and his Syrian army. Once the bloody uprising broke out the nature of the struggle changed: It was no longer between two groups of the Jews but between the Jews and the Syrians. The Hellenistic Jews, except Menelaus and his family members, joined the Hasidic Jews in the rebellion against Antiochus and his Syrian army, and ended the distinction between Hellenists and Hasidim.

Judah, a son of Mattathias, proved himself a military genius who organized networks of an effective military intelligence system and made use of the hilly geographical features of Judea to the best advantage for the Jews. It was a miracle for a few thousand Jewish guerrillas, with no arms except short wooden handles topped by metal heads, slings, sickles and other farm tools, to beat the several times numerically stronger and well-armed Syrian armies. The Jews were making use of captured arms and getting stronger and Antiochus was committing more and more troops, and finally more than half of the armed forces of Syria (1 Maccabees 3:34).

The Jews achieved religious freedom in 164 B.C. but kept fighting until 142 when the Jews finally achieved political independence. Maccabees came to establish the Hasmonaean dynasty, taking its name after Hasmon, their ancestor.

JUDAISM DURING THE HASMONAEAN DYNASTY

The Jews, once again as a cohesive religious people, rededicated the Temple in 165 B.C. The long struggle for independence was over in 142.

In 141 the Great Assembly chose Simon, second son and the only surviving son of Mattathias, to be High Priest, General, and Governor. The title of King as such was avoided, and the two offices of High Priest and the secular ruler were made hereditary in Simon's family. However, Ptolemy, Simon's son-in-law, seditiously plotted to become a vassal Governor to the Greek King in Syria, and killed Simon and Simon's two sons, but failed because the Jews rallied around the only surviving son of Simon, who had escaped death.

John Hyrcanus, son of Simon, ruler from 134 to 104, expanded the country and brought Samaria and Idumaea (Edom) within the domain of Judea. As the war was over the Jews enjoyed peace and prosperity. Hyrcanus, however, was inclined to the Greek notions of extravagant ancestral tombs, luxurious court life and standing armies; moreover, he changed his sons' Jewish names to Greek names. The Levite scribes objected to the territorial expansion because of Jewish exclusivism under the Law which excluded from the chosen the Samaritans and the Edomites. They were aghast at the Hellenizing influence of Hyrcanus and the priests; accordingly, a factional split emerged. Scribes later were known as Pharisee-lawyers or "the Separated," and priests were known as Sadducees or "the Righteous."

Significantly a Greek religious notion crept into Judaism when the meaning of life was questioned in the minds of some Jews. The staggering number of Jews who died in the twenty-five year military struggle against the Greek kings of

Syria raised that age old question. Ironically too, the Jews, winning the religious war, willingly made an important concession to the Greco-Egyptian mysticism in the notion of the survival of soul after death.

Judaism had been singularly concerned with the adherence of the living Jews to the Law and was never concerned itself about the life beyond the grave. Of course the ancient pre-exilic Jews were familiar with the Egyptian notions of after-life for the righteous nobles beyond the grave and the bodily resurrection, but neither the pre-exilic Hebrew beliefs nor Judaism ever adopted such a religious concept of salvation beyond mortality. The Jews were very much like other ancient Semitic peoples of the Middle East who believed in melancholy souls, after death, hovering around shadowy places like Sheol where the burnt children were once offered to Baals. And as times went by after death, such souls evaporated into dimness, if not nothingness.

It was, perhaps, human for the surviving Jews to wish and hope that those Jews who died in the Maccabean war would also share the glorious future of peace. So wrote prophet Daniel: "And many of those who sleep in the dust of the earth shall awake, some to everlasting life, and some to shame and everlasting contempt." (Daniel 12:2.) Speculative debates followed about whether an everlasting life is merely survival of the soul after death, the bodily resurrection, or something else.

Except for the concept of an everlasting life the letters of the Law remained essentially same as before. But the way the Law was practiced and administered during this period was quite different from the practices of Judaism as carried out during the reform years of Ezra.

For the first time in the history of the Jews the priests came to exercise the political power of an independent nation. It was a true theocracy, i.e. a government by the High Priest-King claiming the divine sanction of God and the secular political sovereignty of a nation. In the post-exilic period Governor Nehemiah used to chastise the High Priest and his son who had married a foreign woman. Subsequently the position of the High Priest as the civic and religious leader of the Jews was gradually exalted, but he was never the political sovereign.

In Judea, an independent nation, the nature of various civic and religious organizations went through a drastic transformation. The High Priest-King was a secular ruler in addition to being an anointed representative of God. The Great Assembly and synagogues were no longer civic and religious organizations: The Great Assembly came to be called the Sanhedrin or a Supreme Council of State, composed of the priests and scribes, and was the supreme authority for all political and legal decisions.

The High Priest-King had no limits on his sovereign power over life and death of the Jews as his subjects so long as he had control over the Sanhedrin. It was during the reign of Hyrcanus that the King appointed the priests to important positions of Ambassadors, Generals and other political positions but assigned the scribes to then-minor functions of lawyers, judges and minor temple positions. The more Hyrcanus favored priests over scribes, the more bitter and intense the struggle between the two groups became.

The Sanhedrin was comprised of seventy-one members appointed by the High Priest-King. Under it were two intermediate Sanhedrins, the function of which was to act as the Court of Appeals and the intermediate administrative agencies. Each intermediate Sanhedrin consisted of 23 members. Each member of the Sanhedrin and the intermediate Sanhedrin had three clerks to assist him.

Sanhedrin members sat in a semi-circle, and in front of each member sat three of his clerks, making three lower semicircles. Junior clerks sat in the front semi-circle and the senior clerks took the seats right in front of the Sanhedrin members.

Beneath the Sanhedrins were village or town courts held in the village or town synagogues. Each village or town court consisted of three judges, also appointed by the High Priest-King. The mandate of the Law to replace patriarchs with appointed judges came to be realized (Deuteronomy 16:18-20).

The tenor of Judaism changed completely because of the way Judaism was practiced: Judaism was an educational tool of the Jewish civic and religious autonomy in the absence of political independence during the reform period of Ezra. Nevertheless, Judaism became an integral tool of the political and judicial power in the independent Judea of the Hasmonaean period. Priests had a taste of political power; religion and authority was a fatal combintion; and the Law and a theocracy as holy institutions proved to be an unqualified failure during the Hasmonaean period.

Judaism, a dynamic principle, became frozen to a rigid and static formula, with the Law as the tool of the State. The very intimacy and pervasiveness of the Jewish religious life, according to the Law which was designed to achieve the moral greatness of God, led to defects which were the reverse of its virtues: an intoleration of dissenting opinions, an overextended planning, suspicion and paranoia fostered by a theocracy, the autocratic rule by the High Priest-Kings, life and death struggle among priest-princes for power, fratricide, regicide, corruption, and the exploitation of the ignorant Jews by the priestly and legal experts in violation of the essence of the Hebrew tradition.

Political independence for the Jews was a curse in disguise: The Persian and Greek rules used to free the Jews from the complexity of combining political power and religion, vesting both authorities in the Levite family. The colors and practices of Judaism changed under the varying circumstances. Judaism in the independent Judea caused a maximum of friction among the Jews.

Opposed to the autocratic rules and Hellenizing influence of the priestly rulers were the Pharisee-lawyers, who were close to but were out of power. The rivalry and contest was waged by an out-group of Levites against the in-group of Levites. Alexander Jannaeus, High Priest-King from 103 to 76 B.C., turned out to be a ruthless oriental despot, who simply put to death thousands of Pharisees, and had the captured rebels crucified and the throats of their family members cut in front of the dying rebels while he himself held feasts with his concubines. Pharisees had their day of vengeance on the Sadducees when Salome Alexandra, the wife of Jannaeus and Queen of Judea from 76 to 67 B.C., appointed the leaders of the Pharisees as her advisers.

It became clear that, in a theocracy, one saying, "Let us go and serve other gods," and one criticizing the rule of the High Priest, could not be any different. The Law specifically stipulates that one has to put to death without pity his own brother, son, daughter or friend or any one, except one's parents, for the crime broadly defined.

Cursing a ruler used to be no big thing in the pre-exilic Palestine but the Law was clear that cursing a priest, who was also a ruler, became punishable by death. Furthermore, for contempt of the priests and the judges an offender was to be put to death (Deuteronomy 17:12f.). There were no penalties for taking a bribe (Deuteronomy 16:19). Nearly all ancient Middle Eastern laws were lenient toward government officials and judges for taking bribes.

It is not hard to surmise just what meanings numerous kinds of offerings had for the average Jews during this period. There were burnt offerings, cereal offerings, peace offerings, various sin offerings, guilt offerings, trespass offerings, free offerings, and votive offerings. Some of them were head taxes, inheritance taxes, sales taxes, criminal fines and medical fees payable to the priest-physician in addition to tithes. The Law did not require offerings if a man or a woman masturbated or made love according to the Law, or a woman had normal menstruation; however, in nearly all other cases one had to make an offering of one or another kind.

An average Jewish family of this period lived in a one- or two-room house, built of sunbaked clay-bricks on a limestone foundation. No area of privacy remained that an individual Jew could call his own–all watching and being watched. A combination of the rigid and extensive letter of the Law and a theocracy created incredible situations.

In all ancient nations in which the customary law was conceived as revealed by a god or gods, one who violated even the seemingly most trivial rule had to expect terrible consequences, for he broke the unitary law of a god, not a trivial rule. But such revealed laws were not meant to be enforced by secular enforcing agents but by the little gods who might judge or might overlook.

Every act and utterance of every Jew or group became subject to inquiry and scrutiny by priests and lawyers as public enforcing agents. Theocracy, as government and religion, was not only absolute in the exercise of force but unlimited in its application. The Law no longer represented educational tools, the sense of prideful participation in the Jewish life, and the feeling of renewed life after committing a sin and being forgiven by God.

In a theocracy there was no room for prophets, either Levite or non-Levite, who would raise a voice against the anointed representative of God. In order to enforce the unenforceable letter of the Law and to silence any criticism against the ruling priestly family which was engaged in constant court intrigues and power struggles, snooping and espionage became permeated with only a shadowy distinction between an adherence to the Law and the need for investigating everyone for political reasons. A combination of religion and political authority was stifling Judaism.

The struggle between the Sadducees and the Pharisee lawyers was waged in a subtle and cloaked manner. The Sanhedrin was the arena where members demonstrated how much each member knew the Law better. Lawyers had every reason to exaggerate the complexity and subtlety of the Law. Knowledge of legal technicalities represented power for the lawyers to challenge the priests.

The written letter of the Law was clear. Therefore, some claimed whoever knew more about the past oral interpretation of the Law were more pious people who knew more about the Law, the will of God. "Six days you shall labor, and do all your work; but the seventh day is a sabbath to the Lord your God; in it you shall not do any work. . . ." (Deuteronomy 5:13f.). The letter of the Law seemed to be clear enough, but Moses put to death one who collected sticks on a sabbath day. If one walked leisurely to his farm field on a sabbath day to see if everything was all right, was such a journey considered as a work? How far can one walk away from home according to the Law? Is feeding the cattle on a sabbath day work? Should building fire and cooking be considered work?

The Law demands accurate definitions and no definition can be accurate and "hairsplitting" enough because one or another interpretation determined one's life or death. Priests and lawyers of the Sanhedrin sat in a semi-circle and argued about the merits and demerits of each word and comma. In order to kill an unblemished bird, a priest had to slaughter it by hand in a certain precise way. Only a certain type of knife, honed to perfection, could be used, and the veins in the neck had to be cut precisely so that the bird might bleed properly, and so on.

Some notes were taken but the lawyers and the clerks memorized the seemingly brilliant arguments and interpretations of the Law. Whoever memorized more past oral arguments and decisions were naturally considered better lawyers and more pious persons. In turn these lawyers claimed such oral traditions to be authoritative just as the Law.

This dark period in the Jewish history brought about an important development of the Law. Scribes emerged as professional legal experts. Although most scribes were Levites, in the Book of the Law the function of scribes was never assigned to any particular family. Therefore, non-Levite laymen from wealthy and prominent families could become lawyers. These professional lawyers developed an authoritative interpretation of the Law purely as a matter of technical knowledge. Professional lawyers were bent on transforming the Sanhedrin into more a secular court rather than a strictly religious or theocratic organization.

With the emergence of a legal profession the Law gained its own life. It was the need of the Law itself to create accurate definitions, distinctions, further details, interpretations of each word and further interpretations of each interpretation, which in turn strengthened the legal profession against priestly functions. The legal profession developed an authoritative interpretation of the Law which in turn prompted the rapid growth of judicial customary law accompanied by specific decisions. In short, lawyers kept interpreting the existing laws and making new laws, and at the same time leaving the priests in ignorance of the rapid development of the Law.

One has to either memorize the oral traditions or remain in ignorance of the Law. Being a great lawyer depended on one's analytical mind and capacity to memorize among other things rather than on one's birthright or family lineage. The Sadducees gradually saw the picture and objected to the claim of the Pharisee-lawyers that the oral traditions were equally parts of the God's revelation and parts of the Law. The Sadducees accepted only the written Law as revelation of God.

In order to be loyal and faithful to God one has to know

the Law, the will of God. The implications were clear that a great lawyer was a pious person, and that priests who knew less about the oral traditions might be considered not only ignorant but also less pious Jews, if the proposition of lawyers were accepted. Such was the nature of controversy which accompanied this secular and religious question that it was impossible to settle until one party wrested the control away from the other or gave up a sum total of religious, political, judicial and civic leadership of the Jews, because, in a theocracy, the leadership was indivisible.

It was, however, during the reign of Queen Alexandra that the spiritual office of High Priest and the temporal office of Queen became vested in two different people. The Queen, under the Law, could not become High Priest because of her sex, and Hyracanus II, son of the Queen, was appointed High Priest. But when the Queen died in 67 B.C. Aristobulus II, a younger son of the Queen, forced Hyrcanus II to agree that Aristobulus become the king while Hyrcanus remained High Priest. Antipater, a half Jew known as an Idumaean, offered to help Hyrcanus regain the throne and raised rebel troops, and a civil war followed from 67 to 63 B.C.

Both factions, the priests and the lawyers, appealed to the Roman general Pompey the Great, who had just conquered Syria, for assistance. A theocracy was just rotten-ripe to fall apart: the Levite family was not capable of governing politically or reestablishing the religious consensus. Pompey allowed Aristobulus to remain King, who had bribed Pompey with a magnificent vine wrought in gold, while the latter was cautiously studying the situations in Judea.

In 63 B.C. when Hyrcanus, the High Priest, and the Pharisee-lawyers appealed to Pompey to abolish the kingship, the Roman legions ended the civil war and the political independence of Judea as well by capturing Jerusalem, and placing the Jews under the Roman rule. Aristobulus, his family, and his followers were taken as prisoners to Rome. At every turn in this tragic series of events leading to the loss of political independence thousands of the Jews died fighting.

JUDAISM UNDER ROMAN RULE

The Romans culturally were no different from the Greeks. They were so thoroughly Hellenized that, when the Romans absorbed the Mediterranean world and Asia held by the Greeks, the Romans treated the Hellenistic culture and civilization, already established by the Greeks, as if it were an extension of the indigenous Roman accomplishments. For the Jews too both the Pharisees and the Sadducees appealed to Pompey the Great to abolish the Hasmonaean dynasty altogether and restore peace to Judea, and appeared to be ready for accommodation with the new foreign master.

The Roman control of Judea in 63 B.C., however, did not restore peace to Judea or end the sufferings of the Jews. The causes were two-fold: the insensitive feuds among the Jewish leaders and the civil strife of their Roman master. In this period of the Roman Republic each independent Roman army general conquered territory, ruled the vanquished in a despotic way, and often had to negotiate, through his friends in the Senate in Rome, what rights should be granted over the occupied territories under his command. At times military commanders fought against one another.

Pompey the Great reorganized his conquered territories in Asia into four provinces. Judea, a part of the Roman province of Syria, was placed under the rule of the Roman Governor of Syria, and Pompey left Hyrcanus II, the High Priest, and Antipater, as the civil administrator, in charge of Judea.

In order to advance personal ambitions the Jewish leaders sought opportunities to befriend one or another Roman general. In 55 B.C. M. Licinius Crassus, a notorious Roman general who had become one of the richest in Rome by taking over confiscated properties and by means of usury, bargained with Caesar and Pompey and became Proconsul of Syria. He immediately looted the Temple in Jerusalem and in a subsequent revolt tens of thousands of Jews were sold into slavery. It was the practice of each Roman general to exploit the territory where he was Governor in order to run for the Senate in Rome or the Tribuneship and pay the necessary election expenses. Both Pompey and Crassus were the richest men in the Roman Republic.

In 40 B.C. Antigonus II, a son of the Hasmonaean dynasty, led a revolt for political independence but was crushed and beheaded. It was during these disturbances that the Roman Senate confirmed Herod the Great as King of Judea. The Jewish rebel guerrillas and even outright criminals established strongholds in the hilly countryside. The rumors spread like brushfires, and frantic Jews running up and down the hills exchanged with one another the vision of the end of the world in sight.

But a new era for the known world under the Roman rule and Judea was on the horizon. In Rome the republican government which was characterized by mob rule, a corrupt Senate, and independent-minded army generals, had been exhausted by civil wars, disorder, and fast changing fortunes of each social class. In 31 B.C. the Battle of Actium drove Mark Antony and Cleopatra to suicide. Gaius Octavianus, the winner of the Battle, came to control all the Roman armed forces, and as a capable statesman ushered in the era of the Roman Empire.

Octavianus, the master mind of power politics and administrative organization, tamed the energetic and restless armies, the original benefactor of the Empire. He rejected the army as an instrument of governing even in the conquered territories and undermined the Senate as the power center. The restoration of peace throughout the vast Roman Empire and the establishment of effective imperial administrative machinery and civil service in Rome and the provinces came to preserve the Empire by imposing the Roman peace and respect for law upon the Romans and the conquered peoples.

Octavianus, however, could not do much about the hopelessly primitive Roman religion, except having a Roman general, Marcus Vipsanius Agrippa, build the Pantheon, dedicated to all gods. The construction of the Pantheon, a circular temple employing a massive dome as its roof in the Campus Martius in Rome, was completed in 27 B.C. Romans had about thirty gods of their own and some of the Roman religious festivals had even the pristine orgiastic fertility rites and propitiating rites of the primitive agricultural Roman people. The concepts of immortal soul and afterlife were mundane and strange to the Romans. They were puzzled by the strange mystic theologies of the Greeks in Egypt.

It became, however, the Roman policy to accord the local gods of the territories, occupied by the Romans, the same honors as the original Roman gods. The Egyptians, the Jews, the Greeks, and other foreigners in Rome and in their native lands were free to worship their own gods and build the temples for their own gods.

The Egyptians elevated the new Roman prefects in Egypt and Rome to the status of gods in life as well as after death, just as the Egyptian pharaohs had been. Alexandria in Egypt remained as the religious and literal center of the known Roman world, whereas Rome became the new political center.

The average Romans found the Greco-Egyptian mysticism and religious rites rather attractive and Roman gods were neglected. The Pantheon was to house all gods and accord original Roman gods equal honors with foreign gods.

The Roman religion did not pose a threat to Judaism, but the Roman legal system, which was to challenge Judaism, was emerging from the embryonic stage of growth, and was decisively taking a new direction during this early period of the Roman Empire. The Romans, even when they were a small city-state, displayed a passion for law and order. The

Law of the Twelve Tables (452 B.C.) reduced their customs to a codified law, approved by their tribal leaders. As early as the second century B.C. the Romans built and dedicated Basilicas, i.e. secular court buildings near the Forum or the open-air marketplace. Basilicas were the first court building ever built for the sole purpose of dispensing justice in human history.

In Rome during the reign of Octavianus the architectural splendor of Basilicas was accompanied by the advanced legal system developed by professional lawyers. Lay juries disappeared, and legal procedure gained importance over abstract oration. The office of Praetor (366 B.C.), a trial judge of senatorial rank, was a judge of facts as well as of law. A second Praetor (240 B.C) administered justice in all cases involving foreigners, i.e., including cases between a Roman and a foreigner.

The Roman provincial magistrates governing the conquered lands patterned their edicts in commercial and important criminal cases after the edicts of the Praetor of the foreigners in Rome. Such edicts came to be known as the law of nations.

In Judea, Herod the Great, a son of Antipater, was the King of Judea, under the Roman rule, from 37 to 4 B.C. and proved to be an able administrator and diplomat. He had an Idumaean, a Jewess and a Samaritan among his ten wives in order to appease the country he ruled. He courted the pro-Herod Jewish aristocrats, known as the Herodians. He restored peace and order, and encouraged commerce and trade, while keeping the taxes to a minimum in bad harvest years. He commissioned the great public construction projects, such as open-air stadiums, fortresses, a great harbor at Caesarea to promote shipping trade, and above all the magnificent Herod's temple which took more than eighty years to complete.

The Herod's temple-palace was the imposing complex of

buildings built of cream-colored stones and marble, and had many courtyards and halls for judging and other functions. The dispersed and Hellenized Jews living outside of Judea and the Samaritans admired Herod. Nevertheless, the Jews in Judea hated him for his Hellenism and his assertion that he was a full-blooded Jew, descended from a noble Babylonian Jew, because the Jews had no doubts about his tainted blood of Edomite origin. The Romans considered Herod a Jew and the Jews considered him an Idumaean slave. Herod became suspicious of his mother-in-law, Alexandra, and everyone around him for political plots to overthrow him from the throne; accordingly, he put to death his wife, Mariamne, and three of his sons, and the aged Hyrcanus II, Mariamne's grandfather.

In 4 B.C., when the heartbroken Herod died, his kingdom was divided among his three sons. Archelaus, the eldest son of Herod and his Samaritan wife, inherited the land of Judea and Samaria, but could not put down the rebels. In 6 A.D. the Roman Emperor Octavianus exiled Archelaus to Gaul, and placed Judea and Samaria directly under control of a Roman procurator. But the Roman procurator too could not stamp out the rebels. Galilee was such a rebel stronghold where the Zealots established a network of guerrillas and brigands with concealed daggers. Inevitably the Jews living near such rebel hideouts often became the innocent victims killed on suspicion.

The nature of Roman administration of Judea and Samaria changed fast: Each independent Roman military general used to treat Judea as if it were his own personal estate to be exploited, but the Roman rule transformed into a remarkably efficient administration under Herod the Great and Roman procurators. But the Jews in the countryside never forgot or forgave the earlier tyrannical rules of the independent Roman generals.

The Sanhedrin and synagogues again became the civic and

religious centers for the Jews, but many Jews simply stayed away. The Sanhedrin no longer had the supreme authority to make important political and legal decisions over life and death of the Jews but could "cut off" the unrelenting offenders of the Law from the Jewish community. In Jerusalem and the countryside numerous Jews did not mind being excluded from the Jewish community. Many Jews so rejected formed their own circle and did not miss the mainstream of Jewish life. The Jews did not have much confidence in the moral leadership of the Sanhedrin and its members. Furthermore the Greco-Roman philosophy and mode of living became fashionable.

With the restoration of peace throughout the Roman Empire and the vast network of narrow but paved roads, improved harbors and lighthouses, communications, larger ships and navigational systems, the new commercial opportunities brought profits to the dispersed and Hellenized Jewish traders, merchants, artisans and adventurers. In Babylonia, Egypt, Syria, Turkey, the Mediterranean port cities, and even in faraway Spain, the Jews adapted themselves to the new environment and rose to prominence. Every major city contained a Jewish community, consisting of wealthy merchants, cattle breeders and land owners. The leaders of such Jewish overseas communities were highly respected in Judea. The dispersed Jews, numbering more than a few million, outnumbered the Jews living in Judea. Even a half-Jew was accepted as a full-blooded Jew outside of Judea.

These dispersed Jews paid visits to Jerusalem whenever they could pay for trips, made offerings at the Temple, and made sure the congregation knew how much they were giving in offerings. Theirs were generous thanksgiving and free will offerings, in sacred money, equivalent to the unblemished and fattest sacrifices. Moneychangers at the Temple gates were ready to accommodate them for sacred cash.

It was a time of unprecedented economic prosperity in Jerusalem. The construction of the Herod's temple-palace, commissioned by Herod the Great in 19 B.C., was on such a grand scale that Solomon's Temple-palace could be considered an extremely austere project. In the streets of Jerusalem various peoples intermingled and spoke Greek, Latin, and other dialects. The Roman legionnaires, the bare-chested athletes, the Greek and Roman merchants, dancers, and sellers of aromatics, magic potions, and sour wines busied themselves in the marketplace. The rich lay in the sedans carried by slaves.

A tissue of privilege creating the cleavage between the rich and the poor became visible. The Sadducees held or controlled all the choice pieces of land adjacent to the city walls and the town walls, which brought in enormous revenues but were exempt from tithes and taxes. Of course the writers of the Law were so convinced of the pernicious effects of land ownership that they forbade the priests to inherit land, but the writers were badly mistaken. Later laws stipulated that 48 cities and towns and all lands round about them were assigned to the Levites for the houses and pasture lands for their cattle (Numbers 35; see also Ezekiel 45:1 6).

The book of Jubilees (Leviticus 25) was written by a priest or a lawyer toward the end of the Hasmonaean dynasty. It stressed that the land should be redistributed and all the debts cancelled every fiftieth year. Its author wrote: "The land shall not be sold in perpetuity for the land is mine [God's]; for you are strangers and sojourners with me." (Leviticus 25:23.) The book of Jubilees was merely a blueprint for the future just as the Book of the Law itself was. The book of Jubilees was never accepted by the priestly class and landowners.

Somebody had to pay for the on-going construction of Herod's temple-palace, the luxurious living of the upper-class Jews, and the Roman procurator and his garrison in Jerusalem, and make up the differences created by the vast amount of tax- and tithe-exempt lands. The Jews in the countryside could not see fair play between the affluent and the impoverished, no matter what the letter of the Law might say. Payments fell due and the Jews came to hate the tax collectors wholeheartedly. The poor Jews were compelled to mortgage their houses, cattle, future harvest, and even themselves and families to pay their taxes, tithes, and offerings. They felt betrayed by the Sadducees and the Pharisee-lawyers, who kept setting up and enforcing the new standards of proper conduct and telling the average Jews what were or what were not good and right for them.

An efficient Roman administration and a prosperous urban economic society ironically sharpened the disharmony among the Jews. Such a discord among the Jews in turn prevented the Jews from reviving the religious consensus which had gone to oblivion during the Hasmonaean period. There could not be any civic independence without religious consensus. The Hasmonaean dynasty was a totalitarian regime which upheld monolithic religious unity by authoritarian rules. Once a theocratic dynasty went, the whole social, economic and religious structure of the Jewish society was in a turmoil.

The synagogues during the Hasmonaean dynasty were more judicial and police organizations rather than the local civic centers where the pooling of the labor, agricultural tools and other material resources in plowing and harvesting one field at a time, harvesting and throwing the fields, after the harvest, open to sheep and cattle, were supposed to be arranged.

It was during the earlier post-exilic reform period that religion was a mode of self-sufficient living uniting each Jew with the common life. Each synagogue used to be an intimate group in which the common life of the Jews overlapped the interests of livelihood, family, religion, education and social life. Once the religious consensus was gone under the Hasmonaean dynasty and early Rome rule, the Jews had no one to turn to. Each alienated Jew faced the world alone and found himself too weak to handle the problems and too feeble for the daily ordeal.

Out of feeling helpless some Jews looked inward again, and others sought some way out by withdrawing from the society and retiring to a sort of monastic life. Although seventy-one seats of the Sanhedrin were equally shared by the Sadducees and the Pharisees, the Jews considered the Pharisees the lesser of two evils. The priestly Sadducees seemed to know less about the Law and accepted only the written Law as revelation of God. The Pharisees-lawyers, on the other hand, expounded the oral traditions which were transmitted by word of mouth from father to son, and they knew it by memory, and insisted that the oral traditions were equally revelations of God.

Not all the Pharisees were of the same mind. In fact the Pharisees were a united opposition to the Sadducees, but the religious views of the factions within the Pharisee party were far apart from each other. The followers of Shammai were the Pharisee-lawyers and the followers of Hillel the Elder the Pharisee-rabbis or teachers. Shammai, the stern self-righteous man, demanded a strict adherence to the letter of the Law and the oral traditions. Hillel, a Jewish humanitarian from Babylon, stressed the Spirit of the Law. Lawyers kept juggling the words and the sentences in the Law, and rabbis considered such juggling as the fundamental cause of disharmony in the Jewish society, when the ruling elements lost sight of the spiritual perspective.

The followers of Hillel were, however, far outnumbered by the followers of Shammai; consequently, the Pharisee party represented nothing but the position of lawyers. Most Pharisee teachers were non-Levites and, therefore, lacked "authority" to judge and could not command the popular following.

The oral traditions contributed to the Law in one important way. It was clear that the Law was not interpreted in one exact way. Lawyers disagreed on the meaning of the same letter of the Law. This was not altogether bad because such disagreements gave the Jews of this period a breathing space and left some room for average Jews to make their own choices.

The Pharisee-lawyers, however, were driving the Jews out of the mainstream of religious life rather than drawing them in. They would not eat with a non-Pharisee without ascertaining that the food had been properly tithed. They would find faults with the conduct of non-Pharisees who knew not the law.

Extreme cults sprang up. The Zealots, the militant freedom fighters, hated the Sadducees and the Pharisees for their subservience to and accommodation with the Romans. The Essenes also looked forward to the final battle of God against the forces of Darkness to come. Each Jewish group kept itself apart from other Jews. They refused to eat, socialize or marry with other Jews who did not belong to the same cult. The members of each cultic group professed to love one another but kept the holier-than-thou attitudes toward the Jews of other groups. Each professed to purify the Jewish faith, and at the same time contributed to the disharmony of the Jews.

The worst seemed to be over, and the hope for better and bright days was there. It was not in the depth of despair that the Jewish discords occurred, but with the first gleam of a great hope the Jews violently disagreed with one another on the question of what general direction they should be heading for. An underlying optimism prompted the Jews to believe they deserved a better leadership, which should change things and reconstruct their religious society. At the same time some of the Jews were becoming impatient with the Jewish religious malaise and the aimlessness of their society.

Such was the historical setting in which Jesus was born about 4 B.C. of humble parents from Galilee, the hotbed of the militant Zealots and the land disparaged in Judea and Samaria. It was during the reign of Roman Emperor Octavianus (31 B.C. to A.D. 14) and the last years of Herod the Great, the King of Judea.

CHAPTER V

Jesus and His Teachings

Contrasting views of the authors of the books of Job and Ecclesiastes indicate a great transformation which was taking place in the Jewish spiritual way of thinking and which was equally relevant at the time of Jesus.

JOB AND ECCLESIASTES

The book of Job in the Old Testament is an ancient Hebrew script for a poetic drama with the cast of God, Satan, Job and his friends. The drama raises the millennium-old question why the will of God is inscrutable. If God is just, sensible, and good why doesn't He reward those who are faithful to His will?

No one knows when this drama was written or who wrote it. Job, the central character of the drama, is portrayed as a wealthy and pious nomadic sheikh in the land of Uz. One day God asked Satan what the latter thought of Job's piety and righteousness. Satan said to God that Job would curse God if he were to lose all that he has.

God and Satan proceeded to put Job to a test. Marauders robbed Job of his possessions and a hurricane killed his children. Sickness and unbearable sufferings afflicted Job, and even death became preferable to Job. Job finally protested that he might not be impeccable in the eyes of God but he certainly did not deserve the unendurable pains he was going through.

In this drama his friends argue that God rules the universe sensibly and that if a man were righteous God would automatically reward him with good fortune and that misfortune is invariably the result of God's wrath inflicted upon him for some "sin" committed by him or his ancestors. In the end God appeared to Job but gave no answer to the question.

The question of faith and reward was equally pertinent and relevant at the time of Jesus. The Jews did their best to be loyal and faithful to God during most of the post-exilic period and innumerable Jews laid down their lives for the cause of God. Yet, one could not say that the Jews enjoyed peace, security, and prosperity any more than the Egyptians, the Mesopotamians, the Greeks and the Romans.

Individually also, sharp business practices seemed to pay off, and the rich and powerful seemed to thrive at the expense of the poor and weak. God, as a stern judge, did not seem to be even fair but freakish and devilish and had no concern with men. Such was the skeptical and cynical attitude of the author of Ecclesiastes when he wrote:

> In my vain life I have seen everything; there is a righteous man who perishes in his righteousness, and there is a wicked man who prolongs his life in his evil doing. Be not righteous overmuch, and do not make yourself overwise; why should you destroy yourself? Be not wicked overmuch, neither be a fool; why should you die before your time? (Ecclesiastes 7:15-17.)

There is a wide gulf between Ecclesiastes and Job as far as the spiritual perspective of each author is concerned. The author of Ecclesiastes is not torturously introspective on the self-righteousness of Jews or perfection, moral or otherwise. Blind chance and luck, instead of God's sensible and well-laid plans, seemed to rule man's life, and everything is vanity, "since one fate comes to all, to the righteous and the wicked, to the good and the evil, to the clean and the unclean, to him who sacrifices and him who does not sacrifice." (Ecclesiastes 9:20.)

No one would be startled even if it were claimed the book of Ecclesiastes was written by a Greek philosopher, except for one important respect. In the book of Job, God gave no answer to the ultimate question on the meaning of one's life. In the book of Ecclesiastes the author expressed the unique Judaic faith that one's spiritual commitment itself is the reward of life and there is no other meaning to one's life except, "Fear God, and keep his commandments; for this is the whole duty of man" (Ecclesiastes 12:13), and no one has any right to demand anything of God as the reward even for impeccably righteous conduct and total devotion to God.

The Jews at the time of Jesus did not have a religious consensus. The moral of God giving no answer in the fictitious tale of Job and the spiritual theme underlying Ecclesiastes are identical. On reflection, a religious consensus did not guarantee for the Jews a glorious future of peace and security but was used to provide for the Jews a civic autonomy solely motivated by religion as in the reform years of Ezra. In the absence of political independence the Jews used to be no less happy or cohesive as long as they had spiritual unity; nevertheless, the political independence itself did not strengthen the cohesiveness or well-being of the Jews when they lacked the religious agreement as in the years of the Hasmonaean High Priest-Kings. Equally, economic prosperity itself did not help the harmony and welfare of the Jews any more than political independence.

In the absence of religious consensus the Jews began questioning the merits of Judaism as the ultimate value of the

Jewish life. In the absence of the spiritual unity and civic autonomy, the Law as the core of Judaism had to be reexamined and revitalized or new answers had to be sought. This was the mission of Jesus just as it was for each faction of the Pharisee party, the Sciarii, the Essenes, the Zealots and other large and small cults flourishing at the time of Jesus.

JESUS OF NAZARETH

The Gospels mention little about the life of Jesus, and say nothing at all about his long formative years. His parents were from Nazareth, a bucolic little town of farmers and sheep-raisers in the northern uplands of Galilee, the land furthest removed from both Jerusalem and Samaria, the capitals of the ancient Hebrew kingdoms. Galilee or "Land of pagans" was the fertile but backward land disparaged in Judaea and Samaria. The Zealots in Galilee hated the priests and lawyers in Jerusalem for their impiety in collaborating with the Roman occupation legions. The Jewish aristocrats in Jerusalem considered Galilee the land which nothing good could come out of.

Some traditions suggest that Joseph, an aged carpenter and a widower, had four grownup sons and two daughters before he remarried Mary, a young bride of about sixteen. Joseph and Mary had a donkey, took turns riding it, and moved to Bethlehem, near Jerusalem, where Jesus was born. The name Jesus was a Greek equivalent to the Jewish "Joshua" or "the Lord saves."

Baby Jesus, along with his parents, moved on to Egypt where they went from one Jewish community to another along the Nile valley. Joseph took his family and started back toward Galilee after a few years' stay in Egypt, crossing again that wilderness of Sinai where bandits, leopards and wolves were not uncommon.

Jesus was perhaps at the tender age of three or at most

seven when his parents returned to Galilee, and most of his childhood was spent at Nazareth, where his father's relatives lived. Some of his kinsmen, Zebedees, had fishing boats on the Lake of Galilee only fifteen miles away from Nazareth. The sons of Zebedees, James and John, later became apostles of Jesus.

Jesus, at the age of twelve, first attracted notice by his display of mature learning and wisdom in his arguments of law with the doctors of law in the Temple in Jerusalem. His parents, accompanied by relatives and neighbors, had made the trip of about one hundred miles to Jerusalem from Nazareth to celebrate the Passover.

Every Jewish adult male was to assume religious duties, at the age of thirteen, as a son of the Law, and was supposed to make the trip to Jerusalem each spring for Passover and each fall for the Harvest Feast of the Weeks; hence Jesus might have made many similar trips to Jerusalem. Nevertheless, Jesus perhaps did not have opportunities to have the intensive training on the Law characteristic of lawyers. Being aware how little academic training he had Jesus considered himself and his followers "babes" in the midst of the intellectual giants when he said:

> I thank thee, Father, Lord of heaven and earth, that thou has hidden these things [religious truths] from the wise and understanding and revealed them to babes; yea, Father, for such was thy gracious will. All things [religious truths] have been delivered to me by my Father; and no one knows the Son except the Father, no one knows the Father except *the Son and any one to whom the Son chooses to reveal him.*
>
> (Matthew 11:25-27.)

As "all things have been delivered to him" Jesus felt duty-bound to the public ministry. Jesus was well aware that his every utterance would be scrutinized by the lawyers and priests, and that the danger of death for blasphemy and uncertainties and hardships would be in the way he had chosen. Jesus "was in the wilderness forty days, tempted by Satan." (Mark 1:13.) He pondered his mission, even hesitated to undertake the mission, and finally rose above all the fears and doubts.

At this time John the Baptist was preaching the impending Kingdom of God or messianic age. He evangelized like a prophet born out of season because the canonization of the Book of the Law in the post-exilic Judaea at the turn of the fourth century B.C. ended the period of prophecy, and the Law specified prophecy as blasphemy punishable by death.

John, dressed in haircloth and a leather belt, eating locusts, denounced the moral laxity of just about every ruling element of the society as "a brood of vipers." He baptized all the masses flocking to him in the River Jordan for purification. John did not spare from his denunciation Herod Antipas, the ruler of the Galilee district, for living with his brother's wife; consequently John was put to death.

Once baptised by John, Jesus mustered all the courage he needed to undertake the task and lead himself to a certain death. Jesus reflected on the anxiety, tension, and fear that he felt: "Foxes have holes, and the birds of the air have nests, but the Son of man has nowhere to lay his head." (Matthew 8:20.)

His public ministry itself lasted anywhere from six months to at most two years. Only fragments of his teachings were handed down to us. Yet his ministry of such a short period was to change the course of human history.

Jesus first publicly appeared in Galilee, traveling from town to town and preaching in open fields and in synagogues. His listeners were people of diverse backgrounds, literate and illiterate, fisherman, farmers, sheep-raisers, housewives and prostitutes. There were priests and lawyers among the listeners but they were there to examine the teachings of Jesus.

There could hardly be a meeting of minds between the Teacher and the listeners on the context of the teachings. Jesus meant one thing and an average listener would roll the teaching over his needs, desires or hope or wishful thinking without reflecting on Jesus' penetrating vision and profound thoughts. Many came to see him perform great magic or miracles rather than to listen to him.

Jesus determined that he had to throw the aura of mystery and secrecy over his teachings just as the writers of the Law did to bridge the gap between two conflicting perceptions of God. Once when Jesus was away from the crowds, those who were with him asked about the parables. Jesus said:

> To you has been given the secret of the Kingdom of God, but to those outside everything is in parables; so that they [the multitudes] may indeed see but not perceive, and may indeed hear but not understand: lest they should turn again, and be forgiven.
>
> (Mark 4:10-12.)

Perhaps Jesus never imparted all the secrets even to his apostles. Underneath this teaching of Jesus lay the realistic issue which Jesus had to resolve even before he could deliver the spiritual messages. Performance of sensational magic or miracles, and contradictory but perfectly suitable double meanings attached to each parable or each religious theme were the practical issues which had to be solved before he proceeded to express his spiritual vision and thoughts. Conversely, the teachings of Jesus would not have survived if they were not accompanied by the performance of magic or miracles and the twofold meanings of each moral tale.

Although the Jews at the time of Jesus had opportunities to study the Book of the Law at each local synagogue they were not living in an age when they could have ready access to printing presses, telecommunications and other means of proliferation of information. None of the Jews had a copy of the Book of the Law at home then. The fact that Jesus brought the most abstract religious truths close to the minds of the listeners then was a miracle.

Furthermore, hindsight is always clearer than foresight, and people ages removed from the time of Jesus could more readily understand the teachings of Jesus than his contemporaries. A reader of the New Testament today can readily look back and see the meanings of his teachings in the historical and social context of his time. Jesus was teaching spiritual and moral values not in a vacuum but in view of very specific Judaic practices as affecting the lives and well-being of the Jews of his time. Such was the nature of Jesus' teachings.

FATHER AND SON

Jesus called Yahweh "Father." As a word, Yahweh means "to exist" or "to be actively present." God or Yahweh was called in a variety of ways in the Old Testament: God of Bethel, the Holy One of Israel, Creator, Judge, the God of the Hebrews, Shepherd, Sun, Light, Shade, Husband, Mother-Bird, and so on.

"Father" perhaps sounded more endearing than "mother" in the ancient patriarchal Jewish society. The patriarchal family system as such was disappearing at the time of Jesus. Such a large family system was the luxury of the Levite family and wealthy upper-class Jews. The patriarchal tradition, however, lingered on even in an average Jewish family. The father in an average Jewish family was the chief planner to provide a living for the family, and to lead the family out of crisis and emergencies just as the pre-exilic patriarchs did centuries earlier.

In a society such as the United States God may be called "Mother." God is formless, intangible and invisible. God is neither personal nor a creature of either male or female sex. "Father" is simply an affectionate name in ancient Jewish society just as "Mother" would be in modern society.

Jesus had important reasons to call God "Father" in the most lovable personal relationship. At the time of Jesus the pious Jewish person regarded the Lord of History more in terms of a divine plan working in every event, and regarded the victory of the foreign army or the act of foreign legionnaires massacring the suspected rebel Jews as the righteous judgment of God for disobedience of the Jews to the Law. God allowed the foreign powers to dominate the Jews so that the Jews might renew their faith. Similarly devout Jews attributed family or individual misfortunes, such as the poor living, the blind, crippled, deformed, and deaf, the business failures, the sickness resulting in death, the leperosy, and so on, to some present or past violations of the Law committed by the afflicted or his ancestors. The sick, the mourners and the poor had no one to turn to for sympathy or otherwise. Jesus said:

> He [God] makes his sun rise on the evil and on the good, and sends rain on the just and on the unjust.
>
> (Matthew 5:45.)

Jesus separated Judaism from the elements of judgments and blessings and curses inherent in the primitive religion. God takes part in human affairs but does not take part as a stern judge with swords in his hands. None of the ancient Hebrew prophets ever completely discarded the characteristics of little freakish gods while they stressed the will of the moral and righteous God. The implication was simply overwhelming. It was not the old religion which was to thrive by feeding on each other's fears but the new faith which would be nurtured on the sense of love rising above and overcoming fear.

God was no longer an absolute divine sovereign, knowing and dictating the future, ruling, judging and punishing all nations and individuals, or bestowing favors upon a certain nation, family, or individual as chosen or chosen of the chosen as a matter of foreordination or predestination. God was no longer considered as willful or inscrutable. This perception of God was involved when Jesus said, "All things were delivered to him [Jesus] by my Father."

What Jesus said was clearly in conflict with the Judaic tradition as interpreted by the priests and lawyers of his time but completely in accord with the nature of God as perceived by the writers of the Law, who portrayed God more as the sole moral cause, whose nature was infinitely perfect in love, compassion and forgiveness. So noted the writers on the perfect nature of God: "You [the Hebrews] shall be holy; for I the Lord your God am holy." (Leviticus 19:2.) The finest spiritual and moral essence had already been embedded in Judaism but hidden and shrouded in the letter and oral traditions of the Law and the aura of mystery, capriciousness, and secrecy. Just as generations of the ancient Hebrews were perceiving God and His nature gradually on ever higher moral and spiritual levels, Jesus was no exception.

It is not possible for anyone to truly love some Being who might inflict unbearable punishments on him or his family or people at any moment. Such a Being of terror simply cannot be the one and same moral Being who is holy and perfect. Therefore, Jesus presented the Father as a Being whom an average Jew did not have to fear but truly love. It was that discrepancy Jesus referred to, in which the priests and lawyers of his time were presenting God to average Jews as a monsterous, fearsome, capricious and cruel Being at times, and yet average Jews were told to love that terrifying Being, when Jesus portrayed Pharisee-lawyers as blind guides and described a blind guide leading another blind, both falling into a pit. (Matthew 15:14.)

Even more significant is the Father and Son relationship as understood by the contemporaries of Jesus and the succeeding generations of Christians. Jesus once asked his disciples, "Who do men say that the Son of man is?" The answers of his disciples varied: Elijah, John the Baptist, Jeremiah or one of the prophets reincarnated. "But who do you say that I am?" persisted Jesus. Finally Peter responded, "You are the Christ the Son of the living God." "Then he [Jesus] strictly charged the disciples to tell no one that he was the Christ." (Matthew 16:13-20.)

Contradictory but perfectly suitable double meanings can be attached to this conversation. It can be interpreted in the light of the ardent messianic expectation of the Jews in the first century. The Greek "Christ" or the Hebrew "Messiah" means "anointed one." Moses, Aaron, Kings Saul, David, and Solomon, and all the prophets were anointed ones. Messianic claims were frequent and normal prior to the Babylonian exile; messianic and prophetic claims, however, were treated as blasphemous, punishable by death, in the post-exilic Judea.

It can also be interpreted in the light of the perfect nature of the Father as the sole moral cause. Jesus, more than anyone, knew the Father intimately and His nature and will.

How and in what way did Jesus know the Father intimately, His nature and will? Jesus set forth examples of "infinitely perfect nature" in his Sermon on the Mount and some of them are:

> The Law commands not to kill but "I [Jesus] say to you that every one who is angry with his brother shall be liable to judgment."

> The Law says not to commit adultery but "I say to you that every one who looks at a woman lustfully has already committed adultery with her in his heart."

"If your right eye causes you to sin, pluck out and throw it away; it is better that you lose one of your members than that your whole body be thrown into hell."

The Law commands to love your neighbor and hate your enemy but "I say to you, Love your enemies and pray for those who persecute you, so that you may be sons of your Father who is in heaven." (Matthew 5.)

Just a few of the examples cited above are sufficient for us to see a spiritual theme of Jesus.

Did Jesus believe that anyone but himself would be able to live by these specific standards? As specific standards the above teachings of Jesus are not only nonsensical but also may distort and even harm the growth of a normal personality by forcing everyone to live on the verge of constant guilt trips: an impossible command cannot signify an ethic or a moral or spiritual ideal, and much less a legal rule. Or was Jesus teaching superficial ideals, or was he being unworldly and unrealistic?

On the other hand the teaching of Jesus in its entirety indicates that he was primarily concerned with the widening gap between the practices of the Law on one hand and the moral and spiritual value on the other.

As Jesus observed, the Law which had originated as a spiritual and moral value of the post-exilic Jews turned into merely a technical knowledge, and the excogitated strict construction of the letter of the Law was causing a disharmony among the Jews. The lawyers at the time of Jesus acted as if the legal process operated on its own inherent logic independent of the spiritual and moral compass or yardstick. The priests and lawyers forgot about the Spirit of the Law and did not know God. One certainly cannot love some Being without knowing that Being. Therefore, Jesus was explaining the perfect nature of God in human terms: If God were a human form God would not be angry, would not look at a woman lustfully, and would love enemies and pray for those who persecute him.

"You, therefore, must be perfect, as your heavenly Father is perfect," said Jesus (Matthew 5:48). Jesus seems to be saying to his listeners, "Now you know the Father and His nature and will," and therefore,

> Hear, O Israel: the Lord our God, the Lord is one; You shall love the Lord your God with all your heart, and with all your soul, and with all your mind, and with all your strength . . . [and] love your neighbor as yourself. There is no other commandment greater than these.
>
> (Mark 12:28-32.)

In essense this is the Spirit of the Law, and Jesus equates the Father with the Spirit of the Law and the moral and spiritual perspective of Moses, Elijah, the prophets and the writers of the Law. Jesus said:

> Think not that I have come to abolish the law and the prophets, I have come not to abolish them but to fulfill them. For truly, I say to you, till heaven and earth pass away, not an iota, not a dot, will pass from the law until all is accomplished.
>
> (Matthew 5:17-18.)

In his Sermon on the Mount Jesus conveyed to the listeners the spiritual message without having to point out anyone's spiritual and moral shortcomings or chopping logic like an argumentative lawyer, and got the point across, without saying or suggesting that no one but he had that spiritual and moral perspective which was perfect and was akin to or identical with that of the living God. Said Jesus: "If I glorify myself, my glory is nothing; it is my Father who glorifies me, of whom you say that he is your God. But you have not known him. If I said, I do not know him, I should be a liar like you [Pharisee-lawyers]; but I do know him and I keep his word." (John 8:54f.) Jesus presented the complex subject matter simply enough so that the multitudes would understand.

This spiritual message Jesus conveyed was what the post-exilic Jewish life had generated and the writers of the Law and the prophets preceded him.

Whether Jesus intended or not, the Father-Son relationship had another implication. Prophets prophesied in the name of God in the pre-exilic Hebrew society; writers set forth the Law as revealed to Moses by God; and priests and lawyers of his time rendered their legal opinions and decisions in the name of Moses in the post-exilic Judea. Prophecy in the post-exilic Judea, however, was blasphemy punishable by death; furthermore, Jesus was neither a priest nor a lawyer but a Pharisee-teacher, and did not have authority to express legal opinions in the name of Moses; therefore, in presenting the nature of God and the Spirit of the Law Jesus repeated, "I say unto you. . . ." without any attempt to cite authority to render weight to his teachings. (This approach is simple enough today, but Jesus was treading the thinnest legal technicality of his time which separated life and death.)

Jesus had the unshakable confidence in his spiritual message as the best when he said:

> And then if anyone says to you, "Look, here is the Christ," or, "Look, there he is!" do not believe it. False Christs and false prophets will arise and show signs and wonders, to lead astray, if possible, the elect. But take heed; I have told you all things beforehand.
>
> (Mark 13:21-23.)

The parallel analogy between Jesus and the writers of the Law in this regard is too striking to be overlooked. In debt to the writers and the prophets, Jesus saw no further use for more Christs and prophets, just as the writers who derived their spiritual perspective from the prophets saw no further necessity for prophets in the post-exilic Judea.

Jesus agreed with the writers on the essential need of instilling into the Jews the Godly perspective or spiritual views of life, and that the Law, specifying the objective standards of Jewish conduct, was derived from such Spirit of the Law or the spiritual perspective of the writers. Jesus and the writers agreed in more ways than they differed on spiritual issues, although their differences became magnified as the teachings of Jesus came to collide with the Judaic practices of his time.

"YOUR SINS ARE FORGIVEN"

The priests and lawyers on one hand and Jesus on the other were on a collision course because of Jesus' repeated statement "Your sins are forgiven." "Sin" in the Judaic context meant a violation of any specific provision of the Law. Priests and lawyers pretended they were free of sins because they knew all the details of the Law and lived by the Law.

Average Jews often breached the Law. To begin with, ordinary Jews did not know the particulars of the Law, much less abide by them. Average Jews had to seek legal opinions either from priests or lawyers before they did anything. The counsel of a priest was not reliable because a lawyer would say the oral tradition which had been handed down to him from his father would prove the legal opinion of the priest to be illegal. Lawyers did not agree on the same point. There were liberal lawyers and conservative lawyers. In many cases a lawyer would consult other lawyers and lawyers would disagree with one another on the same issue.

In any case "sins" were never freely forgiven, and it was the requirement of the Law for whoever broke the Law or recovered from any sickness listed in the Law that he make offerings for atonement.

The statement "Your sins are forgiven" would have deprived priests and lawyers of their livelihood to some extent, and added insult to the injury. Jesus placed a blanket coverage of sins over all Jews: by "sin" Jesus meant any human conduct which fell short of the Spirit of the Law, i.e., the infinitely perfect nature of God. In this sense priests and lawyers were sinners very much like any other ordinary Jew. "I have not come to call the righteous, but sinners to repentance," said Jesus (Luke 5:32). In this sense, too, Jesus seemed to make room for a Christian theologian of a later age to advance the doctrine of the original sin. (The doctrine of the original sin advances the theme: Adam's sin corrupted man's whole nature; Adam's guilt for eating a fruit in disobedience to God's commandment and its penalty passes on to thousands of generations of his descendants; and man is born in a state of sin.)

Furthermore, in performing the miracle of healing a paralytic man, Jesus claimed to the lawyers that "you [lawyers] may know that the Son of man has authority on earth to forgive sins." (Mark 2:10.)

The meaning of "authority on earth to forgive sins" is not clear from the context in which Jesus made such a claim. Did he mean to say he has the power to uplift any Jew from hopeless despair and the guilt complex of committing sins and not being able to make offerings for atonement? Jesus healed a paralytic, which was an evidence of a "sin" in the Old Testament context, and he certainly forgave the sin of the paralytic by healing him on the spot. (Whatever Jesus meant by "authority" that authority did not mean the authority of the church to excommunicate or absolve sins and grant indulgences.)

Was Jesus imposing upon the average Jews the guilty feeling of sins more encompassing than what they used to feel? The standards of infinitely perfect nature are much more difficult and extensive, if not impossible, for any one to live up to than the standards of Jewish conduct the Law requires. Was Jesus overlooking or unaware of the potential abuses of the Church power while he was chiding the abuses of the spiritual power by the priests and lawyers of his time?

(Jesus, like the writers, did not subscribe to any psychological analysis of men, either as good or bad. The story of Adam's fall from the Garden of Eden was merely an introduction to the Law in the sense that no one should usurp the power of God to determine right or wrong and take the knowledge of right or wrong, i.e. the Law, into his own hand. Jesus never meant to overturn the Law itself and did not deviate from the Judaic tradition in this regard.)

The meaning of the statement "Your sins are forgiven" becomes clear in the light of the separation of Judaism from the elements of judgments, blessings and curses. Said Jesus:

> "Judge not, that you be not judged . . . Why do you seek the speck in your brother's eye, but do not notice the log that is in your eye?"
>
> (Matthew 7:1,3.)

Once lawyers attempted to set up a trap for Jesus by asking him to pass a judgment on an adulteress. The Jews then were not ready to forgive an adulteress, who was punishable by death under the Law, and the lawyers reminded Jesus of what, in the Law, Moses commanded for the crime of adultery. Said Jesus to them: "Let him who is without sin among you be the first to throw a stone at her." When they went away Jesus said to the woman, "Neither do I condemn you; go, and do not sin again." (John 8:7,11.) Similarly Jesus told a prostitute "your sins are forgiven." (Luke 7:48.)

But Jesus unmistakably stated that "whoever divorces his wife and marries another, commits adultery against her; and if she divorces her husband and marries another, she commits adultery." (Mark 10:11-12.) This teaching of Jesus on divorce was addressed to both husbands and wives. The Jewish wives began claiming the right to divorce. The Roman law was emerging as a formidable foe of Judaism, just as the Greco-Roman philosophy always challenged Judaism.

In all the ancient semitic law codes of the Hebrews, Babylonians and Assyrians only the husband could divorce, whereas in the settled agricultural societies, such as Rome, Greece and Egypt, the wife could reserve the sole right of divorce by marriage contract.

Furthermore, the idea of permanence was not basic to the Jewish marriages before the Babylonian exile and even at the time of Jesus. A rich Jewish man could marry as many wives as he could afford and divorce a wife at his pleasure and convenience without any legal obligation to give or provide anything for the departing wife. It was under the Roman legal system that the status of Jewish women gradually improved. The Romans promoted the permanence and integrity of monogamous marriage and the family system by protecting the legal rights of the wife and the rights of offspring of such a monogamous marriage.

The Roman law recognized an option on the part of a prospective wife to choose either a regular or a free marriage. A wife under a free marriage could remain on her own without passing into her husband's family; in such a free marriage the husband did not acquire any right over the property of his wife; and the wife had to support herself and did not inherit her husband's property if the husband died without a will.

Upper-class Jewish women, influenced by Roman law and custom, began claiming the right to divorce their husbands and remarry. (As happened repeatedly in the Jewish history, the Jews adapted themselves to changing reality by filling up the loopholes in the Law in a preposterous way: the Jewish women claimed the right to divorce because the Law was silent on such right of the Jewish women to divorce. In rude fact, the writers of the Law did not have to specify because it was too obvious that the semitic family system and polygamy, which regarded wives as the properties of the husbands, would not allow the wives to divorce husbands.)

In reality too, an adultery by a wealthy Jewish man or woman was the legal process of marriage, divorce and remarriage and an adultery by a poor Jewish man or woman was an adultery, punishable by death under the Law. Jesus, of course, did not overlook such a nebulous distinction, which meant life for one and death for another for an identical act.

Nevertheless, if the teaching of Jesus on divorce were meant to be a specific moral value it would be superficial for Jesus to forgive an adulteress and a common prostitute but not forgive divorcees, and refuse to pass judgments on adultery and prostitution but to do so on divorce. Jesus was teaching that marriage is not an arrangement between a man and property for convenience but a moral commitment between a man and a woman. At the same time he refused to pass judgments on specific cases of adultery and prostitution. Jesus was not teaching that a man and his wife should go to their graves locked up in an impossible marriage in spite of incompatible personalities, sexual incompatibility or other irreconcilable differences, or create a living hell for themselves.

Jesus was interested neither in giving specific moral values beyond and above the Law nor in rendering judgments on specific cases, but in showing the spiritual point of evaluating one's own moral choice. On this point as on other spiritual issues Jesus is free of inconsistencies or unpredictableness. (If Jesus were asked about specific values such as the right of a master discharging his employees for one reason or another, a parent spanking his children, polygamy, breaking up of a betrothal, a practice of renewing the six-year period of slavery, and other daily occurrences in his time, would he have approved any of those practices?)

Then what did Jesus mean by the statement "Your sins are forgiven"? The threat to the Jewish society solely motivated by religion which Jesus feared was the sense of judgments held by self-righteous Jews against the seemingly unrighteous or unconventional Jews. In Judea at the time of Jesus the insecure atmosphere was artifically created to encourage a Jew to relate only his righteous deeds and the unrighteous deeds of others.

Each Jew judged every other Jew for ancestry to ascertain if the other's pure Jewishness was not tainted with the blood of Samaritan, Edomite, or any other dubious origin, Levite or not, wealthy or not, i.e. blessed or not, ignorant farmer or not, what sect of Judaism the other Jew belonged to, and so on. Inevitably too, a majority evaluated the unconventional Jews with suspicion and used the weight of numbers and religion to reject them. This possibility never troubled the writers of the Law, who set forth numerous "cut off" provisions to exclude and banish the unorthodox Jews and the Jews of questionable heritage from the Jewish community. The convictions of the writers in this regard led to what has been called Judaic "exclusivism."

As Jesus perceived, the entrenched group of lawyers turned the spiritual (more correctly demonic) sense of judgments into the earthly power to judge, plan, manage, and manipulate every aspect of the life of each Jew under the penalty of "cut off." Said Jesus:

> What do you think? If a man has a hundred sheep, and one of them has gone astray, does he not leave the ninety-nine on the hills and go in search of the one that went astray? And if he finds it, truly, I say to you, he rejoices over it more than over the ninety-nine that never went astray. So it is not the will of my Father who is in heaven that one of these little ones should perish.
>
> (Matthew 18:12-14.)

In the parlance of today's language Jesus stated the spiritual function of drawing all Jews into the mainstream of the society but denied any spiritual authority to keep judging, excluding, and driving any Jew out of the mainstream. When Peter asked Jesus, "Lord, how often shall my brother sin against me, and I forgive him? As many as seven times?" Jesus said, "I do not say to you seven times, but seventy times seven." (Matthew 18:21-22.) It was inclusiveness rather than exclusiveness which Jesus was teaching as a fundamental spiritual function.

Various religious cults sprang up, and many Jews not only stayed away from the Temple but also hated the priests and lawyers, who failed to see why the rejected Jews were no longer minding about being excluded. The priests and lawyers were bogged down to solve the legal problems as they arose at various levels as the answers to the immediate problems at hand but rarely dealt with underlying problems. Jesus made the canniest observation of the lawsuit-happy Jewish society of his time:

> So if you are offering your gift at the altar, and there remember that your brother has something against you, leave your gift there before the altar and go; first be reconciled to your brother, and then come and offer your gift. Make friends quickly with your accuser, while you are going with him to court, lest your accuser hand you over to the judge, and the judge to the guard, and you be put in prison; truly, I say to you, you will never get out till you have paid the last penny.
>
> (Matthew 5:23-26.)

Ambiguity and obscurity in the letter of the Law, the oral traditions, which nearly all the average Jews did not know, legal formalities and technicalities resulting in a maximum of delay, a long period of mental irritation to the parties in a lawsuit, and the need of each lawyer to demonstrate novel ideas beyond and above those of his fellow lawyers rendered the outcome of the legal process short of justice but capricious, unpredictable, and uncertain. No matter what, Jesus seems to be saying, those lawyers will make you lawsuit-happy but will not make you one bit better off by going to court.

Very significant is his teaching that the Law was not the direct revelation of God but was man-made. When the lawyers pointed out to Jesus that his followers were not observing the sabbath by plucking ears of grain, Jesus said to them, "The sabbath was made for man, not man for the sabbath; so the Son of man is lord even of the sabbath." (Mark 2:28.) The proper observation of the sabbath under the penalty of death was one of the most important rules in the Law. "The Law" could be easily substituted for "the sabbath" in the context in which Jesus spoke, as if to read, "The Law was made for man, not man for the Law."

Jesus, also, set aside all the dietary laws on the ground that the Spirit of the Law is to promote harmony and welfare among the Jews without creating worse evils of social and spiritual outcasts for violating insignificant dietary laws. Jesus clearly disregarded the notion of the Law as verbally given by God. The strength in the teachings of Jesus stems from that clear distinction between exactly what is the fundamental and absolute source and what are the derivatives and relative.

(Only in hindsight, it should be recalled that modern scientific developments initially brought about incredible confusion among the churches and Christian theologians as well as among Jewish theologians with respect to the literal truthfulness of the creation story and the notion of the Book of the Law as verbally revealed.)

An important question, however, remains unanswered: Who forgives one's sins in the context of "Your sins are forgiven"? For Jesus the spiritual and moral value stems from each individual's spiritual perspective of his life. If one tries hard to bring his perspective close to the nature of God it will be reflected in his character, intention, and attitude. Before one says anything or takes an action he has to check it out from his perspective. Only one's perspective can forgive his own ill behavior, actions or utterances. Of course one can repent and constantly try to bring his perspective closer to the nature of God.

For Jesus the Law or its interpretation has to conform to the spiritual and moral value but the spiritual and moral value has to go further than where the Law leaves off. Such was the spiritual meaning of the parable of the prodigal son. A son demanded and received from his father his legal share of inheritance and moved away only to spend extravagantly his share in loose living. This son, in need and desperation, came back to his father, who ordered his servants,

> Bring quickly the best robe, and put it on him; and put a ring on his hand, and shoes on his feet; and bring the fatted calf and kill it, and let us eat and make merry, for this my son was dead, and is alive again; he was lost, and is found. (Luke 15:22-24.)

The legal rule, applied to this moral tale, was taken from the Sumerian legal code, which was more than two thousand years old at the time of Jesus. Once the father gave the legal share to a son, the father had the right to disown his son and did not have to receive him as his son, but could ask him to leave, or give him a few meals and some pocket money to tidy himself up and ask him to leave, or employ him as a hired servant. The father was dealing with the profound spiritual and moral choices beyond and above the legal requirements by forgiving and welcoming his son as he did.

Jesus taught each listener to become a moral legislator and a moral judge of his own thoughts, deeds, and utterances. No teachings of Jesus suggest even remotely that it is the church function to legislate, judge and absolve sins in any way while he was directly challenging the Temple and priestly function to legislate, judge, and forgive sins. Therefore, a blanket coverage of sin and the repeated statement of Jesus, "Your sins are forgiven," had the subtlest meaning, in view of the Judaic practices of his time, as a direct challenge to the practices of the priests and lawyers of his time.

It was the Judaic tradition of the post-exilic period that the Law and morality were completely fused, and that there were no moral choices for any Jew to make outside of the Law. Nothing is outside of legal valuations according to the Judaic practices; nevertheless, Jesus taught that there is and should be a wide range of moral choices beyond and above the Law, that the interpretation of the Law itself must come under moral valuations, and that nothing is outside of spiritual and moral valuations. It is the teaching of Jesus that one cannot embrace and adhere to the spiritual perspective because of threats of exclusion, enforcement, penalties or judgments, but because of his willingness to embrace and love the Godly perspective as his.

As Jesus observed the Jewish society of his time, ordinary Jews had to resign into the hands of a group of lawyers who made decisions for each Jew and average Jews had no room to make choices, moral or otherwise. It was the relation between those who knew the Law and those who did not know. Of course there was a spiritual and moral distinction between obedience to the Law, the will of God, and obedience to the will of another human being, and that distinction became more visible when the lawyers used the Law as the tools to realize private gains. It was to the advantage of the lawyers to bring as many aspects of individual lives as possible under legal valuations, and none of what was happening in Judea escaped the observation of Jesus.

Jesus was not teaching a blanket coverage of sin to make austere beings out of average Jews and make them feel all the more guilty by falling short of the perfect nature of God, but to restore moral and spiritual choices to them and restore self-esteem to the average Jews, free of a guilt complex for not being able to or unwilling to make offerings and for not knowing the particulars of the Law. It was the teaching of Jesus that one must be able to forgive himself and make moral choices according to his individual perspective, and have self-esteem before he can forgive and love others, when Jesus said: "He who is forgiven little, loves little." (Luke 7:48.)

Jesus was telling his listeners not to let lawyers decipher what the Law was and make decisions for them but to make moral choices for themselves. In this sense Jesus clearly differed from the writers and the Jewish leaders of his time: Jesus was denying the exclusive right of the Levite family to codify the Law and decode what the Law was.

"LOVE"

The spiritual and moral value, one's spiritual views of life, the Godly perspective, moral choices, and so on, no matter how one may designate them mean, according to the teachings of Jesus, one and same thing, that is the subjective standard which each individual holds for himself. Jesus summed up the content of that subjective standard in the single word *love.*

Needless to point out, no society can exist and function if each individual acted his own way according to his own subjective views of life. The great commandment should be cited here once more:

> . . . You shall love the Lord your God with all your heart, and with all your soul, and with all your mind, and with all your strength . . . [and] love your neighbor as yourself. There is no other commandment greater than these.
>
> (Mark 12:30-31.)

These passages of the Law quoted by Jesus state the spiritual value (Deuteronomy 6:4-5 and Leviticus 19:18). For Jesus spiritual and moral values are two dimensions of man's perception of the nature of God. Jesus expressed the mutuality of the relationship between a Jew and the Jewish society and what quality such a relationship should be.

"Love the Lord your God with all your heart" and "Love your neighbor as yourself" are not separate commandments but one and same commandment. Religion and morality are inseparable. "Love your neighbor as yourself" carries with it the meaning "Love the Lord your God with all your heart," and vice versa. Jesus simply asserted a spiritualization of morality, subjective standards of Jewish conduct, just as the writers of the Law stated a spiritualization of the Law, objective standards of Jewish conduct.

While showing infinite perfection Jesus taught how one could translate one's spiritual value into the moral choices in the living world of reality. Jesus stated the yardstick of measuring moral values of right or wrong in the following teachings:

> Judge not, that you be not judged. For with the judgment you pronounce you will be judged, and the measure you give will be the measure you get.
>
> (Matthew 7:1-2.)

> So whatever you wish that men would do to you, do so to them; for this is the law and the prophets.
>
> (Matthew 7:12.)

> Judge not, and you will not be judged, condemn not, and you will not be condemned; forgive, and you will be forgiven; give, and it will be given to you; good measure, pressed down, shaken together, running over, will be put

into your lap. For the measure you give will be measure you get back.

(Luke 6:37-38.)

The only sentence which requires explanation is "good measure pressed down, shaken together." It refers to the quantity of grain poured into a measuring jar as a dry measure of value like paper currency of today, and the teaching means that one should not try to shortchange others as he would not wish to be shortchanged.

A reader should note how many times the words "you" and "measure" were repeated. Simply Jesus asks each of his listeners what are your needs and desires and teaches that as one would know his needs and desires, then he should be able to measure spiritual and moral values of right or wrong.

The spiritual and moral value begins with the knowledge of the needs and desires of the self. It is neither self-denial nor uselessness of men's pursuits of happiness on earth. Again it should be stressed that Jesus is not teaching specific objective values, but the yardstick of spiritual and moral values which centers around one's needs and desires. It is a common sense or a general sense of right or wrong. As one comes to have the yardstick he can measure innumerable spiritual and moral values: "Don't cheat as you would wish not to be cheated," "help a drowning man as you would wish to be helped when drowning," "place yourself in his shoes," and so on.

Jesus is not assuming human nature is basically egoistic or altruistic, depraved and sinful or good, social or antisocial, natural or unnatural, or any other scientific or philosophical speculations and conclusions about human nature. A spiritual perspective, however, is not innate in human nature but acquired.

Jesus does not assume that human desires and urges for food, sex and other material and emotional needs are either animalistic and bad or good, or that human wants and desires might stand in the way of attaining the spiritual and moral value. On the contrary there are enough material resources for every one to satisfy his necessities if every Jew upheld the Godly perspective and learned to share the material resources.

The yardstick of moral values cannot exist apart from one's needs, urges, desires, and impulses. Jesus, on the other hand, recognizes that one's wants and desires will change as the mode of living changes. One's needs and urges in times of war cannot be the same as those in times of peace. One's needs and desires are relative to time, place and circumstances, and to the society of which one is a member. The yardstick itself is not a fixed and calculable one but a relative one, and it is the Judaic tradition that God is the Lord of History, determining right or wrong only in the historical and social circumstances, and this phase of Jesus' teaching did not deviate from the Judaic tradition.

The yardstick draws the moral minimum in the living world of reality. Jesus said the most Godly thing for any one to do is to lay his life for his friends and there is no greater love than this, and that kind of sacrifice for others is by far over and above the line the yardstick draws. Jesus leaves a wide and flexible lattitude in which each individual can make moral choices and exercise free will, according to his spiritual perspective under diverse circumstances. Every problem or situation presents many possible or probable moral choices as was the case in the parable of the prodigal son.

Jesus did not seek uniform human conduct measured by the yardstick, because uniformity renders spirituality and morality meaningless. Yet the needs, urges and desires of the Jews are alike in some fundamental ways because they live in the same society at the same time and face the same humane problems of emotional insecurity, oppression of the suspected rebel Jews by the Roman occupation legionnaires, heavy taxation, alienated feelings, and so on. Therefore, objective standards of conduct, the moral minimum or the Law, no matter what one may call it, will depend on the probability of consensus and will become evident. It is Jesus's teaching that the Law must be continuously responsive to the needs and desires of the people, and sensitive to the spiritual and moral value of the Jews.

Furthermore, as each Jew tries to be closer to the perfect nature of God the Law itself will become self-enforcing to a great extent, and the need for legal valuations and judgments will be kept to a minimum.

At this point it is appropriate to examine the Judaic tradition that God is the Lord of History determining right or wrong. As Jesus rejected the notion of nations, tribes, families and individuals being judged, punished or favored by God, God as the Lord of History is not the Lord of judging but strictly a moral Being who shows right or wrong in the historical and social conditions.

In the Old Testament context God personally did not determine right or wrong. It was the prophets and the writers of the Law who, in the name of God, made such value judgments retrospectively on the actions and behaviors of their pre-exilic ancestors. Jesus does not question the need for the elite or leaders of the Jews of each generation to point out the new direction in the light of past mistakes. Equally Jesus did not object to the need for objective standards of conduct as such, and Jesus certainly did not seek to uproot the Law but to return it to the original intent and spiritual vigor of the writers.

In the mutuality between a Jew and the Jewish society of his time, Jesus sadly observed that the priests and lawyers were legislating away every aspect of the life of each Jew, leaving no room for an average Jew to make moral choices, and its consequence was tragic. Jesus chastized lawyers because "you shut the kingdom of heaven against men." (Matthew 23:13.)

Furthermore, the Law and the individual spiritual and moral value were no longer interacting, or mutually supportive of each other. Jesus was pointing out a two-way street between the willingness of Jews to uphold the Law and the socio-economic and spiritual benefits which the Law could deliver to the Jews or the Jewish society. Once the perception of the people that the Law is working for them is shaken, the Law is merely a tool to beat the people, who in turn would try to beat the Law. Jesus perceived the mistake of the writers of the Law in stressing uniform conduct and righteousness at the expense of morality and religion.

What Jesus pointed out was the difference between a wide range of moral choices enjoyed by the pre-exilic Hebrews under the customs on one hand and the mechanical details observed by the Jews and the free will denied to average Jews under the codified Law according to the Judaic practices of his time. The national saga and the Old Testament books of prophets clearly indicate a pendulum swinging violently from one extreme of rather "stiff-necked" and ill-disciplined spontaneous freedom of the pre-exilic Hebrews to another extreme of rigidly well-disciplined and highly regimented life of the post-exilic Jews. Jesus, indicating the shortcomings of one extreme, was not urging a full swing back to the other extreme. In spite of the simplicity which the teachings of Jesus might seem to have on the surface he pointed out with great clarity and razor-blade sharpness and precision spiritual issues involved in so complicated a subject matter.

What is absolutely true according to Jesus is that each individual has to have spiritual and moral views of life and try constantly to bring that perspective ever closer to that of God. Otherwise, Jesus takes a relativist stand on all specific values and the yardstick of such moral values itself, and Jesus urges the listeners to discard the self-righteous attitude but have self-doubts about their own rights and give the maximum benefit of doubt to their adversary. An ordinary Jew, furthermore, does not have to run to a priest or lawyer for legal opinions on every action or decision he has to make: A choice made by a third party cannot be one's own moral choice. For this relativism the teachings of Jesus are not filled with fiery self-righteousness or the ferreting out abuses and impiety everywhere.

The yardstick does not represent either conservatism, masculine virtues, feminine virtues, superficial sentimentality or religious escapism, but merely transforms the spiritual sense of love into earthly and realistic meanings, without which men cannot live together, without which each individual cannot perceive the meaning of his life, without which no institution can justify the reasons for its existence and remain viable.

Jesus taught that a harmonious society must be ruled according to both the Law as the minimum objective standard of conduct and to moral choices left to individuals. Why was the Jewish society of his time, ruled strictly according to the Law alone, creating disharmony, emotional insecurity, alienation, and spiritual malaise?

Jesus was not the only one who was asking that question. Otherwise, numerous cults would not have flourished in Judea at the time of Jesus. Hillel the Elder felt deeply the necessity to systematize the interpretation of the Law and began teaching ethical norms of common decency and the need for loving concern of each Jew for others about twenty-five years before the birth of Jesus. Jesus drew upon and crystalized the essence of the ancient Hebrew tradition which had been reasserted.

The teachings of Jesus on the perfect nature of God and the yardstick were also meant to state a spiritual platform broad enough for all pious Jews easily to stand on. Jesus never doubted that the Jews were in a special relationship to God because the Jews were the first people to search for the spiritual and moral value in the midst of successive tragedies in the ancient Hebrew history, and the answers to their spiritual search for right or wrong was slowly but surely unfolding among the Hebrews, and that in their historical and social context.

The teaching of Jesus on inclusiveness, coupled with the perfect nature of the Father, eventually extended the concept of "neighbor" to all peoples including the Samaritans, the Greeks and the Romans.

KINGDOM OF HEAVEN

The primary teaching of Jesus centers around the Kingdom of God or the Kingdom of Heaven.

The Jews at the time of Jesus believed in the messianic age and the earthly Kingdom of God in which God's promise is fulfilled. They believed God would inflict His wrath upon the Greeks and the Romans and vindicate divine judgments. But one foreign master replaced another and these foreign masters became prosperous instead of being punished adequately.

At the beginning of his public ministry in Galilee Jesus tried to point out gently the misconception of divine judgments held by his contemporaries and said:

> And there were many lepers in Israel in the time of the prophet Eli'sha; and none of them was cleansed, but only Na'aman the Syrian.
>
> (Luke 4:27.)

Why only the Syrian? This was not what the Jews in Galilee wanted to hear. They became furious and chased Jesus out of the Synagogue and the city.

On the other hand Jesus seemed to talk about future events or the end of the world. A few parables of Jesus seemed to describe the Kingdom of God in terms of Heaven and Hell:

> So it will be at the close of the age. The angels will come out and separate the evil from the righteous, and throw them into the furnace of fire; there men will weep and gnash their teeth.
>
> (Matthew 13:49-50.)

> Truly, I say to you, in the new world, when the Son of man [Jesus] shall sit on his glorious throne, you [apostles] who have followed me will also sit on twelve thrones, judging the twelve tribes of Israel.
>
> (Matthew 19:28.)

Jesus seemed to be urging the listeners to distribute all of their possessions among the impoverished, to forget about their families and to follow him to the new Kingdom of God. (Since the second coming of Christ and the earthly Kingdom of God had failed to materialize, such a Kingdom came to be considered a place where the souls gather, very much like the pantheon. The angels of several ranks would examine each soul, admit outright some to Heaven, keep others in purgatory, and turn the rest away to Hell as portrayed in Dante Alighieri's *Divine Comedy.*)

The multitudes of Jews, who were forced to live in fear, anxiety, tension, and loneliness, held out the hope of personal immortality and some mystic union with God for salvation in this life or in a life after death or preferably in both worlds as a reward for being loyal to the will of God. A sort of moral support was needed for those Jews who, without such support, felt that they were powerless to face the world alone and its daily ordeal. The Jews, except for the affluent priestly class, were seeking souls for themselves and they could not see or believe any other way. The Prophet Ezekiel, during the Babylonian exile, wrote so vividly:

> Thus says the Lord God: Behold, I will open your graves, and raise you from graves, O my people; and I will bring you home into the land of Israel. And you shall know that I am the Lord, when I open your graves, and raise you from your graves, O my people.
>
> (Ezekiel 37:12-13.)

According to the teachings of Jesus the spiritual reality has no meaning apart from human existence and vice versa. Was he teaching that the spiritual reality and human existence are inseparable and recognizing at the same time the exceptional realm of spiritual reality altogether removed from human existence? Or was he teaching about the God of the Dead as well as the God of the Living?

The mother of the sons of Zeb'edee, the kinsmen of Jesus, pleaded with Jesus so that her two sons might sit "one at your right hand and one at your left, in your Kingdom." Jesus answered, "You do not know what you are asking." (Matthew 20:21-22.)

Jesus told a number of parables about the Kingdom of God. The parable of the sower concerns seeds which fall on good soil, not on the path or the rocky ground, and later yield grain. A grain of mustard seed, the smallest of all seeds, grows up to be "the greatest of shrubs and becomes a tree, so that the birds of the air come and make nests in its branches." (Matthew 13:32.) Also, the Kingdom is like a lamp brought in to be put on a stand, not under a bushel, or under a bed. The Kingdom is like one's healthy eye. These and other parables which Jesus told about the Kingdom of God are simply not suitable to explain heaven and hell.

The supernatural had little part in his moral tales or his teachings, which conveyed more earthly meanings. Jesus also said, "If you have faith as a grain of mustard seed, you will say to this mountain, 'Move hence to yonder place,' it will move; and nothing will be impossible for you.'" (Matthew 17:20.)

Is Jesus teaching about the almighty power of God to perform miracles? In the teachings of Jesus there is hardly any reference to the miracles God performed through Moses. The crowd who gathered around Jesus had heard enough of disoriented words from priests and lawyers; accordingly, words did not mean much any more to them at the time of Jesus. The crowds gathered to see Jesus perform miracles and signs from God rather than to listen to him. The Jews considered miracles and signs a confirmation of the authority of any one to speak for God. There were no meetings of minds between Jesus and his listeners: "An evil and adulterous generation seeks for a sign," said Jesus. (Matthew 12:39.) It was the worn-out Jewish generation who would rather live in illusion of wishful thinking than face the truth. (Matthew 13:15.)

Then what did Jesus mean by the Kingdom of God? It is necessary for us to see the setting of Jewish society in which Jesus was preaching the Kingdom of God.

Who were the rivals of Judaism at the time of Jesus? Baals or little gods or high places dedicated to Baals no longer existed in Judea. Witchcraft, sorcery and similar practices associated with Baals and other animated gods had been extinct for a long time in the post-exilic Judea. In the post-exilic Judea the excessive zeal of religious reformers, extensive planning reflected in the Law, subsequent regimentation of the Jewish society and abuses of a spiritual power by a theocratic dynasty achieved one of the original objectives intended by the writers of the Law, i.e. a complete purification of the ancient Hebrew faith in one God only.

Baals, high places and the priests and prophets of Baals used to threaten the ancient Hebrew faith in the pre-exilic Hebrew society. The Jews of the post-exilic Judea were thoroughly indoctrinated that the only thing which mattered was absolute obedience to the Law. The Jews were not ready to embrace the Greco-Roman "Baals" and the primitive religions of the Greco-Roman world.

Judaism itself, however, was a rival to Judaism. Judaic beliefs in the mystic sense did not deliver what God was said to have promised: a glorious future which the prophets and the writers of the Law dramatized for the average Jews. The priests and lawyers could no longer deny messianic beliefs and various beliefs in bizarre millennia held by the Jews at the time of Jesus. Once Judaism was understood in the Messianic beliefs and millennia the Spirit of the Law lost its relevancy to Judaism.

Furthermore, at the time of Jesus, various Greco-Roman philosophical schools and the Roman legal system, not only as technical knowledge but also as moral and ethical principles, could readily threaten Judaism. They were new little gods. In sending his apostles out for missionary works Jesus gave them "authority over the unclean spirits." (Mark 6:7.)

The unclean spirits, according to Luke, are "demons." (Luke 9:1.) So wrote Luke about Judas who betrayed Jesus: "Then Satan entered Judas called Iscariot." (Luke 22:3.) Jesus once cajoled Peter Satan (March 8:33.) "Satan" or "demons" carried meanings more in terms of the adversary or undesirable ways of thinking or impulses. "Satan" or "demons" did not mean Baals, animated gods, or little spirits once worshipped by the Semitic peoples. Various Greco-Roman philosophical ways of thinking and the Roman legal system as technical knowledge and ethical values could become ready alternatives to Judaism to those Jews who were living outside of Judea and those Jews in Judea who, disillusioned about the practices of Judaism, lost confidence in the Levite family, the priests and lawyers, and the Temple.

Jesus perceived two dimensions of the world men live in: the real world and what one thinks the real world is. This perception of Jesus separates the modern world from the ancient world of little gods.

In the ancient world of little gods the real world was not constant or stable. Plague, floods, earthquakes, droughts, locusts, and other natural disasters used to change the real world overnight. As the ancient people perceived, the real world itself did not seem to exist, but little spirits seemed to present a mirage to the ancient men; therefore, the perception of the world by the ancients depended on the way they believed in little gods and the characteristics of gods.

Jesus taught: What one thinks the real world is depends on his views of life. It was a very difficult religious concept for the contemporaries of Jesus to understand and an easy concept for the modern people to grasp. A few crude but simple modern examples will illustrate this point.

One who had been discharged by a corporation would readily embrace survival as his perspective. He would raise many questions to himself: Why did I stick my neck out on this or that project without going along with the rest? The time is bad and the middle management is expendable; whatever. Confidence and self-esteem reaches the lowest point.

Job hunting can be both physically and emotionally tiring. The wife and children are invariably affected. Initial numbness turns into fear of uncertainty and insecurity, fear into anger, and anger into anxiety and loneliness. He is alone in the world. In the process his marriage may fail or mature. The world he is in seemed to change rapidly not because the real world changes that rapidly but his perception of the world changes rapidly. He used to perceive a world made of people with families and with a clear identity with the employer each proudly works for.

After discharge, he comes to see only numbers or cash values rather than the people and human values and sees the cash value of the bottom line as the measure of everything.

Once on a radio-telephone talk show in Boston about a

year ago, a young man of about thirty years old was boasting of his sexual conquests. He claimed to have made love to more than three hundred different women in the period of two years. He made eye contact with women in the supermarkets, department stores, and night clubs. An eye contact could tell him immediately if a certain woman was willing. He developed and refined all sorts of techniques. The point is his perspective on the meaning of life. All the dimensions of the world except one was unreal to him.

A teenage girl is escorted to a prom by her date, and she imagines her escort to be her most admired singer and the school ballroom to be in the ephemeral make-believe world of Hollywood.

In many parts of large cities some of the youth have survival in the crudest sense as their perspective. The world they see is not human society but a jungle. The old women with handbags or the old men with social security money are ready for preying.

There are numerous perspectives one can embrace today. One, on drugs and alcohol, sees the world one way and another, glued to the television tube only, sees the world another way. One's profession tends to affect his perspective considerably. An economist tends to be an economic determinist, and a sociologist a sociological determinist, a lawyer a legal determinist, and so on.

As mentioned in the earlier chapters diverse philosophical schools also considered various criteria as the moral standard. Invariably each of these criteria presents an adherer with a certain moral perspective of looking at the world surrounding him. One may also hold a mixed bag of perspectives and the assumption is that life is too difficult and too complex and cannot be reduced to a simple formula.

The Kingdom of God is this world in which one can interact with his fellow men, not the next world, seen through one's spiritual views of life from within. This process of viewing the world from one's Godly perspective is precisely the spiritual reality of the Kingdom of God, and immortal and eternal is that spiritual perspective. In this sense the Kingdom of God is not only what one thinks the real world is but also what he thinks the real world should be: It is a unique integration of idealism and realism. One's spiritual view of life is the source of that power capable of generating and guiding his intelligence, and emotions.

The ancient Hebrews attributed one's wisdom, ideas, thinking, will, emotions, attitudes and even change of heart to God. The dialogue between God and a man was more than a literary format. In this sense too God was depicted as the sole moral cause for all effects to follow. Jesus said, "The Kingdom of God is not coming with signs to be observed; nor will they say, 'Lo, here it is!' or 'There!' for behold, the Kingdom of God is in the midst of you." (Luke 17:21).

In what way is the Kingdom of God different from other kingdoms? Various perspectives also present worlds other than the real world: the kingdom of money, the kingdom of efficiency and utility, the kingdom of survival, the kingdom of reason, the kingdom of will, the kingdom of experience, and so on. Each of them contains a certain amount of truth, with emphasis on one or another aspect of human life and society.

Philosophical perspectives, however, do not originate in religion and do not purify the measure of moral compass in a spiritual sense; accordingly, philosophical perspectives are based on reasoning and speculation rather than on the actual life of historic men. On the other hand, the spiritual and moral values manifested in the Bible are rigid but not static, love of fellow men not love of knowledge, obscure but very much full of life, often illogical, unreasonable and preposterous but real, and very determined but multifaceted. Above all, the historic Hebrews, out of sufferings and deaths, tell us what is the ultimate value which the generations of the Hebrews considered worthy for men to pursue.

Of course, philosophical studies on one or another aspect of individual life and society enrich our lives by enabling us to understand those aspects of our lives and society. Yet the actual life of historic men is not simply multi-faceted; life itself is beyond reasoning.

Only in the Kingdom of God are human existence and the spiritual reality completely fused, and one can see the meaning of life, because the spiritual value and moral value are not two separate elements but merely two dimensions of man's perception of the nature of God. Life is not the reward of one's spiritual commitment to moral choices but one's commitment itself.

In the familiar parables of Jesus on sheep and goats, if one feeds the hungry, gives drink to the thirsty, welcomes a stranger, clothes the naked, visits the sick and the one in prison, Jesus said, "As you did it to one of the least of these my brethren, you did it to me" (Matthew 25:40.)

Jesus did not teach that spiritual and moral faculties are innate in human nature. There is no logical or rational reason for a man to love his fellow man as himself. One's experience and human history may prove the teaching of Jesus to be false and unreal. Yet the ultimate meaning of one's existence cannot be determined if one goes by reasoning, experience, logic, intuition, fancy, wisdom or any other philosophical criteria alone. In all philosophical, psychological and scientific speculations the spiritual reality and human existence have to be separated, thus reducing one's life to melancholy existence without any meaning. In the Kingdom of God one can be conscious of his life without obliterating the distinction between living and mere breathing.

The Kingdom of God is here for whoever seeks (Matthew 7:7). Eternal is that spiritual perspective as one tries to make the ever imperfect world a little better place to live in because that world seen through one's spiritual perspective from within was the Kingdom perceived by the ancients and the medievals, is the same Kingdom seen by the moderns, and will be the same Kingdom to be perceived by future generations.

Jesus was concerned with the pernicious effects of family and property upon one's spiritual views of life.

Jesus perceived his followers would face religious persecutions, and said, "And brother will deliver up brother to death, and the father his child, and children will rise against parents and have them put to death; and you will be hated by all for my name's sake." (Mark 13:12.) Jesus was referring to specific provisions of the Law, which said:

> If your brother, the son of your mother, or your son, or your daughter, or the wife of your bosom, or your friend who is as your own soul, entices you secretly, saying, "Let us go and serve other gods," which neither you nor your fathers have known, . . . you shall not yield to him or listen to him, nor shall your eye pity him, nor shall you spare him, nor shall you conceal him; but you should kill him; your hands shall be first against him to put him to death, and afterwards the hands of all the people. You shall stone him to death with stones, because he sought to draw you away from the Lord your God. . . .
>
> (Deuteronomy 13:6-10.)

> . . . if there are many unfaithful fellows in one of the cities you shall surely put the inhabitants of that city to the sword, destroying it utterly, all who are in it and its cattle, with the edge of the sword. . . .
>
> (Deuteronomy 13:15.)

In order to be absolutely obedient to the Law, the writers of the Law stipulated stern measures in the Law to stamp out Baals, little gods, and unorthodox Jews. Jesus dreaded the consequences of religious persecutions against his followers. Although Jesus himself was crucified, the Jewish religious persecution against his followers was carried out on a very limited scale, not because the orthodox Jews were generously inclined toward the unconventional Christian Jews, but because the absence of religious consensus among the Jews themselves was obliterating the distinction between conventional and unconventional Jews. (It was an ironic twist of history in which the Jews often suffered religious persecutions at the hands of the followers of Jesus.)

On property also, Jesus did not preach any specific kind of economic or social system but he did not disparage the material needs of men. It was the teaching of Jesus that one cannot love his fellow men in fear of one's own material and physical security, and Jesus said:

> Do not be anxious about your life, what you shall eat or what you shall drink, nor about your body, what you shall put on. . . . But seek first the kingdom and his [God's] righteousness, and all these things [the material needs] shall be yours as well. Therefore, do not be anxious about tomorrow, for tomorrow will be anxious for itself. Let the day's own trouble be sufficient for the day.
>
> (Matthew 6:25-34.)

When Jesus taught his followers to love enemies he was urging his followers to rise above fear of enemies and to have the courage to love. The issue of war or peace was irrelevant to the people in the known world of the Roman Empire, including the Jews. The Roman peace, one of the longest eras of peace known in human history, was well underway at the time of Jesus. Jesus had no reason to address the issue of war or peace.

His pacifistic teaching of "Love your enemies" was spoken to the Jews who were lauding the proud but totally senseless

Jewish defiance against the Roman Empire. A reader of the Gospels will detect the same noble sense of defiance in Jesus as well as in the writers of the Law. Jesus, very much like the writers of the Law, did not believe the Jews should remain weak. Jesus was teaching the Jews about the surest way to defy and win instead of the proud but senseless and weak way to defy and self-destroy.

The difference between Jesus and his contemporary Jews lay not in defiance or courage as such but in kinds of defiance and courage. Needless to say, absolute pacifism is not a specific value expressed in his Sermon on the Mount, but it is a part of the spiritual perspective Jesus teaches. He was not teaching one should be weak or meek; on the contrary, one's self-esteem, stemming from his spiritual perspective enables him to be strong and rise above fear and hatred in the face of insults and provocations and to do all he can to stop a chain of retribution.

Jesus was merely pointing out the senselessness of the Jewish defiance against manifold forces which were not within the control of the Jews; nevertheless, Jesus believed in the ability of the Jews to reshape infinitely their future and channel all the Jewish national energy into the new direction. Jesus was teaching the pacifistic attitude in the presence of the Roman legionnaires in Judea and Galilee, and had no illusion that the Jewish spiritual perspective was infinitely superior to Roman arms or any other arms.

Jesus, however, is not original or unique in preaching about the pacifistic attitude. The Prophet Jeremiah urged King Zedekiah of Judah and the Hebrews of his time to rise above fear and hatred and stop a senseless defiance and warmongering against the Babylonian Empire. Yet the teaching of Jesus was such a difficult pill to swallow for the Jews who had lost a political independence. The proud but politically weak Jews found in the urgent sense of defiance their emotional outlet for hopeless despair and weakness.

For Jesus all that mattered was a religious consensus or a religious and civic independence. No military or political power can take that religious and civic independence away from the Jews or any other people, and one should not mind turning his cheek one bit. (The Jews proved time and time again in the course of history that the Jewish Spirit could not be quelled by massive persecutions and displays of raw power inflicted upon them.) One does not have to step on the dog droppings on the sidewalk if he is willing to walk around, and Jesus did not mean any differently when he said, "Do not resist one who is evil." (Matthew 5:39.) Indomitable human wills to uphold each different version of absolute righteousness clash in each violent defiance or war, which is invariably tragic in retrospect.

Jesus seems to be teaching love in terms of indifference or apathy toward those who are absolutely incapable of sharing human values. In sending his disciples out for missionary works Jesus instructed them: "And wherever they do not receive you, when you leave that town shake off the dust from your feet as a testimony against them." (Luke 9:5.) Jesus was equally convinced that there would be always someone who would refuse to share human values. It was in Galilee, where Jesus grew up and began his public ministry, that militant Zealots and nationalists were defying the Roman legionnaires and claiming a toll of lives every year at the time of Jesus.

On reflection, the teachings of Jesus in this and preceding chapters not only shed the limelight on the personality of Jesus but also enable us to visualize the formative years of Jesus which the Gospels say little about.

As a reader finishes reading the Old Testament and starts reading the teachings of Jesus in the New Testament he cannot help noticing that Jesus' teachings remind him of the calm sea waters under the warm spring sun following the tidal waves of the stormy weather: Tenderness, gentleness, determination, inner restraint, serenity, quietism, and peace color Jesus' teachings as if the Kingdom of God represents those qualities. His teachings were never doom-ridden, overly pessimistic or agonizingly introspective. There were political causes that gave to the ancient Hebrew prophets a tone of extreme righteousness and a tone of bitterness.

In the teachings of Jesus gentle persuasions replace willful urgings. Jesus did not make verbal assaults on the listeners to discipline rigorously their will or feel duty-bound religiously or to resign to the will and power of God. Jesus made simple points out of the complex subjects as if in a simple conversation between one man and another.

Jesus' teachings sound strangely so modern and represent truly a new era leaving behind an old one. Yet his teachings have meanings in the historical and social context of the ancient Hebrew life and the religious theme underlying his teachings is purely Judaic. Jesus did not have the slightest intention of breaking away from the Judaic tradition but of revitalizing Judaism and having the Judaic practices conform to the original spiritual vigor which the writers of the Law aspired to.

The teachings of Jesus lack that passionate vigor which are common in modern evangelical, fundamentalist and revivalist preaching in which the confession, repentence, and conversion are characterized by ecstasy, convulsions, hysteria or the chanting of religious formulas and songs.

Jesus' sermons and parables would not have caused any listener to rise weeping or moaning from his seat. His sermons and parables simply could not be accompanied by hand, leg or body gestures to emphasize the absolute truthfulness of such sermons or parables. Jesus must have spoken in a soft monotone in an easy-going style, telling stories or parables but avoiding verbalism in a passionate zeal in stressing the positive spiritual and moral meanings of his teachings. The context of his sermons and parables could not be delivered in any other way.

Jesus did not hide his disagreements and his indignations against the Judaic practices of his day, yet even in doing so his wits and charms seem to unveil a model of tolerance and compassion in him rather than a sharp sternness. Said Jesus, "Every sin and blasphemy will be forgiven men, but the blasphemy against the Spirit will not be forgiven. And whoever says a word against the Son of man will be forgiven; but whoever speaks against the Holy Spirit will not be forgiven, either in this age or in the age to come." (Matthew 12:31f.)

Jesus was bent on refining and purifying rather than deviating from Judaic traditions. Being quite tolerant of every sin, blasphemy, and dissenting opinions and even bad words about himself, the only thing Jesus did not tolerate was the "blasphemy against the Spirit." Who did, in the teachings of Jesus, speak against the Spirit and what was exactly "the blasphemy against the Spirit?" To put the question in another way, wasn't the Book of the Law a product of the writers' perception of the Kingdom of God?

CHAPTER VI

Changing Manifestations of Judeo-Christian Faith

FREEDOM FROM THE LAW

Jesus, on the cross at Golgatha, cried with a loud voice, "My God, my God, why hast thou forsaken me?" (Mark 15:34.) The multitudes of Jews, for whom he was laying down his life, were crying for his blood.

His dejected and frightened followers did not run away from Jerusalem to their native Galilee to resume the fishermen's job. Years later St. Paul wrote about the physical resurrection of Jesus, that "he [Jesus] appeared to Cephas [Peter], and then to the twelve [apostles]" and "then he appeared to more than five hundred brethren at one time." (1 Corinthians 15:6f.) Paul perhaps described it so clearly in order to convince the Greeks and the Romans who were skeptical about immortality and bodily resurrection.

Whatever happened will never be known but the story of Christ's resurrection underscored the beginning and subsequent rapid expansion of the Christian community. All of

Jesus' disciples were Jews and the early Christians were Jews, who went to the Temple and also abided by the Law. They were different from other Jews only in the sense that the Christian Jews believed that the Messiah, expected by all Jews, had actually come in Jesus. The Christian Jews started to share a love feast in memory of the Last Supper. They became known as the sect of the Nazarenes, one of many sects within Judaism.

Members of this early Christian sect sold their possessions and turned the proceeds of the sale to the common treasury of the sect. When Ananias and his wife tried to hide and keep part of the proceeds from the sale of their house Peter chastised them for a lie to God and they fell down and died. Members of the sect shared their meals at common tables and the apostles used to serve the tables, but later decided to devote themselves to prayer and ministry instead of serving the tables. Such were the humble beginnings of the Church.

From the very beginning of Christianity the Greek philosophy was deeply embedded in its theology. The fourth Gospel, written about the year 100, begins with the statement: "In the beginning was the Word, the Word was with God, and the Word was God." (John 1:1.) "Word" or "reason" stems from the Greek term *logos,* by which Plato and other Greek philosophers for centuries had been claiming certain truths to be self-evident without being able to state why.

When many Hellenized Jews and Gentiles joined the sect of Nazarenes they did not care to adhere strictly to the Law, and Stephen and his followers boldly insisted that Jesus had freed his followers from their obligation to the Law, and called the meeting place of early Christians "the synagogue of the Freedmen." (Acts 6:9.) Stephen was stoned to death in Jerusalem and became the first Christian martyr. Some Christians moved out of Jerusalem and began spreading the gospels to the Samaritans and to the Gentiles.

The speed with which Christianity spread through the Greco-Roman world is beyond comprehension. The Churches of Antioch, Alexandria and Rome were founded before St. Paul launched his missionary work. Of all apostles St. Paul is known as the apostle to the Gentiles. In Alexandria, Egypt, about seventy Jewish scholars had already translated the Old Testament into Greek, which came to be known as the Septuagint or "the seventy" in Latin, well before the time of St. Paul.

The crucial question was whether or not the Christian Jews living in the Greco-Roman world and the Gentile Christians there should abide by the Law. The initial controversy centered around circumcision and dietary laws. The Christian Jews of Jerusalem believed that all Christians must abide by the Law.

To Paul, Jesus suffered to free Jews and mankind from the burden of the Law, Jesus and his teachings took the place of the Law, and Christians did not have to live by the Law. Peter perhaps perceived that this theological difference, which occurred in Jerusalem about the year 50, between Paul and the Christian Jews of Jerusalem was then insignificant in reality: The decision to accept the Samaritan and Gentile converts had already been made contrary to the Law; circumcision was a custom neither unique to the Jews nor well observed by the Jews; and dietary laws were ignored by Jesus.

Furthermore, Hellenistic Christian Jews and the Gentile Christians in the Greco-Roman world were willing to and had to abide by the local Roman law, and the Christian Jews of Jerusalem had to abide by the Law, which the Roman Empire recognized as the local law of Judea. Although either answer to the crucial question made little practical difference to the Christian Jews then, it should be noted that Paul provided a single most important answer in the history of Christianity.

That difference between Paul and the Christian Jews of Jerusalem on the question was identical with the difference between later Christian flexibility and Judaic rigidity. Christianity readily moved into the Greco-Roman world and the Christians of each locality accepted the local Roman law as if to accept the dictum "if you go to Rome follow the Roman law," but Judaism drew away from the Greco-Roman world by not being able to uphold the local Roman law on top of the Law.

The real difference lay in the fact that one was only born into Judaism under the Law and anyone could be converted into Christianity. In any event Pauline flexibility enabled Christianity to develop into a universal religion, and in turn Greco-Roman philosophy and the Roman legal system were ready to nurture the Christian Church as a universal church.

Although the Romans respected local customs and religions to the extent they affected only local people, the Romans, ruling the whole known world, were in no position to take into consideration the religious differences of different peoples involved in disputes. Therefore, the Roman law sought justice by consideration of strictly secular concepts of fair dealings, equity, faithfulness to commitments, common sense and equality. It was one universal law of nature or right reason, applicable to all men, unchangeable and eternal.

Tragic events followed shortly. The Zealots revolted against the Romans in 66. All the Jews and even Idumaeans came to the aid of the Zealots. The bandits freely roamed around in Judea, plundered and ravaged the villages and towns, and often massacred the villagers. Some husbands killed wives and children so that they might not be abused or sold to slavery.

There were factions among the Jewish fighters inside the walls of Jerusalem. The Zealots killed the priests and lawyers whom they used to hate. Each faction kept killing members of other factions. The Jewish rebellion was born out of the impatience of average Jews with their own religious malaise and the lack of confidence in their elders as much as out of the sense of defiance against the Romans. In any event the Romans watched and waited in anticipation that the Jews would kill one another. Over a million Jews were either killed or starved to death during this hopeless uprising of the Jews against Rome (66-73).

When the Jewish resistance finally ended, the Romans massacred the old and known partisans and sold the young into slavery. The Jewish fighters who had surrendered to the Romans were thrown to beasts and gladiatorial combats in Caesarea. The Temple was destroyed; Jerusalem and the outlying areas were in utter desolation. (How painfully did Jesus understand the bitter and defiant mood of the Jews of his time and its consequences. His teachings also revealed the premonition that the Jewish national malaise was irreversible and would inevitably invite appalling horrors and sufferings as happened.)

The Christian Jews found shelter in a small town of Pella beyond the Jordan River and survived the destruction, and then moved to Aleppo in Syria. The Christian Jews denied the divinity of Jesus or virgin birth or the supremacy of the teachings of Jesus over the Mosaic Law, and parted with the mainstream of the Christian Chruch. The Second Advent of Christ not coming to realization, the Christian Jews reverted to the Judaic beliefs in the sense that they refused to create souls for themselves by any stretch of imagination or fancy or place hopes above the present life.

The Roman legionnaires carried away the candlestick and the sacred Ark of the Law from the Temple in Jerusalem. The Jews made another desperate stand against the Romans from 132 to 135 but were crushed again. Judea was made into a Roman colony called Syria Palestina, and Jerusalem was barred to the Jews under the penalty of death, and it ended

Jewish life in Palestine until 1948 when Israel became independent.

MORE DETAILED LAW

The destruction of the Temple, however, brought about fundamental changes in the practice of Judaism. It should be recalled that the Book of the Law was, in part, written to establish a Levite theocracy. The destruction of the Temple set aside the prerogatives of the Levite family as the leaders of the Jews, and broke down thoroughly the power of the priests and lawyers, who had asserted domination over the entire aspects of the post-exilic Jewish life.

All the provisions of the Law in regard to sacrifices and rituals at the Temple were swept away. No priest could take advantage of the strict hygienic laws. The Law as a legal system enforceable by the State was brought to oblivion. As the Law was no longer a system to be enforced the Law as religious canons left no room for abuses. As the theocracy, the priestly class and lawyers were gone the Jews came to have no intermediary between themselves and God. Rabbis are teachers, not priests or practioners of the Law, and as such rabbis are not middlemen between Jews and God.

To the Jews barred from Jerusalem under the penalty of death, the Law came to represent the Jewish spiritual and moral imperatives, the Temple, the homeland and the way of the Jewish life.

There used to be two major factions of the Pharisee party: Levite and non-Levite lawyers and lay teachers. Teachers or rabbis who were religious liberals and laymen became the new leaders of the Jews after destruction of the Temple and organized a Council of Teachers at the Judean coastal town of Jabneh which was to perform the role of the defunct Sanhedrin, the Supreme Council of State. The Council of Teachers differed from the Sanhedrin in one fundamental way: The Sanhedrin relied on authority to enforce, but the Council of Teachers played the role of educators and arbitrators to pursuade, and made their opinions not mandatory but acceptable to the parties on the volition of the parties involved in a dispute.

Rabbis Johannan ben Zakkai and Gamaliel and their followers at Jabneh also toiled collecting mountains of the oral traditions, i.e. the opinions of the Teachers from the time of Hillel the Elder. Thus, the Mishnah (Instruction), a commentary on the Law, was completed by Rabbi Judah about A.D. 200. Further interpretation of the Mishnah resulted in another commentary called the Gemara (Supplement), which was completed in Palestine by the beginning of the 5th century; its more detailed version was completed in Babylonia by the beginning of the 6th century. The Mishnah and the Gemara form the Talmud (Learning), which is more a Jewish encyclopedia covering Jewish history and Jewish accomplishments in mathematics, medicine, philosophy as well as Law.

For the Law the Talmud is a record of elaborate debates. The parties to a dispute state facts, the teaching Rabbis cite the appropriate Mishnah and Gemara provisions, the students of the Law raise questions on a point of law, and each teaching Rabbi expresses his opinion. More often than not the Rabbis disagree on the same point of law, and one or another Rabbi gets embarrassed for not having done his homework.

As arguments develop, one or another party to the dispute gets embarrassed for failing to disclose a certain pertinent fact essential to a dispute. The exact conversation exchanged by the parties in the transaction must be restated, for even one or two words often may change the color of the pending case. Reasoning is based on case law just like case laws in the United States. The names of about one hundred Rabbis were mentioned and each Rabbi's opinion as well as the majority opinions of Rabbis in each case were preserved in the Talmud. The study, teaching and judging of the Talmud was a rigorous, highly self-disciplined and well-organized form of education.

Ezra's contribution to the Jewish life cannot be overemphasized in three important respects. Ezra placed a stop to the millennium-old questions of "wherefores" and "whys" about the meaning of one's life, the inevitable destiny of the Jews, and the relationship of God with Jews individually and as a group not in any mystic sense but only in terms of objective standards of the Jewish conduct and the pure Jewishness manifested in the Law and later the Talmud.

Secondly, the Book of the Law, developing into the highly complex Talmud, enabled the Jews to adapt themselves to subtle legal nuances, the imperatives of modernity. (Why are the children born of the Jewish fathers and non-Jewish mothers "bastards" and the children born of the non-Jewish fathers and the Jewish mothers "Jews"? This logical inconsistency, particularly in view of the Jewish patriarchal and genealogy systems, indicates the adaptation of the Law to the historical reality, not to logical consistency or reasonableness.)

Indeed the Jewish intellectuals of the 5th and 6th centuries could readily reconcile to any complex society of the 20th century as they would not consider the complex laws of the modern 20th century any more complicated than the Talmud.

Thirdly, the Judaic emphasis on education helped the multitudes of Jews to become politically very mature. The Jewish educational process to bring "sons" or "students" of the Law or the Talmud to the perception of Judaism adaptable to changing reality could be measured over the entire span of the Jewish history after Ezra, i.e., about 2400 years.

The above aspect of the development of the Law is significant because the Law was not considered as "revealed" in the Old Testament context and that was one of the points Jesus had clearly made. (But Christian theologians considered the

Law as "revealed" as late as in the 19th century. Some professors were expelled from the Divinity Schools for teaching that Moses did not write the Book of the Law, even in the United States of the early 20th century.)

In any event the Jews were discarding and leaving behind the concepts of the unchangeable and eternal revealed Law and absolute right or wrong when the Christians and the Greco-Roman philosophers and lawyers had just begun to marvel at the concept of the Law, unchangeable, eternal and universal, based on logical consistency and reason. Thus, early in their history, the Jews learned to be matter-of-fact and to doubt and know.

Dispersed in the Greco-Roman world the Jews encountered many legal restrictions of the Christian kingdoms against them: prohibiting Jews to hold public offices, hire Christian domestics, or charge high rates of interest to Christians; cancelling debts owed to Jews by Christians; mandating Jews to wear special badges or garments and to live in a restricted area; feudal system barring Jews from owning land and feudal guilds excluding Jews from industry; and the list goes on. It fostered the Jewish attitudes of doubts about the local Romano-Germanic laws throughout the Medieval period, and even to this day, and such skeptical attitudes coupled with the Judaic inspiration and propensity for perfection and the Judaic emphasis on education perhaps helped the Jews to become creative in many fields of human endeavor.

The Jews, forced to live in a restricted area of big cities, lived according to the Talmud. The Jews were less law-abiding from the Gentile point of view. The ways the Jews and the Gentiles interpreted the law differed: For the Jews who narrowly interpreted the written laws, the consideration to adapt to reality and meticulously sharp factual distinctions were far more important than logical and rational consistency; and for the Gentiles, broad generalizations and principles, logical consistency and systematic reasoning counted.

Besides, survival preceded local legality, which had placed the Jews outside of the local laws. It was simply a staggering load for any Jew to strictly adhere to the Talmud within the Jewish community, and the local law outside the Jewish community. They could not take any law, including the Talmud, to be universal, unchangeable and eternal. Every word in the Talmud represented every inch of the homeland, and the Talmud the homeland they could carry on their back. It became the symbol of what the Jewish life should be and the destiny the Jews could shape for themselves in defiance of all the odds and all the elements which threatened to humiliate and destroy them.

When a Jew inevitably commits a "sin," i.e. a violation of the Talmud, he is being silly or capricious for not knowing what is good for him but not in the Christian sense based on the depravity and original sin of mankind.

Whenever crises or persecutions face the Jews, all the differences, and dissentions, such as are prevalent among the orthodox, conservative and reform Jews of today, disappear. In the face of crises and persecutions the Jews become alive by upholding the Spirit of the Law, exercising their moral choices far beyond what the letters of the Law and the Talmud call for, and stick together.

The Jews could not be immune from the influence of the Greco-Roman philosophy and the Roman jurisprudence which reshaped the modern family system of the Jews and the status of the Jewish women. Numerous great Jewish minds attempted to place their faith upon a rational basis, but stopped short of being swallowed up by the Greco-Roman philosophy or Roman jurisprudence. Various words and arguments were used but invariably the stopper was the Spirit of the Law, which could not be explained away rationally. The unique relationship of Jews with God, i.e. the Spirit of the Law, inspires and disciplines the Jews in bad times and remains dormant in times of peace and prosperity.

EARLY CHRISTIANITY

Early Christians had neither time nor aptitude for a theological construction of the teachings of Jesus. Even St. Peter contradicted the teachings of Jesus by proclaiming that "he [Jesus] is the one ordained by God to be judge of the living and the dead." (Acts 10:42.)

As far as objective standards of conduct were concerned early Christians left the matter to the local Roman laws. Christianity, freed from the Law, rendered the teachings of Jesus sterile in the Greco-Roman world. The teachings of Jesus in the historical and social context of the ancient Hebrews could least appeal to the Gentile Romans and Greeks of that time who knew nothing about the ancient Hebrew history and the practices of Judaism. The teachings of Jesus, addressed to specific Judaic practices of his time, were not appealing to the Greco-Romans who had never known the rigid and extensive Law as a pervasive guide of their lives; therefore, the spiritual and moral values espoused by Jesus in the historical and social circumstances of the ancient Hebrews could not be meaningful in the Greco-Roman world. Even the early followers of Jesus found the teachings of Jesus "a hard thing" for any one to listen to and parted with Jesus (John 6:60-66).

The Roman law, on the other hand, had nothing to do with religion. The giant Empire was in no position and had no reason to stress the spiritual and moral standards of conduct for diversified groups of the peoples in its vast domain, or to legislate every aspect of the life of each citizen.

It was Greco-Roman philosophy which began theorizing moral standards based on logic and reason. It seemed as if early Christians did not have anything new to offer in that regard. Thus, early in the history of Christianity, the spiritual value in the personality cult of Jesus and the moral value in terms of Greco-Roman philosophy and jurisprudence came to be separated, and such a separation resulted in a change in the moral as well as the spiritual context of Christianity as shall be noted in ensuing chapters.

Early Christians had to solve the urgent practical problems at hand. Some Christians wished to die only after the Second Advent of Christ and were worried they might not be raised to Heaven if they died sooner, and other Christians saw no need for earning a living in anticipation of the imminent Second Advent of Christ. Should a Christian divorce his or her pagan spouse? Should the Greco-Roman women, without veils, be allowed to pray in the church? Should the church members be allowed to bring law suits before the secular courts? And so on.

In the process of opening up the Church to the Gentiles and the Jews alike, all kinds of people, drunkards, women-chasers, educated Jews, illiterate Gentiles and slaves, and others, were brought precariously together by the early Christians, who had to promise something to everybody. When Paul received a report that a Christian was living with his father's wife, Paul denounced immorality of that kind as, "not found even among pagans," and instructed the Christians of Corinth to "drive out the wicked person among you." (1 Corinthians 5:13.) (This banishment or expulsion order of Paul later came to serve as a basis for the church doctrine of excommunication.)

Early Christians concentrated on the personality cult of Jesus, and had to explain the teachings of Jesus in the way the Greeks and Romans could readily understand. The Gentiles in the congregation would become quiet when virgin birth, resurrection, heaven and hell, angels and demons, and miracles were mentioned but restless, boisterous or yawning when the teachings of Jesus were mentioned.

Some Greek philosophers considered St. Paul a "babbler" preaching foreign divinities (Acts 17:18). Some Christian Jews in the same congregation would not accept virgin birth and divinity of Christ, others would question the supremacy of the teachings of Christ over the Law and Christ over Moses, and others would insist that Jesus, a heavenly being, was incapable of suffering or feeling physical pains on the cross and denied his incarnation. The Gentile converts retained customs and notions from previous beliefs, particularly the Greco-Egyptian notions of bodily resurrection and afterlife.

"Now there are varieties of gifts, but the same Spirit," said St. Paul adapting to the diversified group of the early Christians, each looking for what he wants; "to one is given through the Spirit the utterance of wisdom, and to another the utterance of knowledge according to the same Spirit, to another faith by the same Spirit, to another gifts of healing by the one Spirit, to another the working of miracles, to another prophecy, to another the ability to distinguish between spirits. . . ." (1 Corinthians 12:4-11.)

Virgin birth, resurrection, heaven and hell, and various miracles had become established facts for centuries before the church fathers in the 4th and 5th centuries began constructing the Christian creeds and dogmas. The aura of mystical features which the ardent followers of Jesus showered upon Jesus came to overshadow his teachings. Teachings of Jesus were of secondary importance and myth in the Gospels became far more significant.

A great number of the earliest Gentile Christians in Egypt and Syria were Gnostics who blended Christianity with rather imaginative oriental philosophical and religious tenets about knowledge of the mystical hierarchy of the invisible world as the key to personal salvation in the afterlife.

Alexandria in Egypt was the religious and intellectual center of the world. The Egyptian notions of resurrection and afterlife for the kings and nobles were forced upon the religiously skeptical Greek and Roman rulers in Egypt and Syria, and such religious notions were gradually gaining factual authority in the Greco-Roman world well before the time of Jesus. The benefits of resurrection and afterlife were extended to the common people under Christianity. Mysticism opened the door for Christianity to the labyrinth of fancy and imagination as an integral part of early Christianity. The exorcist ceremony of driving out the demons from some Christians and miraculous recovery of the sick and physical resurrection of the dead were deemed and praised wonderful Christian victories over the demons and death.

Early church fathers also had to solve two other major problems: an organizational problem of the fast-expanding Church and the political relationship between the Church and the secular Roman Emperor, a "god." The inability of early Christians to respect Roman family customs, the local customs and the Roman temple worship services which were no more than modern-day patriotic gestures led to persecutions against early Christians by the Romans.

Some Christians questioned if it was sinful for them to pay taxes to the pagan emperor or if they should live by the Roman customs based on the superstitious religions of the Empire. These early Christians were black-or-white spiritualists who dichotomized everything into either Christian or pagan. Christians were persecuted not only by the Emperor Nero but also Emperors like Marcus Aurelius (161-180) and Diocletian (284-305), great statesmen of integrity, who perceived the danger of the divided loyalty of Christians to the Emperor and the Church.

In 313 the Emperor Constantine proclaimed equal rights for all religions and restored to the Christians their confiscated property. Christianity flourished under the imperial policy of religious toleration and emerged as the dominant religion of the Empire. Before the battle of the Milvian Bridge, near Rome, Constantine was said to have seen a cross and a victory sign in the sky and his victory was attributed to the Christian God.

Constantine perhaps was not a Christian in his lifetime and did not single out Christianity for favor. Christ was given an equal footing with other gods in the Roman pantheon. Constantine personally worshipped Jupiter, the supreme Roman god, and identified God the Father with Jupiter and Zeus. He was head of every religious sect within the Empire, and scrutinized the major activities of each religious sect.

Pagan Constantine had to preside over the Christian Church council. Greek theologians from Alexandria in Egypt, Athanasius and Arius, were engaged in a bitter controversy over the nature of the Father and the Son. In the scheme of Neo-Platonic Philosophy, Athanasius insisted Father and Son were of the same essence, while Arius maintained that they were of different substances. Each side tried to win the favor of Emperor Constantine, who did not know what the controversy was all about. Constantine valued Greek learning which presented opposite and diverse views without savage attacks upon each other, and did not see any reason why the Christians should be divided by the arguments for or against hypothetical and philosophical assumptions which the Gospels did not set forth.

He summoned the first world-wide church council to meet at Nicaea in 325. Of about eighteen hundred bishops in the known Christian world, about three hundred bishops and seventeen hundred clerical assistants to bishops attended the Council of Nicaea, which agreed on a creed favorable to Athanasius. The Council itself was an imposing demonstration of the world-wide church organization which would not accept any inferior position for the Church. The Church was an ally for the time being but was emerging as a potential rival to the Empire.

The ascetic and selfless Christians began establishing communities of Hermits or monks in Egypt, and Athanasius introduced into Rome the ideals and practices of monastic life and Neo-Platonism which renounced the pleasures of wine, sex, and marriage, and the desires and appetites of the flesh, and identified every pleasure with guilt.

The Creed, pronounced at the Council of Nicaea, merely touched upon the tip of an iceberg in the speculative labyrinth, and did not resolve anything by labelling Arius and his followers heretics. Christ was definitely declared to be both God and man.

Fierce arguments followed. Some denied that Mary was the "Mother of God" because no one should logically precede Jesus, God, and that the divine nature of Jesus was derived not from Mary but from the Father. Some questioned exactly when the Spirit of God descended upon Jesus, at the conception or his baptism, and others questioned exactly when the Spirit of God did leave Jesus, disabling him from performing more miracles on the cross, and so on. Pope Leo the Great (440-461) dictated the Council of Chalcedon (451) to declare his solution of the two natures of Christ, divine and human, perfectly blended in Jesus Christ.

The Council of Toledo (589) declared that the Holy Ghost proceeds from the Father and the Son (i.e. not just from the Father). It was rather a tragic fact that first episcopal warfare was waged against so-called schismatic sects and exterminated tens of thousands of "heretics" in the course of these arguments. As early Christians and Medieval Christians were ultimately dependent on the personality cult of Jesus or a historical person, they felt they had to come to a definite conclusion on every fine "hairsplitting" point in the speculative abyss. ("Hairsplitting" distinctions were made on the tangible and specific points of the Law in Judaism and on the intangible points of conjecture in Christianity.)

Early local churches used to be independent until it became legal for Christians to openly worship, and the bishops, called papas, as apostalic successors were distinguished among the clergy. Gradually the bishops of the Greater Metropolitan sees were recognized. The Bishop of Rome became prestigious because Rome was the imperial capital and the Roman See had the largest revenue. Then the imperial capital was moved to Milan and then to Constantinople. With the removal of imperial capital the prestige of the Roman See fluctuated but the Bishop of Rome became finally recognized as the successor to Peter during the papacy of Celestine I (422-432).

Eastern Christianity in Constantinople grew up in the cultural context of Byzantine civilization and later became less related to the Church in the West. Leo the Great refused to recognize the supremacy of the patriarch of Constantinople in the Church. Christendom looked up to the Roman See as its center.

(Although the Bishop of Rome was no longer merely one of the bishops it was not until the 11th century that the Bishop of Rome represented the centralized medieval papacy and came to pronounce upon church dogmas, to oversee ordinary diocesan affairs of other bishops, and to collect money from all episcopal jurisdictions.)

When Constantine recognized the right of Christians to worship openly, the Roman Empire was already declining. The Roman aristocrats were no exception to the tendency to follow the lead of the emperor only so long as the emperor was capable and good. Then there was Emperor Commodus (180-192), the beloved son of Marcus Aurelius and his beautiful but amorous wife Faustina. Commodus was proud of his Herculean physical strength in fighting fierce wild beasts before the applauding Romans in the arena; otherwise, he spent his time in large harems of girls and boys or in shedding the noble blood of the senate. He was strangled to death by a gladiatorial wrestler at the instigation of Commodus' concubine Marcia and her Praetorian conspirators. The army deserters were turning out to be highway robbers, and the Roman legal system began favoring the wealthy and distorting justice. Pax Romana, which had lasted for more than two centuries, came to an end.

Both the Roman armies and the Roman administrators betrayed the Empire in the face of the increased pressure from the Germanic tribes and the vigorous Persians. The Roman military commanders and generals indulged in the role of deposing and installing the "barracks emperors" and the Roman administrators were busily engaged in exploiting the people by building up bureaucratic hierarchies. Reform-minded Emperors Diocletian and Constantine could not reverse the decline.

The Romans were tired under the heavy burden of government, defense, and the erratic taxation. The Romans levied taxes on the basis of the assessed value of the land, not on the size of each lot. Roman administrators exercised discretion in assessing and the tax burden fell heaviest on small landowners. Unable to support the tax burden small farmers turned their land over to rich patrons. The senators, ex-magistrates, military commanders and generals were such rich patrons, holding large estates. Each patron then negotiated with the local tax administrators, the governing class of each town, for a lesser amount of tax and protected his clients. The tax administrators came to be squeezed by the central government and the patrons. The Roman coins were becoming worthless, and taxes were collected in kind. The tax administrators could not raise enough taxes as alloted by the Emperor and had to make up the deficit from their own fortunes.

The giant Empire was falling not because of the losses in battles but because of its own inability to redirect the national energy and cope with problems. The giant Empire was simply drifting aimlessly and petering out.

Either a Roman noble had a stately palace with all the luxury or a have-not Roman commoner, being kept idle, had to rely on an allowance of bread, bacon, corn, oil, free baths, and free public amusements provided by the Empire. The Roman law, built up by the greatest professional lawyers anywhere in history, ceased to be the principled guide of the Romans: Every local magistrate was spewing edicts.

On the other hand the Church was gaining strength. The Vulgate Latin translation of the Bible was made by the turn of the 5th century by St. Jerome. Each local church began chiming the bells.

The 4th and 5th centuries were the era of the "wandering of peoples." The repeated invasions into northern Europe of fierce Asiatic hordes forced the entire race of Germanic tribes to cross the Rhine River westward and move into the Roman Empire, carving out territories. Barbarian Germanic tribes in northern Europe considered a brave death in battle the highest virtue: They believed the souls of brave men killed in action were brought by angelic warrior maidens and welcomed in the Hall of Woden, the father of all Germanic gods. Even the souls in the Hall of Woden would fight for entertainment except when they banqueted with Woden. Angles, Alamannis, Saxons, Franks, Lombards, Suevis, Burgundians, Goths, Vikings, Vandals were some of the large Germanic tribes.

The turn of the 5th century marked the historic transition from the Greco-Roman era to the nascent Romano-Germanic tradition of the West. The Germanic tribes were moving into every part of Europe and the Roman Empire in the West came to an end in 476 when an Ostrogoth chieftain deposed Romulus Augustulus, the last Roman Emperor in the West.

ST. AUGUSTINE OF HIPPO

St. Augustine, at the juncture of historical transition, looked back to Christianity, not as formulated by Jesus but as interpreted in the light of Neo-Platonism, the Greek philosophical and religious doctrines, and formulated his thoughts adaptable to the new era of the Romano-Germanic tradition.

No authentic picture of this greatest theologian of the Church has come down to us. A manuscript portrait, drawn shortly after his death, depicts him as a short and chubby man with a black beard, dark skin and piercing eyes. He was the only Church Father who wrote his own *Confessions.*

Born the son of a pagan father and a Christian mother in Thagaste (in today's Algeria), Augustine as a child was as mischievous as any one of his age could be and brilliant at the same time. He began living with a Carthaginian mistress at the age of fifteen. While rejoicing in a life of various vices he also sought after an eternal and pure truth.

While young, Augustine was a Manichee, who believed in dualism, i.e. a perception of everything in the universe in terms of an eternal conflict between two kingdoms of good and evil, or light and darkness, or human spirit and body: The appetites for meat and the desires for sex and other bodily urges are evils, the creation of Satan, which must be subjugated by the human spirit, the creation of God.

At the age of twenty-nine he left Carthage for Rome. Shortly he was a teacher of Rhetoric in Milan, where he met St. Ambrose, the Bishop of Milan. Augustine began reading Neo-Platonic Greek philosophy. One day he heard a child chanting "Take up, read. . . ." When Augustine opened the Scripture it read, ". . . not in reveling and drunkeness, not in debauchery and licentiousness, not in quarelling and jealousy. But put on the Lord Jesus Christ and make no provision for the flesh to gratify its desires." (Romans 13:13-14.) Augustine let his mistress go, embraced Christianity and was baptized by Ambrose at the age of thirty-three. Four years later he was a priest and four more years later Bishop of Hippo (Today's Bone, Algeria), the office he served for about thirty-five years.

In an age of total anarchy and theological diversity Augustine was authoritarian and belligerent against whoever disagreed with him. There was no gentleness or modesty but vehement intensity in his absolute convictions. He died at the age of seventy-four in 430 when the Vandals besieged the city of Hippo.

Augustine, in his book *The City of God,* refuted the pagan charges that the Roman disaster came about because of the imperial adoption of Christianity and the abandonment of the Roman gods and the pristine Roman virtues, and that pacifistic Christianity was responsible for the decline of the Empire and the sack of Rome by the west Goths under their leader Alaric in 410.

Augustine's grim views of the total depravity and the sinfulness of human nature were partly autobiographical and partly descriptive of the rule of force, greed, corruption and despotism everywhere, the symptoms of the total anarchical transition period in which he lived and in which Western Europe was passing once and for all into the political and military control of the barbarian invaders, ushering in the new Romano-Germanic era of the 6th through 9th centuries.

Augustinian theology was a hybrid growth of the Judaic concept of Godly judgments, Neo-Platonism highly tinted with Egyptian mysticism, and Manichaeism. Neo-Platonism, originated in Alexandria, Egypt, more than a century earlier and spread to the known Roman world, was Greek philosophical and religious doctrine based on Plato's dichotomy of Idea and Matter. Its chief concern was not the objective standards of human conduct or the life in this world but how the multitudes of human souls, who readily indulge in sensual and depraved pleasures, might return to God by asceticism, purification, and mortification of the bodily appetites and sometimes by magic and incantations, which might enable the human souls to go through an all-pervading mystical experience of ecstasy and feel the ultimate reality of the universe. Augustine enumerated and attributed many mystical experiences and miracles which occurred in Africa to the relics of St. Stephen, the first Christian Martyr.

Augustine separated spirit and flesh, and divided the worldy interests of flesh and the other-worldly spiritual interests. (As noted already, these two interests were separated as Christianity freed itself from the Law and moved into the Greco-Roman world.) The contest of these two interests manifests in many ways: the earthly appetites of the lower human nature against the spiritual salvation; human pleasures against asceticism and unworldliness; the ruined city of Rome against the ultimate historical destiny of the Church, the City of God; the earthly kingdoms against the Christian commonwealth guided and ruled by the clergy, i.e. the City of God; human existence against selfless spiritual life; the kings of the living against the God of the eternal life on earth and heaven.

The dualism of good and evil and the historical struggle between flesh and spirit closely parallel the corresponding concepts in the cult of Manichaeism in which Augustine was brought up prior to his conversion to Christianity. The doctrines of predestination and salvation only through the grace of God were the necessary corollaries of his doctrine of the original sin.

Needless to mention, Augustine's view of human nature and the doctrine of original sin were implied neither in Judaism nor in the teachings of Jesus. The Augustinian division of flesh and soul was the about-face of Judaism and the teachings of Jesus. Judaism fused the Law and religion, and denied moral choices to the multitudes. Jesus fused morality and religion, taught the need for the interaction of the Law with morality and restored moral choices to the multitudes. St. Paul separated the Law and religion; subsequently the Greco-Roman philosophy and the Roman jurisprudence theorized objective standards of human conduct and Christianity came to be solely concerned with the mystic personality cult of Jesus. St. Augustine found a new dichotomy and an eternal conflict between flesh and spiritual salvation.

(Augustine's view of human nature was made the cardinal doctrine of Reformation Protestantism, notably by John Calvin, and Augustine's view of the future role of the Church was accepted by the Catholic Church. Augustine's City of God was reverting to the Hasmonaean theocracy which the Jews had discarded centuries earlier. There is hardly any resemblance between the teachings of Jesus and Augustinian theology, and it becomes later evident particularly when Calvinism, influenced by Augustinian theology, rejects and denies Free Will, the cardinal teaching of Jesus.)

It should be noted, however, that the church-state relationship in Europe of the fifth century and the subsequent early Medieval Age imposed Augustinian views upon the Christians. Why did the highly civilized Greco-Roman people have to obey the rule of force imposed by the Roman generals and the invading barbaric general-kings? There was no answer except that general-kings were the instruments of God's wrath on earth and that despotism and the use of force in government was the divinely appointed remedy for sin as in the Old Testament, the concept from which Jesus clearly dissociated himself.

Furthermore, in the development of Judaism it was the clerical or rabbinical function to see to it that objective standards of conduct specified in the Law were observed by the Jews, but in Christianity objective standards of conduct were spelled out in the Roman laws and the function of enforcing the laws belonged to whoever had the military control over the land and the people. Under the circumstances Augustine was actually defining the glorious future in store for the Christians and the function of the Church in a grand scale of the City of God, a historical destiny of the Church in which a

Christian commonwealth guided by the clergy would inevitably replace all earthly kingdoms.

MEDIEVAL CHRISTIANITY

Toward the end of the 5th century the Frankish King Clovis (466-511) was engaged in a great battle against the confederation of Germanic tribes. In this battle he invoked the God of his Christian bride (who was later canonized as St. Clotilda), and defeated the enemy. His immediate conversion to Christianity won him support of the Church. Although Clovis was the first Germanic king to embrace Christianity almost all Germanic tribes had Christians among them. Many of the Germanic people who had been living west of the Rhine River (i.e. the Roman Empire) adopted Christianity. They used to be hired as mercenaries by the Roman Empire. Furthermore, as the Germanic tribes captured the Romans for slavery, some of the captives were Christians, who worked diligently to convert the captors for salvation.

The Frankish Kingdom, then considered merely as one of the barbaric kingdoms, came to be recognized as a kingdom within the Roman Empire (more correctly the Eastern Roman Empire with its capital in Constantinople), opened the way to wide conquests of the former domains of the Roman Empire in the West from other Germanic peoples, and eased the pain of a slow but steady transition to the Germanic rule from the Roman rule. By slow and almost imperceptible degrees the Germanic tribes seized the Roman territories and began establishing an Empire in place of the dissolved Roman Empire in the West. The Franks came to rule over the entire area of Western Christendom except for the British Isles, ruled by the Anglo-Saxons and their enemies, and Italy, under the rule of the Lombards and their rivals.

The Dark Ages, following the collapse of the Western Roman Empire, were certainly turbulent but did not prolong total anarchy. Each victorious Germanic king distributed the occupied territory among his chiefs and each chief parceled out his holdings among his retainers or the chiefs of the clans, who controlled distribution of fields and left pastures and forests for common use. The Germanic people loved to drink beer, and discussed all matters of importance at drunken feasts. Their clothing for men and women was alike and tightly fitting and was made of animal skins. Each man was content to be married with only one wife, and was devoted to the family life, and women were respected. An adulteress, however, was stripped naked and whipped in public. The father had the right to but rarely let the newborn baby die of exposure even if displeased with the baby for one reason or another.

Although there had been a considerable social distinction between German and Roman, the Franks in today's France and Belgium readily intermarried with local Romans and mingled with local people, and Latinized even their language. The Saxons and Alamanni, however, remained in today's Germany, retained the German tongue, and had fewer opportunities to intermingle with the Romans. It was Germanic custom for a man to steal a wife from another tribe or buy one within the same tribe. The captives and the losers in gambling who could not pay off debts became serfs. Sons became warriors, at an early age, the status of which meant a complete independence from the paternal authority.

Members of each Germanic tribe lived according to their own tribal customs. Thor, among innumerable Germanic gods, was god of thunder or law and order. Thor's day (i.e. Thursday) was the trial date. The Germanic customs were not written down because they did not know how to write. They were willing to let the local Romanized inhabitants live by the Roman law.

The Germanic tribes were anxious to be civilized with the

help of the Christian clergy and monks. Some of the Germanic kings wished to put a mixture of Roman law and the Germanic customs into writing with the aid of the Christian clergy and monks. The Roman law and the Germanic customs inevitably influenced each other, and the result was a variety of hybrid Romanesque laws.

The Germanic kings readily recognized the Emperor of the Eastern Roman Empire as their overlord, though only nominally. Diversified Romano-Germanic customary laws became applicable to Germanic and non-Germanic subjects and adapted to the needs of each locality.

Augustine's City of God was steadily on the rise. The Germanic invasions initially created a political power vacuum in many parts of Europe. Furthermore, the people came to look up to the local church and local clergy rather than the alien rulers. The Germanic rulers were willing to let the clergy act as the local administrators and judicial arbitrators.

The pontificate of Pope Gregory the Great (590-604) was marked by zeal in propagating Christianity in Europe and England and bringing back into the Christian fold the Arians of Italy and Spain, the diehard followers of "heretical" Arius, who eventually became reconciled to the Church.

Born in Rome of a wealthy patrician family Gregory used all of his personal wealth to found monasteries and for other religious purposes. A man of medium height, bald head, brown eyes, a hooked nose and bearded chin, Gregory the Great was a man of common sense. Once sought for his opinion on the sinfulness of taking a bath on the Sabbath day Gregory told the pious Christians that he would not approve of bathing as a pleasure on any day but would not forbid it as cleansing even on the Lord's day. He did not wish to be Pope but was elected unanimously.

Once elected, Pope Gregory, the first monk ever to be so elected, administered the vast church estates honestly, and allotted the revenues, in equal shares, for the bishop, the clergy, the church buildings and the relief of the impoverished and the hungry.

He spread the doctrines of St. Augustine throughout Christendom, along with the popular notions of angels, demons, miracles, hellfire and the use of allegory. Warlike Germanic tribes had to compromise their Germanic virtues of honor, pride, adverturism, violence and danger with the Christian virtues of humility, conscience, repentance, kindliness, and peace in the new mysticism and put the peaceful Kingdom of God in place of the chivalrous Hall of Woden.

Although Gregory forcefully stated his view that even a wicked secular ruler was entitled to obedience from his subjects and secular rulers were answerable only to God and their conscience, he was obliged to assume the role of the Emperor in the West in order to counterbalance the prestige of the Church in Constantinople, and such a secular role of Gregory became the basis for later claims of the Church to temporal powers.

A cleric forged a document called the Donation of Constantine whereby, centuries earlier, Emperor Constantine supposedly had given Pope Silvester the city of Rome and its surrounding areas in gratitude for a miraculous recovery from leprosy. Forged documents used to impress the illiterate Germanic rulers were no rarity then, and the authenticity of the deed of gift went unquestioned. Also another questionable donation was made to the Church by Pepin the Short, the Frankish King, who granted land around Ravenna to the Pope, which helped the rise of papal monarchy; consequently, central Italy came directly under the temporal rule of the papacy in 756.

Charles the Great (768-814), the Frankish King, conquered a wide area of Europe including today's France, Germany and Italy and emerged as the master of Germanic world. The Holy Roman Empire was in the making by 800.

Charles, a towering stocky man of fun and gaity with a spark of playful amusement in large glassy eyes, was a bulldozer-like warrior whose physical vigor could not be exhausted in his exercise of swimming, hunting, womanizing and annual military campaigns personally directed by him. Charles, an illiterate himself, encouraged education for Germanic peoples and established a Palace School, and a library to collect old manuscripts. The clergy and monks were the civilizers who also had to prepare minute imperial edicts for the correction of official abuses and management of his estates.

Charles, a zealous promoter of Christianity but a cold calculator, insisted however on his supremacy over the Church, decided on church dogmas, compelled the cathedrals to elect his nominees as bishops, made appointments to church offices, regarded the Pope merely an honorable figure among his Frankish bishops, who were to pray for the success of the Emperor in conducting the affairs of both Empire and Church, and considered the clergy and monks to be relatively corruption-free servants. No pope of this period questioned the Emperor's lordship over the papacy.

In 843 the Holy Roman Empire was divided among three grandsons of Charles: one part eventually evolved into France, another part into Germany, and the third part, comprising the remnants, into the Holy Roman Empire.

The spread of medieval feudalism weakened the Frankish kingdoms. Feudalism was accompanied by an impressive ceremony called homage, which created a sort of contractual relationship of the Lord and a vassal for mutual obligations of aid and support. Each vassal of the Lord King held a city or villages and adjoining lands. In return for the land thus granted the vassal had to organize his men into units, each of which was charged with a required number of armed knights attended by a requisite number of sergeants and squires. A knight in turn as lord would subdivide his domain, and each tenant would provide a certain number of armed men to serve the lord. Each tenant also paid dues to the lord.

Each lord had legal jurisdiction over his tenants, and each tenant over his undertenants. The land kept subdividing until the bottom was taken up by serfs. Each tenant owed allegiance to the lord to whom homage had been made. Kings and feudal lords gave their tenants charters or verbal understandings which set forth the rights of tenants. (The Magna Carta in England, 1215, was one such charter.) Many feudal lords of this age were illiterate and had to sign, on charters, their names by a cross.

A feudal landholding was also bestowed in return for public service and other services the king in his court required. The Kings consulted bishops, abbots and other vassals in deciding important affairs of the state, issuing decrees, or in instructing retainers in the royal court on how to handle new classes of cases. Bishops and abbots were also granted feudal landholdings for their services and they were feudal lords. The donations of lands by the Germanic kings and their vassals to local churches were generous. The lordships were made hereditary; accordingly, the king could not take away the customary rights of his vassals or the rights granted to his subjects by the previous kings.

The kings inherited kingdoms but the vassals of the kingdom had the right to choose and install the new king. The election process was vague and the idea was that the king's son would ordinarily succeed the king but the new king had to be acceptable to the vassals.

Royal authority weakened because the king neither had any more land to give nor could he increase royal revenue. A king or an emperor could not exercise absolute authority over the entire kingdom, and his authority was exercised only within the confines of his small personal estates.

Bishops and abbots as feudal lords relied on the kings or secular feudal lords, not the pope, for protection to maintain

their domains and fiefs. This meant that bishops and abbo and the church properties came under control of kings c feudal lords, who exercised the power of lay investiture tc confer the office of bishop or abbot on successive incumbents of a bishopric or abbey. Bishops and abbots were worldly rulers independent of the papacy just as the dukes and counts were independent of kings and emperor.

Each lord exercised the power of Justice, including the power to impose the death penalty. Each locality had its own laws, and there were more than one thousand different hybrid Romanesque laws throughout Western Europe, and a traveler found a different law at each new horse stop. Some were written but most laws remained unwritten customs. Dukes, counts or other lords did not dispense justice. Each court was formed by a small number of freemen, like today's jury, who were clergy and landholders appointed by a duke (the tribal chief), a count (Emperor's appointee), a bishop or an abbot.

While grassroot churches were gaining strength locally everywhere, the papacy itself lost its effectiveness. About the middle of the 9th century a frustrated Frankish cleric produced (forged) the Isidorean Decretals, whereby the popes of the early Church supposedly commanded the direct responsibilities of bishops to the pope. Subsequent arguments for the sovereign authority of the pope were in vain. In the 10th century the papacy was a "pornocracy" controlled by the amorous mother and daughter team of Theodra and Marozia, mistress of Pope Sergius III and mother of Pope John XI.

Saxon kings, particuarly Otto the Great (936-973) in Germany, began asserting strong royal power. Pope John XII (955-964), known as the Boy Pope, elected at the age of eighteen, secured the aid of Otto to defend the papal states against Berengar II, the King of Italy. John crowned Otto as the Holy Roman Emperor. In 962 Otto exacted from the papacy the so-called Ottonian privilege, whereby the Emperor was free to choose and have only his nominee elected as

Pope. Thus the pope was no more than a German bishop. (In order to tightly control secular and spiritual authorities within his Empire, Otto divided and fragmented Germany into numerous petty feudal lay and clerical principalities, which hindered the unity of Germany until the 19th century and which aroused an extreme nationalistic aspiration in Germany of the 19th and 20th centuries.) Church offices were bought and sold and it was hard to distinguish the clergy from secular offices.

It was during this period that monasticism became an important institution. Various monastic orders came into being in the 10th and 11th centuries. Whenever a new monastic order was established the initial vigorous yearning of its adherents for spiritual perfection served as a wave of protest and reform against the worldlinesss of the church as well as the secular rulers. The Cluniac monastic order was unique in the sense that, instead of each monastery being independent, all Cluniac monasteries were subordinated to the abbot of the mother monastery at Cluny in the duchy of Burgundy. The Cluniac order spread effectively the reform ideals for celibacy of the clergy, papal election by an electoral college of cardinals, and opposition to lay investiture and simony.

In the 9th and 10th centuries the northmen in the North and the Saracens, Wendy and Magyars in the East threatened again to reduce Europe to a state of anarchy. The first millennium after Christ was approaching and the Christians throughout Europe exchanged the visions about the imminent end of the world.

The most atrocious and destructive new invaders were the Vikings, who sailed down in their slim, long and speedy boats by sea and riverways and set beachheads on the coasts of the Caspian and Black Seas, England, France, Germany, Spain, North Africa and Italy, looting and plundering. These northern Germanic tribes were simple-minded enough to become

mercenaries for whoever paid them with silver and gold. The Vikings fought against the Vikings.

The Vikings came down fiercely but became very submissive when and where they decided to settle down. Their chieftains married local princesses, embraced Christianity, readily adapted themselves to local customs wherever they decided to live and became assimilated into the native population, and their homeland itself became Christianized with the establishment of bishoprics and monasteries.

Popes and Emperors had been engaged in sporadic contests for supremacy ever since the revival of the Holy Roman Empire in 962. A steady rise in the power of the pope was inevitable, provided the right man came along. Such a man was Hildebrand, the Cluniac monk, who became Pope Gregory VII in 1073. Gregory, short and obese with sparkling eyes, was a son of an Italian farmer. Bishops were used to German pontiffs, not Italian. Gregory had to overcome the initial protests of German bishops, put the papacy in order, and claim the supremacy and independence of the centralized papacy and the right of the pope to appoint, depose and transfer bishops. Gregory's inconclusive struggles with Henry IV, the young Emperor, left his reform tasks incomplete.

As mentioned earlier the Church was highly decentralized until the 11th century; accordingly, a variety of Germanic customs crept into local ecclesiastical laws. In many localities the medieval trial by ordeal was executed often at the most solemn moment of the Mass. In some cases the accused had to place his hand into a pot of boiling water and take out a stone or carry a hot iron in the aisle. If his hand healed clean within three days he was declared innocent.

Trial by combat was the method of adjudicating legal disputes by personal combat between the parties or their appointed champions. No other legal method was recognized for the settlement of a lawsuit involving recovery of the land. Even the churches authorized judicial combat to decide the ownership of disputed church properties. The practice of duelling and the trial by the ordeal of cold water were also common. Germanic superstitions and ethics of deciding honor and valor were an integral part of Medieval Christianity.

Then came a rather odd phenomenon, taking place in the city of Bologna in northern Italy in the last decade of the 11th century. Ambitious young men from nearly every corner of Europe came to Bologna to study law. Eventually these students formed an autonomous student council, which established the first University in Christian Europe, and appointed, evaluated and discharged professors. Irenerius, a brilliant young lawyer, began lecturing on Justinian's law texts.

Centuries earlier, Justinian, the Eastern Roman Emperor (572-565), was bent on reviving a universal Roman Empire with Christianity as the religion of such an empire, and reestablishing the absolute power of the Emperor. In pursuit of this ambitious policy of a highly centralized empire Justinian also needed a uniform legal system. The Justinian code was the collection of ancient Roman constitutions (Codex Justinianus, 529), opinions of the ancient Roman jurists (the Digest, 533) and his own legislation (the Novellae, 565).

Clearly emerging were the ideas that one uniform law must be applicable to all peoples in the wide geographical area and that a centralized and powerful administration must tame the diversities of feudalism.

Upon graduation from the University of Bologna, young men with their diplomas pondered their career. One's preference depended on the individual observation of which of two, the Church or the state, would offer a better career. Those who went to work for the church became "canonists" and those for the state "civilians." Several universities, dedicated solely to the study of law, sprang up in northern Italy and they were given charters of privileges by Popes and Emperors.

An obscure monk named Gratian, at the University of Bologna, toiled and completed the compilation and systematic arrangement of Papal decrees known as the *Decretum* (1140), which was given an official sanction in 1234 and made a part of subsequent canon laws. The church courts administered justice according to such canon laws, which were binding on all persons in Europe until the Reformation.

Canonists studied the papal decrees which had decided particular law cases and laid down general rules of law. The Justinian code presented an ideal model for the divine right of the Pope, the centralized church and a uniform ecclesiastical law. Canonists launched a general attack upon diversified customary laws and feudal decentralization.

In theology too, an effort to systematize and interpret the Bible in a uniform way culminated in the *Sentences* (1159) by Peter Lombard, Bishop of Paris, which made theology distinct from canon law. The Popes of this period were prepared to maintain the centralized papacy against the diversities which feudalism represented.

The Lateran councils forbade usury and the clerical sanction of trials by ordeals and duels. Canon lawyers of this age were bold enough in endeavoring to bridge the gap between law and morals. Classical Roman law principles of faithfulness to commitments, fair play, equity over technical legal distinctions, interpretation of the laws on the basis of common sense, reason, and logical consistency underscored the canonist theories of contracts, the women's right to inherit land and chattel, less formal but speedy trial procedure, imprisonment of criminals instead of capital punishment; and such underlying classical Roman law principles of canon law later helped modernize commercial and maritime laws.

Although canonists and civilians received nearly identical Roman law training, civilians understandably sided with the secular rulers and canonists with the primacy of the Pope. This contest was not decided by debates but by a monumental historical event.

Pope Urban II (1088-1099) proclaimed the First Crusade (1096-1099) for the recovery of the Holy Land of Palestine from the pagan Muslims, and an almost continuous crusading movement followed for nearly two centuries.

The Crusades presented wartime profit opportunities to the people in large towns, who in turn also found opportunities to exclude the feudal lord's authority from the affairs of each town. The townspeople formed an association to achieve their goal of becoming independent with their own army and courts. Merchants and artisans formed their associations. Each association hired an able outsider, impartial to conflicting interests of the leading families of the town or the interests of the leading merchants or artisans.

These associations, efficiently administered, found the road to prosperity, and towns became communes or independent cities. Associations formed a league to further their political influence, and eventually forced kings to grant charters to cities and towns, which in turn enacted laws, set up courts and even controlled prices.

The Crusades also resulted in an enormous increase in the wealth, power and prestige of the Church and papacy. Chartres Cathedral, the Cathedral of Notre Dame, Amiens Cathedral and the Cathedral of Toledo were built.

A universal supremacy of the papacy came close to full realization by the time Pope Innocent III (1193-1216) equated the pontifical authority with the greater light of the Sun and royal power with the lesser light of the Moon, and accepted secular kingdoms as fiefs of the Church.

The Church owned one-third of European soil, and the popes of this period made and deposed kings. Kings simply could not refuse to place the pope's nominees in key secular government positions. Feudal royal government machinery could work without kings because able archbishops and bishops could run secular governments as if they were managers running estates for absentee landlords. Archbishops, bishops, and other clerics were devoted to a system of universal law and order and kings were subject to that law and order.

Innocent III, a young and brilliant administrator and autocratic man of decisive nature, appeared to be an ideal man tailored to be the Pope of this Age. He reorganized the Papal chancery, placed secular states under the moral guidance of the Papacy, legislated by issuing thousands of decrees, and personified the High Priest-King of Europe. The Fourth Lateran Council, invoked by Innocent, proclaimed among other things the sacraments of the Eucharist, penance and communion, and the dogma of Transubstantiation.

Inspired to reunite the Roman Church and the Eastern Church in Constantinople, Innocent III inaugurated the Fourth Crusade. He promised the redemption of sins to all who should serve in the crusade personally a year or by a substitute two years. The crusaders, who were supposed to render every assistance to the Eastern Church, sacked and looted Constantinople in 1204 so atrociously and thoroughly that a separation of both Churches became permanent.

Pope Gregory IX (1227-1241), a relative of Innocent III, established the Inquisition against heretics. The Inquisition warrants against heresy reached into every corner of Europe. Any opposition to the church doctrine or papal decrees was considered pagan. Monks of a single-minded devotion and of self-righteous integrity had no reason to think the actions of the Papacy anything but holy and began working ruthlessly as servants of the holy inquisition against the political foes of the Pope.

It was during this period of the universal supremacy of the papacy that Catholic monks and scholars were contented to read the writings of the early Church Fathers and ancient Greco-Roman philosophers, and scholarship was judged by one's ability to cite ancient authorities to lend weight to his opinions and beat an adversary in a public disputation or play upon words rather than by the originality or creativeness of one's thoughts. This led to the Medieval Scholastics.

ST. THOMAS AQUINAS

The Prince of Scholastics was St. Thomas Aquinas (1225-74). The "Apostheosis of St. Thomas Aquinas" by the 15th century painter Benozzo Gozzoli portrays Thomas in a sitting position taller than men of average height. Thomas looks so heavy, and his bloated round face with a wide forehead and a straight long nose is far from being handsome or sharp looking.

Thomas, an absent-minded professor, was born in 1225 as a son of the Lombard nobility. He was related to about half of the European royal families. Ordained a priest about 1250 and awarded a doctorate in theology in 1256, he was professor of philosophy at the University of Paris throughout his life. When some of his students shouted about a winged ox flying over the sky, Thomas searched the skies for the ox; thereafter, the name of the Dumb Ox stuck to him. Anything but dumb was he, who was the advisor to every Pope and was eagerly sought after by kings for opinions.

Early in the 13th century the philosophical writings of Aristotle together with the commentaries of Averroes and other Arabian scholars became available. Aristotle's writings seemed to uphold the position of Averroeists that empirical truth and philosophical truth could refute theological teachings. Averroeism threatened the integrity and supremacy of "revealed" truths such as the creation story, yet to reject or ignore Aristotle was neither effective nor desirable.

The reading of Aristotle was banned off and on at European universities and the Church initially allowed only monasteries to study Aristotle's works.

Before the time of Thomas the theology and philosophy of St. Augustine prevailed unquestioned. Augustine taught that man must search for truth with intuition or the inner world of ideas through a mystical experience of ecstasy rather than upon reason or sense experience. In the parlance of today's language either one believes or does not believe and one can-not arrive at the spiritual truth by thinking.

There was another dimension to the controversy over Aver-roeism. Augustine was no less a man of intense conviction in his religious way of thinking than a mystic who arrived at his doctrinal analysis on intuition or ecstasy. The writers of the Law, Plato and Augustine, and Jesus to a lesser extent, shared the view that not many men are endowed with abilities to grasp religious or philosophical truths: One great prophet, one philosopher-king, one spiritual prince or one Christ can perceive that truth, and the multitudes of lesser human souls can not perceive but only feel; therefore, lesser souls simply must follow the leader on intuition or ecstasy.

The Aristotelian philosophy, however, made every man a rational animal who was capable of comprehending truth. Therefore, the controversy involved the right to disagree with the orthodox views and questioned the right of the Church to impose its creeds and dogmas upon all Christians.

Thomas struck a compromise by saying that certain truths, like the incarnation, are known only through revelation; truths about material things only through sense experience; and other truths, such as the existence of God, through both reason and revelation.

The characteristic part of Thomas' theology is his theory of law. He classified law into four different kinds.

First, the Eternal Law is based on the reason of the al-mighty and willful God, Creator of the universe and a judge of every individual, family, tribe and nation.

Second, Natural Law is the divine reason implanted in cre-ated things. An example of this is the rational nature of men to live in society, to procreate and educate children, and to seek the truth and develop intelligence.

Eternal Law is Thomas' perception of the attributes of

God. Natural Law is a restatement of the ancient Greek philosophy. These concepts were perfectly respectable in the Medieval Age when abstract theories did not have to be proved on the basis of human experiences or scientific investigations.

Third, Divine Law is "revealed" law. Specific provisions in the Book of the Law and the teachings of Jesus as specific commands are revelations, i.e. a gift of God's grace rather than a discovery by human reason.

Fourth, Human Law is a derivative from Natural Law, i.e. the unaided human reason. The unaided human reason is the divine reason implanted in human beings. Plato, Aristotle, and the Stoic philosophers and Roman lawyers to whom Scholastics owed their theological and philosophical views were invariably pagans.

What Thomas meant was that even a pagan king had divine reason implanted in him and his subjects should not disobey such a pagan king, and that the Church should not judge and depose a king by branding him as a pagan. "Pagans" often were Christians but political foes of the Pope and there was rather a nebulous distinction between a "pagan" and a "Christian."

Whether or not Thomas' classification of Law is valid today is not important, but his theory is significant in two important respects.

First, Medieval Christianity relied for its moral context on Greco-Roman philosophy and Roman law. Thomas attempted to draw a line between the realm of reason and the realm of faith based on "revealed" truths. This point will be mentioned later.

Second, his moderate stand on pagan rulers was meant to warn against the power of the Medieval Church to *judge* one king to be a Christian and brand another to be a pagan or heretic on account of divorce and other disobedience to the Church, including political disobedience. Indeed he was urging moral restraint on the Church power to judge and excommunicate at the time when the imposing structure of the Medieval Church was beginning to crack.

Thomas died in 1274 at the age of forty-nine, and no one would guess how much the Church would miss him at the time of gathering storms.

PAVING THE WAY FOR REFORMATION

Pope Boniface VIII (1294-1303) was the last pope to assert universal authority. Boniface, a noted canon lawyer, forced his predecessor, Pope Celestine V, a hermit saint, to resign from the Papacy and kept aged and harmless Celestine in wretched misery until his death. Handsome, rude, and vain, Boniface wore imperial dress on occasions, and acted as Pope and Caesar at the same time, and claimed the absolute superiority of the papacy over secular rulers.

King Philip IV, known as Philip the Fair because of his handsome blond features, plotted to kidnap the Pope for a trial as a common criminal on French soil for forbidding the clergy to pay taxes to the King and other disagreements, and dispatched his chancellor, William de Nogaret, and his cohorts for the mission. Nogaret and a small group of anti-pope Italians led by Sciarra Colonna took Boniface prisoner in the estate of the Gaetani family at Anagni and abused him with threats and blows for three days. Nogaret and his cohorts were put to flight by the townspeople of Anagni who belatedly discovered them as aliens. Boniface died shortly of shock and humiliation, and the nature of the papacy was never the same again.

In the Medieval Age the divine right of the Pope and the divine right of the kings were often hotly contested. Such controversies centered around many practical issues arising at various intervals of the Medieval period. It would have been improbable for the kings to survive had all the land held by churchmen been exempt from feudal rents, and equally impossible for the Church to function without property. The Church claimed rights to exact papal taxes, to seize heretics' property, to disqualify heretics from secular offices, to discipline rulers, to approve international treaties and agreements as they were vital to peace, to try ecclesiastical cases in the church courts, and to decide what was or was not an ecclesiastical matter.

As much as property and revenue of the State or the Church were involved, the line between an ecclesiastical matter and a secular matter could not be drawn without taking into consideration the relative strengths of the Church and State. The borderline cases involved a debtor pledging to the Church the land on which he owed money to others, lay tenants holding church lands, collusive land gifts to the Church which enabled the donor to avoid feudal service, small landowners surrendering to the church free land and receiving it back with tenancy for life, and other similar cases.

Philip the Fair induced Pope Clement V (1305-1314) to move the seat of papacy to Avignon in southern France. Rome, without the pope, lost the business that flowed from the streams of pilgrims and priests, and was gradually reduced to an anarchic poverty-stricken city during the Avignon papacy (1309-1377).

The Avignon papacy, on the other hand, could not raise revenues because it could not derive incomes from the church properties in Italy; accordingly, the Pope created new offices for sale, and a buyer of a bishopric had to pay as much as one-half of the first year's earnings. The papacy also derived revenue from the sale of indulgences and other collections, and papal collectors kept portions for themselves.

The Romans clamored for the return of the papacy to Rome. In 1378, under threats of violence, the Roman mob forced the conclave to elect an Italian pope, resulting in the election of Urban VI. Urban tried to restrain the extravagant life of cardinals and their influence on the papacy, and the

Pope and the cardinals never got along well; therefore, the French cardinals, more than two-thirds of the college of cardinals, had second thoughts and elected Clement VII, thus reestablishing the Avignonese line papacy (1378-1423) against the Roman line of the papacy (1378-1415).

The spectacle of two or three rival popes carrying on political chicanery against one another did not advance the eminence of the papacy. The turn of events led the 14th and 15th century popes to be preoccupied with secular politics rather than with spiritual leadership. It was during this period of papacy when popes, cardinals and bishops became proverbial for their pomp and self-indulgence. Some of them were rascals and profligates.

The people in Europe of this period exchanged with one another various versions of the life of Pope Joan. Joan, an English girl, fell in love with a Benedictine monk. The couple fled to Athens where the monk died. The grief-stricken Joan disguised herself as a man and became a monk, and later a cardinal. Elected in 855 as Pope John VIII, Joan's secret became unmasked when she died in childbirth during a papal procession. The religious writers of the Renaissance period polished this scenario painstakingly and turned various versions of it into pornographies and anti-papal propaganda. This allegory was symptomatic of the absurd age.

The 14th century was indeed the age of religious contradictions. While the Black Death and the Hundred Years' War created the popular need to seek souls, anticlerical writers included lay men and women as well as clergy and religious writers. Yet the local priests and monks worked as ever to lighten the burden of the poor and weak and to preserve a semblance of civic order centering around each local church.

John Wycliffe (1320-1384), an English theologian and onetime Professor at Oxford, took a theological stand, later almost identically taken by Martin Luther. John Huss (1369-1415), a Professor at the University of Prague, denounced the sale of indulgences, and professed the supreme authority of the Bible over the primacy of the pope. He was tried and condemned by the Church Council and was executed. The underlying forces that led to the eruption of the Reformation of the sixteenth century had already begun to mushroom.

It was during this period of the papacy too that trade and commerce, initially stimulated during the years of the Crusades, accelerated the growth of the mercantile class, independent commercial cities in Italy and other parts of Europe, shipbuilding and the science of navigation.

The Hundred Years' War of 1337-1453 was not a continuous war but an on-and-off struggle between England and France until England gave up all its possessions on the European continent. Far more devastating than war, plague and unprecedented agonies of death swept Europe.

The Black Death of 1347-1352 claimed one-third to one-half of the population in Europe and Asia, and depleted the labor markets. Serfs became peddlers and hired laborers, and feudal lords had to compete for labor by raising the price of labor and giving serfs economic independence. Payment of wages for labor was not only detrimental to feudal lords but also to the land-rich Church. Debt-ridden feudal lords and their retainers became mercenaries hired by England and France during the War and often plundered towns and villages.

In the early 14th century Berthold Schwarz, a German monk, invented a method of propelling projectiles by use of gunpowder, and ushered in a revolution in weaponry, setting apart the Modern Age from the Medieval Age. The subsequent advent of cannon became destructive to the feudal castles in Europe by the end of the 14th century.

In 1450 Johann Gutenberg invented the printing press, and shortly thereafter the Mazarin Bible was printed in Germany. The Church could no longer restrict the availability of the Bible to priests and monks: the Vulgate was translated into each national language and was read by laymen as well as the clergy.

The Hundred Years' War strengthened the kings in England and France. The kings jammed through Parliament in England and the Estate-General in France such war measures as generous budgets for the prosecution of the war, the power to tax, and other war powers to mobilize labor, to control trade, prices and wages, and to issue decrees and ordinances. The peasants revolted in England and Europe but were put down ruthlessly. The French soil, on which the War was waged, became desolate. Impoverished peasants and disbanded mercenaries turned out to be bands of looters.

New forces were seething and surging beneath the surface of Medieval church life. France emerged the first modern nation by placing all military forces under the King's command and by granting the King the right to impose taxes directly upon the people, instead of collecting small rents from feudal lords.

The kings of France and England asserted the independence of the State and national law and national courts from supreme papal jurisdiction. The temporal jurisdiction of the ecclesiastical courts came under attack. Kings began building imposing courthouses and some courtrooms were three hundred feet long and one hundred feet wide. Kings abolished the temporal jurisdiction of the ecclesiastical courts in Europe in the 15th and 16th centuries.

Pope Innocent VIII (1484-1492), good-looking and personable but corrupt, openly recognized his illegitimate children and dined publicly with ladies. Italian barons revolted and the Pope invited French intervention (and Italy would not regain full independence until the end of the 19th century). The event weakened even further the medieval papacy and the Holy Roman Empire, which were slowly turning out to be relics of the bygone era.

Pope Julius II (1503-1513), an able reformer, attempted to

remove abuses in the Church but such attempts were too late to reverse the tide at the beginning of the Reformation. The close kin and ambitious women favored by the popes relegated the spiritual prerogatives of the college of the cardinals to a nominal one.

Retrospectively, in spite of the abuses and excesses of the medieval centralized papacy, the Church brought Germanic tribes into the fold of Christian faith. It is hard to imagine how the early medieval men in Europe could have survived if the local churches had not helped the Germanic tribal customs to be Romanized and if the civic order had not centered around each local church. The bishops and local clergy were de facto municipal governments. With the aid of local churches and clergy highly flexible and democratic Romanesque customary laws of every description developed and adapted to each locality and constantly changing conditions in Western Europe during the long Medieval period. These customary laws proceeded from the needs and desires of the people in each locality in order to regulate their civic and family life.

The Church contributed immensely to bringing about a unique cultural framework in which the Roman love of order and authority were fully expressed, and various Roman law principles were adopted by canonists, as well as the Greek conceptions of natural law, Judaic concepts of protecting the oppressed and the poor, Germanic customs limiting the power of the kings and emperors and setting forth the rights of vassals, tenants and undertenants, and their mutual obligations. Their rights and mutual obligations were rarely put into writing and the customary laws governing them were more often than not merely intricate sets of understandings.

Yet such customary laws were self-enforcing to a great extent, and left room for individuals to exercise their moral choices on the basis of Christian attitude of fairness and good will. It was indeed in the finest moral tradition of the West.

This aspect of the medieval cultural framework is all the more remarkable in the light of the feudal arrangement of society based on a military framework, and the democratic traditions survived a long period of grave emergency situations created by external invasions in the absence of the centralized authorities.

It is an ironical twist of history, however, that the Church helped to create the diversities of feudalism which stood in the way of the primacy of the papacy. The Church attempted to discard medieval feudalism and stood against the forces of diversity, and such efforts of the Church came to be manifested in the unrestrained secular authority of the centralized papacy over secular rulers, the holy inquisitions against every dissent, heretics, and the Jews and holy crusades against the Arab Muslims and even against the Eastern Christian Church. In the end the medieval society itself was changing radically and the socio-economic and political forces once nurtured by the Church were moving out of control of the medieval papacy.

CHURCHES WITHIN THE MODERN SOCIAL FRAMEWORK

The Modern Age was well on the way by the turn of the 16th century. The Churchmen no longer had the monopoly of learning; accordingly, laymen began studying the ancient literatures, reinterpreting the Bible and the Church creeds and dogmas, and creating new ideas.

The spirit of the Renaissance prevailed throughout the 14th and 15th centuries and came to be manifested in the theory of Niccolo Machiavelli (1469-1527) on the nation-state system coupled with nationalism: A prince should be concerned only with power and success in political actions and should not take into consideration the traditional moral right or wrong. Whatever works is moral and a private sense of right or wrong has no relevance to the conduct of princely affairs: The end justifies the means and cruel, treacherous, cunning or faithless royal policies are justified to achieve political ends. Machiavelli knew clearly the papacy had prevented a strong unified Italy from emerging under a strong–more correctly a despotic–king, and his princely hero was Cesare Borgia, a one-time cardinal and the illegitimate son of the villainous Pope Alexander VI.

Machiavelli was merely stating the rules of the Iron and Blood Age which was well under way. The rapidly changing fabric of European society strengthened royal power in France, Spain and England at the expense of the feudal nobility and the clergy. The discovery of America and the navigation to the Far East opened up the trade routes through the Atlantic and Pacific Oceans. The commercial and financial supremacy of Italian port cities of Pisa, Genoa, and Venice controlling the Mediterranean trade routes was becoming less significant.

Money was gradually becoming important. Merchants profited by supplying the Crusaders with provisions, and amassed fortunes by providing supplies to the armies of England and France during the Hundred Years' War. Merchants were necessarily the allies of kings, not the feudal lords. The energetic merchants were rich enough and were willing to take risks, and to venture into far-off markets for greater profits. As they came to know the markets they were anxious to control production. They liked neither feudal boundaries nor local guilds, markets and ports monopolized by cities and feudal lords, which kept the cost of products high and ate into the profits of merchants. In some cases wealthy merchant families dominated town and city governments and guilds. The medieval knights and sergeants and squires no longer had roles to play in the Modern Age and became the bands of brigands.

The "eternal law," "divine law," "natural law," and "human law" were axioms of medieval intellectualism, but those laws were no more than frigid medieval logic during the anarchic transition period. In many parts of Europe self-help, lynching at the nearest tree and other primitive Germanic summary procedures came to be re-employed in a state of chaos. If the king could restore peace and order the law would be of secondary importance. The new rising merchants would rather see administration of justice and military power concentrated in the hands of the king, not only because peace and order were favorable for trade but also because they did not have to make payoffs to various local elements.

Remarkable are the views of Martin Luther and John Calvin, the Reformation leaders, so closely parallel with those of their contemporary philosophers. The similarity of their views depended on the changing socio-economic and political conditions rather than on theology or philosophy.

The Reformation leaders held the belief that secular rulers were the vicars of God, and obedience to secular rulers was a virtue commanded by Jesus and St. Paul. Luther and Calvin believed in the depravity of human nature, original sin, and the blanket coverage of sinfulness traceable to St. Augustine. Their concept of sinfulness was based on the personal beliefs of an anarchic transition period, and was different from that of St. Paul who needed to replace the Law with the blanket coverage of sin and Grace of God in the process of transplanting Christianity into the Greco-Roman world.

The Medieval Scholastics also moved away from Augustinian doctrines of original sin and predestination because the Scholastics did not overlook the contradiction that, if man's nature were depraved and sinful, human reason embedded in nature could not be all that good. Luther and Calvin perceived Scholastic philosophy as a rival, not a supporter, of faith. In this sense the Protestant Reformation was reverting to Augustinian theology, much more authoritarian than Medieval Scholasticism.

It is appropriate to examine here the theological questions of Free Will and the Grace of God which became a religious battleground during the Reformation. Christian theologians had tried to make the doctrines of Grace and Free Will compatible ever since Augustine. Simply stated, is a man endowed with some qualities, i.e. free will, to make moral choices? If so, can he make moral choices without the divine favor or Grace of God? To rephrase the question, can a man initiate the process of salvation by good deeds alone? No, the process of salvation by good deeds alone ignores the Grace of God. If one's good deeds alone do not count, then. . . .

Is there any neutralizer to make the Grace of God and Free Will compatible? Augustine found such a neutralizer in the doctrine of predestination. Calvin, however, clearly perceived the contradiction in Augustinian logic. Even if the predestined Elect, true Christians, solely consisted of those on whom Grace of God had descended, those Christians were still endowed with qualities to make moral choices. Augustine thought so, but Calvin rejected such a notion as a heresy for disregarding the Grace of God.

To Calvin the doctrine of predestination cannot be the neutralizer to make Free Will and the Grace of God compatible. Why? Logically, if one affirms the Grace of God and rejects Free Will, he is a Christian who rejects moral choices or good deeds; conversely, if he affirms Free Will but rejects Grace, he may do all the good deeds but still remain a pagan.

Why not say, then, that the Grace of God and Free Will act concurrently? It means that whatever a true Christian does is a good deed. Clearly, Free Will and the Grace of God are like water and oil which do not mix either with or without the neutralizer.

Then, why not say that Grace and Free Will must cooperate. That means, if a man with Free Will is allowed to cooperate with God, even a pagan with Free Will may go along with God. Clearly it is a heresy to separate Grace and Free Will and to profess that Free Will is more important than Grace.

Calvin flatly denied Free Will: The multitudes are not capable of making a moral choice; Free Will will enable the multitudes to take only a sinful and depraved course, not a moral choice; and a good deed and salvation are possible only because of Grace of God.

The arguments went around in circles endlessly. The Catholic Church and Luther, however, recognized Free Will without resolving the contradictory nature of the controversy. Calvin, unlike Luther, was endowed with the sense of clear-cut logic and his theology left no loose ends.

In order to understand or simplify the controversy one has to uncloak the cloaked controversy. The vital question in this controversy is who bestows the Grace of God, God or the Church? If a reader places the role of the Church properly in this controversy, then Free Will and Grace become compatible even without the neutralizer. In reality it was a controversy over the role of the Church as an intermediary between man and God: A direct relationship between man and God negates the need for man to rely on an intermediary, the Church; and conversely, the Church cannot recognize a direct relationship between man and God, which negates the need for a church hierarchy. (As noted already, for the Jews, this controversy was resolved at the time of the destruction of the Temple: neither rabbis nor synagogues are intermediaries between Jews and God.)

Calvin stressed the consequences of the fallen nature of man and denied Free Will. Free Will will be exercised exclusively by the theocratic hierarchy and the rest of humanity must simply follow as told. If one recognized Free Will for everyone there would be no role for the authority of the church to decide what were the truths.

One today would find the logic surrounding the controversy merely interesting, but in Medieval and early Modern Europe one was damned as a heretic if he were one step out of the way. No one today would dare guess how many heretics were created by this controversy surrounding Grace and Free Will, excommunicated, put in dungeons or to the stake and burnt. The orthodox Catholic stand is the Dominican doctrine of Grace: Good deeds are meaningless unless performed in a state of Grace. One can attain a state of Grace only through the sacraments administered by the Catholic Church. No matter what, the question remains unresolved.

As mentioned already, Augustine deviated considerably from the cardinal teaching of Jesus on the spiritual meaning of moral choices. Calvinism flatly rejected the fundamental teaching of Jesus.

Calvinism was more theocratic in the Old Testament context than Augustine or the mellowed-down doctrines of the Medieval Catholic Church, and Calvinism had nothing to do with the wide latitude of moral choices Jesus espoused for average Jews.

Lutheranism and Calvinism were a united front against Catholicism; in contrast to Calvinism, however, Lutheranism was more tolerant of dissenting opinions and accepted Free Will. The Catholic Church disapproved of Calvin, but Calvinism was more conservative than Augustinian theology. Luther exalted the secular prince over the church hierarchy; however, Calvin had no doubts about the march of God in a theocratic state in which the secular princes were to be properly subordinated to the guidance and control of the theocratic hierarchy. Perhaps the only difference between Catholicism and Calvinism was a theocracy either under the Catholic Church hierarchy or the Calvinist Church hierarchy.

Although the Reformation leaders were to replace the fraudulent medieval church with the new system of laymen, Calvin did not incline toward representative principles or liberalism. The Calvinist church government was represented by twelve lay elders and six clericals, but lay elders were to serve as censors to inspect and enforce a wide range of individual conduct at home from the dress code and proper sexual conduct to forbidden acts of dancing and card playing. The lay elders hardly participated in administration of church affairs, and the Calvinist form of church government readily developed into a theocracy, if given opportunities, in Geneva, Scotland and even in Boston.

Protestant Churches as well as the Catholic Church had to find their places within the emerging modern social framework. Reformation leaders found the success of their reform movements depend upon the support of secular princes. Secular princes wanted to be heads of the Church in Protestant countries and decide what were pure religious doctrines.

None of the Reformation leaders including Luther ever anticipated such a monstrous arrangement of making secular rulers as heads of the Churches who regarded the national Church as the cement of national consciousness rather than an individual spiritual experience. But a formation of the new social framework was not up to the Reformation leaders. State Churches emerged in England, Denmark, Norway, Sweden, Brandenburg and other parts of today's Germany. Even in France, Louis XIV regarded the Catholic Church in France as the national church rather than a part of a universal church. Calvinism was designed to establish a universal theocratic church and none of the secular princes found it attractive to build a national church on the basis of Calvinism; therefore, all State churches in Europe were Lutheran and none Calvinist.

Protestant justification by faith would have eliminated the priestly offices as intermediary between God and man as in the Judaism of the Christian era, but in Protestant countries, the Catholic priestly offices in each country were made priestly offices of the State. The Church hierarchy which the Reformation leaders considered unnecessary intermediaries between individuals and God remained intact, under the pope in Catholicism and under the kings in European Protestant countries.

Calvinism was less mystical than Lutheranism. It called worldly success a Christian duty, emphasized the virtues of thrift and hardwork, and sanctioned interest charges. Calvin realistically recognized that usury had been firmly established in European countries notwithstanding the canon law against it and that usury in combination with the rising trade and economic expansion was irreversible.

Once the unity of the Church was broken a growing number of sectarian Churches inevitably sprang up. Initial reform zeal and the brotherly love and care of each new Church was always attractive, and weakened the Catholic Church, rich but already weak—a highly undesirable combination for the iron and blood age of the new nation-state system.

The absolute power of kings did not remain responsible for long. In the 14th and 15th centuries religious reformers protested against the heretical popes for laying waste to the Church; however, in the 16th and 17th centuries philosophers and religious reformers protested against despotic secular rulers for laying waste to the state and the church. Early modern man, coming out of medievalism, had yet to establish the new social framework.

The Catholic Church too recognized the urgent need for reform within the Church. In the mid-16th century the Society of Jesus was founded under the papal auspices. The Jesuit order spearheaded reform within, and Rome became the center of universal inquisition. An index of forbidden books was drawn up. The Jesuit order was unique in the sense that they were activists, unlike hermit monks of the Medieval Age. Unlike the medieval monastic orders whose members withdrew from the world, Jesuits were to actively intervene in secular affairs for Godly purposes. As its founder was a Spanish general, the head of the Jesuits was called

General, not Abbott. Pope Sixtus V (1585-1590), an able leader, purged the Curia of irregularities, reorganized the church government and put the church finances on a sound basis.

The Catholic Reform movement within developed into the movement against the Protestant Reformation. This Counter-Reformation triumphed in the religious wars in France of the late 16th century.

The Thirty Years' War of 1618-1648, the final religious war between Catholic and Protestant Europe, turned into dynastic family struggles to decide family quarrels or expand territories and domains for the victorious royal families. The War, waged on German soil, ravaged Germany, and inflicted appalling devastation and suffering on the civilian population. The War did not resolve religious issues but proved that brute and raw force counted in international relations and relegated the powerless Holy Roman Empire and the papacy to insignificant levels in the modern framework of international power politics.

Modern national consciousness, aspirations and greed for territorial gains won an upper hand over the embittered religious issues during the War. The German population diminished so much during the War that secular princes were happy to have as many subjects as possible whether Catholic or Protestant. In France, Protestants were deprived of the right to hold any public office, and Protestant children, at the age of seven, had to make a choice on faith. Once a child of seven years old declared he would be a Catholic, any parent attempting to reconvert that child was punishable by imprisonment.

The tide, however, was against the Catholic Church in Europe in spite of the efforts of Popes Innocent XI and XII, Clement XI and Benedict XIV, to stem anti-clericalism. The Jesuit order began to meddle in secular politics, and also began making use of its worldwide organization for worldwide trading and banking activities; consequently, it was expelled not only from England, but also Catholic France and Portugal and other European countries. The Jesuits were aggressive entrepreneurs in making money and spending money in building high schools and colleges throughout the world.

In the 17th century all the great thinkers gave unity to the system of natural law which was to limit the absolute power of the kings. The natural law was defined as a dictate of right reason, as the laws of human nature, as self-evident truths, and so on, depending on the philosopher who defined it. They considered royal power to be derived from the consent of the people and the king was answerable to God and was subject to natural law. The natural law concept of the 17th century hardly deviated from the pre-Christian Greek Stoic notion of natural law.

Radical changes in European society had to be accompanied by the new philosophy and the new laws or drastic modifications of old ones. Some customs or laws had to prescribe the limit of the new royal power, the limit of the new parliamentary power, the rights of old nobilities, the rights of Catholic clergy, the rights of Protestant churches, the rights of merchants, and the rights of peasants, the relationship of church and state, the relationship of king and parliament, and various other relationships within the new social framework. Diverse relationships could not be left vague and badly framed, intentionally or otherwise, indefinitely. While things were unsettled, the old power elements attempted desperately to hold on to what they used to enjoy and the new ones strived to wrest as much control as possible away from the old ones.

Kings looked back to the divine right of the pope and the absolutism of the medieval papacy. Royal assumption of such power had to be brought about at the expense of others, and opposition to royal absolutism took its own course in each country. In France the King was allied with the old nobility and the Catholic clergy, and all opposition to royal absolutism seemed to be crushed easily; in the end, an abrupt change erupted in the French Revolution (1789-1799).

In England the transition was much more protracted, extending over the entire 17th century, but much less violent than in France because in England, where a centralized feudalism prevailed, such a development was achieved in modifying the medieval system. The trend was clear: Each party allied with other parties as their interests dictated to have a larger role or limit the roles of others within the new social framework.

The Bill of Rights in England (1689), Bill of Rights in American (1791) and the natural rights of men to life, liberty, and property prescribed the limits beyond which even the absolute sovereignty of the state might not rightfully go.

In France of the 18th century philosophers reexamined their thinking. Progress in natural science stimulated social science by applying the scientific method to all aspects of human society and individuals. French philosophers of this period, like English philosophers of the 17th century, were no longer speculating but analyzing the psychological mechanism of the human animal. Psychology, economics, law and philosophy all came under the influence of reason. They reexamined previously accepted axioms of self-evident truths from the new point of rationalism.

The long rules of Cardinals Duc de Richelieu (Chief minister to Louis XIII, 1624-42) and Jules Mazarin (Chief minister to Louis XIII and XIV 1642-61) and the reign of King Louis XIV (1643-1715) made self-evident truths of Frenchmen to be nothing more than incongruous abstractions. Philosophers suggested specific ways in which the evils of modern absolutism might be remedied. The separation of three branches of the government and checks and balances among them, religious toleration, and other features of modern political democracy were gradually theorized.

French philosophers believed that reason provided an absolute standard of right or wrong for human conduct and social institutions. The rationalism of the 18th century rejected not only the lawlessness of kings in France but also the privileges of nobilities who kept governing towns and provinces as though they were under feudalism. Each lord had the right to charge tolls on goods passing through his domain, to requisition all the tongues and other delectable parts of animals killed for food, to carry on the monopoly business of town mills and bakery, and to collect other feudal dues from the peasants.

The nobility filled all the offices at the royal court. Even royal stable boys were nobles. All the military commanders and high-ranking officers were from noble families. Cardinals, bishops, abbots and other responsible clerical ranks came from the nobility. One, of course, could buy the status of nobility. Each year hundreds of Frenchmen bought the status of nobility at a fixed price payable to the king. (After the French Revolution it was said that every doorman in Paris was a duke in disguise.) Those who could read Latin aspired to become civil servants either for the king or the local lord.

Rational truths of "liberty, equality and fraternity" symbolized the revolt of reason against entrenched medieval institutions and political absolutism in France. Before the French Revolution three hundred and sixty systems of laws in France, which had been carried over from the medieval period, were still in effect and one-fifth of the French soil, held by the Catholic Church, was exempt from taxes. Therefore, it all seemed so logical and rational to do away with what ran against rational truths.

The French Revolution culminated, among other things, in the Napoleonic Code, modeled after the ancient Justinian code, which replaced the diverse provincial and local laws. The Napoleonic code became a model for nearly every European state which aspired to centralized administration and one uniform law in each new nation-state. Only England rejected the Justinian code and its influence.

The Catholic Church, the traditional ally of French kings, became the greatest victim of the Revolution. Napoleon confiscated properties which had been the Church's for centuries, and issued religious toleration for Protestants and Jews. The clergy lost their feudal estates.

In 1799 Napoleon's forces seized the Papal States, and eventually the Papal States was reduced to Vatican City.

In a sharp contrast to the war which ravaged continental Europe a totally different scenario was taking place in early 19th century England. A rapid progress in industralization was coupled with a wave of new inventions for modern mass production systems in England at the turn of the 19th century. Capitalism as an economic system was a spin-off of natural law. In England philosophers considered "the greatest happiness of the greatest number" as the measure of determining the utility of legislation; consequently, a hands-off policy of the government in economic activities, a trade free of tariff restrictions, and a market free of legal restrictions and monopolies, industries free of legal controls, in theory, were to produce a natural harmony of various human interests.

Such a non-interference by the government and parliament in the sphere of private business activities seemed to be best for the rising commercial and industrial middle class and the economic interest of England. At the same time, it was not only to free modern Englishmen from the feudal bondage of status and enable them to engage in free economic activities, but also to limit the absolute power of Parliament, which was largely made up of landed gentry.

Capitalism as a principle of natural law was to keep government out of individuals' economic activities. Individuals knew their own interests best, and if legislators and government kept their hands off the natural operation of economic laws, such a non-interference would bring about a natural harmony among the people.

Soon the self-evident truths of natural law and the rational truths of the 18th century began crumbling under the unpredictable direction which the French Revolution was taking. In France and Germany philosophers were aghast at the direction which the French Revolution took.

Rational visions of "liberty, equality and fraternity" became warped and distorted in the manic egoism of Robespierre and Napoleon, and resulted in terrorism, glorification of war against weaker nations, millions of deaths, scars of ravage and waste everywhere on a single man's whim, and wretched poverty of peasants and villagers. Human existence seemed so meaningless and human lives seemed stupid and insignificant accidents.

Pope Pius VI (1775-1799) died in Valence, France, where he was taken a year earlier. Napoleon had Pope Pius VII (1800-1823) arrested and held as prisoner for nearly five years from 1809 to 1814. Even Protestants throughout Europe showed sympathy for the Catholic church. Philosophers revolted against reason in the Romanticism, nationalism, and idealism of the 19th century which idealized the religious past and stressed the common emotions and the spirit of the nation as the ultimate value to life.

Such Romantic philosophy was more than temporary sympathy for the Catholic Church or a backlash against reason, and proved to be a sort of persistent nationalistic aspiration: for the Germans and Italians to unify and create belatedly new nation states in the late 19th century; for other peoples to gain self-determination; for the industrial nations to gain foreign markets in Africa and elsewhere; for the industrial nations with poor natural resources to gain territories with resources; for each nation to defend with arms the right of the nation in the fluctuating international rivalry situations;

for the colonial peoples to gain political independence; and so on.

Extreme nationalism coupled with various economic and political motivations contributed greatly to the causes of World Wars I, II, and probably III before the close of this century.

A totally new force within the new social framework was growing: In the early Modern Age the clash between the infant modern science and the aged Christian theology was just beginning. Threatened with torture, Galileo (1564-1642) recanted his discovery before the ecclesiastical court. Copernicus, Galileo, Kepler, Newton, Darwin, and a wave of scientists sought truths on highly rational and empirical scientific methods. Modern science, unlike philosophy and religion, was a tangible and visible force reshaping the material lives of the moderns. Modern scientists never meant to be critical of tradition and religiously oriented concepts but did not want their scientific endeavors hampered by any assumptions, traditionally religious or otherwise.

The Christian world as well as the Jewish world felt a tremendous impact from the new science. Yet the impact of science upon the Jewish faith was much less than that upon the Christian faith because the Jews could readily accept scientific concepts and at the same time look upon the Law and the Talmud as magnificient Jewish spiritual and moral accomplishments.

The teachings of Jesus on the other hand, taken out of the historical and social context, were no longer timeless and realistic values but largely superficial. Furthermore, the teachings of Jesus became largely overshadowed by the Greco-Roman philosophy and Roman jurisprudence. Augustinian theology, Calvinism, and the church creeds and dogmas also rendered insignificant the awe-inspiring spiritual and moral messages of Jesus.

Therefore, the Protestant churches as well as the Catholic

Church were in no position to accept modern science, which could place every aspect of Christian miracles, "revelations" and Christian creeds and dogmas in jeopardy, because Christianity had no unique moral values apart from Greco-Roman philosophy and Roman jurisprudence and had no spiritual repository apart from Christian miracles and "revelations." The Catholic Church as well as the Protestant Churches stuck to literal interpretation of the Bible and the creeds and dogmas: As in the Medieval Age, the churches in the Modern Age kept cultivating dogmatism and conformism. The new science was merely an infant growing.

CHRISTIANITY IN THE AGE OF SCIENTISM

As early as 1802 in England a law was passed to forbid hiring pauper children of less than nine years of age for work in the cotton mills and other employment practices. Royal Commissions reported appalling work conditions for children of six and seven who had to work twelve hours each day in the textile factories. Novels and simple lay literature depicted incredible conditions for women and children in factories and the coal mines.

Philosophers and lawyers used to believe in natural law on the basis of rationalism, not in terms of a revealed law. The philosophers who believed in natural law in 17th century Europe included mathematicians and an international lawyer. Lawyers especially knew nothing of a revealed law. In the 17th and 18th centuries philosophers were questioning whether timelessness or invariability itself was the sole criterion to test truth, and they were realizing that changes coincident with progress seemed to nullify unchangeability as the test of truth. When lawyers realized that the natural law of capitalism brought about the grim excesses of utilitarian ethics, they readily discarded the concept of natural law, unchangeable and eternal.

Some lawyers of the early Modern Age had advanced the theory that a law has nothing to do with morality and the law of the political sovereign must be obeyed even if that law commands what is morally wrong and forbids what is morally right. This precept was suitable to a self-sufficient legal science. The lawyers were ready to handle changing socioeconomic conditions by legislation, and philosophers were insistent that most legislation was bad because laws tended to be merely obstacles to the natural course the natural laws of economy take or the survival of the fittest takes.

Philosophers and lawyers gradually fell away. Lawyers were not the only ones who reacted against timeless truths and abstract philosophy, but such a reaction against unchangeable natural truths and abstract philosophy was becoming a clear trend throughout Europe of the mid-19th century. The industrial revolution accelerated out of the invention of the spinning jenny (1764), the condensing steam engine (1765), the power loom (1785), the electric motor (1822) and other devices. The people in Europe turned their thoughts in the direction of tangible matters: industry, trade and a life on earth. Everywhere the small manual technique of production in each individual house was giving way to the machine technique of mass production in factories. Lawyers came to scoff at philosophical abstractions, and had to correct inhuman conditions and social ills which the natural law of capitalism and its manufacturing centers brought about, and explore possibilities for the health and better working conditions of the citizens.

As the industrialization progressed industrialists and big merchants expanded their political influence, and began manipulating legislation. Government and business became two basic power centers; accordingly, the demand heated up for the Government to rule business or business to rule the Government. Lawyers who were the products of landed gentry felt no particular love for the new riches and the rising industrialists and merchants. Workingmen who were solely concerned with wages and work conditions readily allied with landed gentry. Philosophers supported the expanding influence of the rising industrialists and merchants.

In the mid-19th century philosophers had to concede and recognize the growing side-effects which theoretically perfect natural laws of economy and a self-regulating competitive system had brought about. Dogmas and absolute principles came to mean less than fact-finding investigations. Investigation of facts replaced speculative knowledge which was based on reason and fancy. Scientific specialists no longer talked about principles but factual data. Social sciences of economics, sociology and psychology became new partners of legal science. Social scientists were interested in fact-finding investigations, not in the eternal and unchangeable principles.

New scientists, unlike the philosophers, came to believe in the unlimited ability of legislation to bring about adjustments and readjustments of complex and often antagonistic human wants and interests, and to plan infinite possibilities for the needs and desires of the citizens from the cradle to the grave. All man-made laws came to be known as positive law in contrast to natural law.

Modern relativism, averse to dogmas and absolute principles, pulled the rug out from under the church concepts of "revealed" law and natural law, eternal and unchangeable. Changing social policies, rules of implementation, and procedural laws came to count more than substantive right or wrong.

Ironically, the conservative and authoritarian Calvinism and Protestant adherence to the Augustinian doctrine of original sin had a wide-ranging influence upon modern societies from modern distrust of human nature to distrust of power, secular or religious. Equally, the rights of Protestant Churches to question, disagree, and excoriate the Medieval

Church underscored growing modern democratic trends to doubt, dissent and criticize secular as well as religious institutions. Such democratic trends are inclined to modifications, compromises and concessions but are averse to the doctrinal rigidity characteristic of church creeds and dogmas.

Marxism, on the other hand, is the product of thoroughgoing rationalism and scientific analysis, the truths of which are readily embraced by the people in industrially backward countries, who traditionally upheld the concept of absolute truths and never became familiar with modern scientism and relativism. For this reason Marxism is very much like the natural law and the revealed law of Christianity in one fundamental way.

Marx and Lenin believed in infinite possibilities for men and human institutions to solve all the problems of human interests and societies. The eternal and unchangeable principle of Marxism and infallibility of the communist party are akin to the self-evident truths of the natural law and the revealed law of Christianity. Marxist doctrines, like Christian revelations, leave no room for modifications, compromises or concessions. Marxist writings are no less scripture to the communists than the creeds and dogmas are to Christians.

Communism, as an economic system, will prove, if it has not proved already, an inefficient flop. But communism as an ascetically superior moral insight, however, has worked miracles in the communist countries and many developing countries. For the impoverished and hungry a political democracy is a luxury which they have never known and can do without. For the communists and the nationalists in the developing countries a social democracy, which communists portray in terms of such minimum human needs as the jobs, public health, the roof over the head, and daily bread, signifies moral criteria.

The political democrats in the developing countries hold themselves back from exploring and adopting even the constructive aspects of social democracy; consequently, the result is votes in rigged elections but no bread or job for the have-nots, the absolute majority, in each of the developing countries. The have-nots merely trade in mud huts and farm life for urban ghettos and factory life and find no compensation for rapid changes in their lives, the breakdown of traditional values, and the impersonal urban life they find themselves in.

In most developing countries the constructive and long-term effectiveness and benefits of political democracy get easily reduced to oblivion and only the weakness and disorders of political democracy get magnified. Political opposition by demagoguery and muckraking, political changes by a series of coups d'etat, a few sheikhs eating off black gold or other natural resources of the country, magnificent church buildings, and mercenary military and police forces represent too weak an alternative to the raw communist moral criteria.

Marxism as a sort of realistic as well as romantic moral exhortation for the future in the developing countries demands faith, and commitment to intolerant scientific doctrines and dogmas for overriding goals, and hopes for the inevitable future. The zealous machinery of the communist party is mobilized to plan, mold, and manipulate the morality of the masses.

Modern theologians, also greatly influenced by modern rationalism, have been belatedly reconsidering the ethical aspects of the Judeo-Christian faith, focusing attention on various social problems. In this endeavor the churches and theologians have been well behind the time and cannot excel modern social scientists. Furthermore, such an endeavor is necessarily limited to minor social ills which extensive modern social legislation has yet to cover.

The onslaught of the tidal waves of modern relativism, laws and social scientism has been corroding the fabric of traditional beliefs. In challenging this attack against traditional beliefs, the Catholic Church made the dogma of the

Immaculate Conception and the Virgin Birth an article of faith in 1854.

Pope Pius IX (1864-1878) challenged defiantly modern civilization itself in the encyclical of December 8, 1864. He asserted the right of the Church to control all culture, science, and the educational system, and repudiated religious toleration and freedom, liberalism, and contemporary civilization.

In 1870 the Vatican Council acknowledged the infallibility of the Pope.

Leo XIII (1878-1903) attempted to narrow the gap between the Church and modern society and the gap between Catholicism and scientism, but such an attempt toward modernism was scoffed at by his successor, Pius X (1903-1914).

The long pontificate of Pius XII (1939-1958) was a modern tragedy: The pope was silent during World War II when man's unprecedented inhumanity against the Jews and other racial minorities was perpetrated at the heart of Christian Europe.

The brief pontificate of John XXIII (1958-1963) underscored a remarkable change in the Church. The Second Vatican Council, convened in 1962, appraised the role of Christianity in the modern world. Even the representatives of the Russian Orthodox Church were invited as observers to the Council. Subsequently the Church did away with the Index of Forbidden Books and the Office of Inquisition.

Be that as it may, the gulf between absolute truths of modern scientism and relativism and the absolute religious truths of creeds and dogmas has been widening, and no serious attempt has been made to bridge the gap; accordingly, two sets of truths have been made incompatible and the ever-widening rift is neither a desirable combination nor a healthy predicament for modern men to be in. What is left of traditional beliefs, which could give an individual the meaning of his life and guide the course of his life in modern society, and what are the contemporary implications of the Christian faith?

EPILOGUE

Contemporary Implications

It is not a part of the original purpose of this book to state the contemporary implications of the Judeo-Christian faith. But, after having surveyed man's changing perceptions of God, fragmentary aspects of our lives in the modern world may be examined profitably in this concluding chapter so that each reader may think further about modern meanings of his faith.

When big criminal cases are tried in this country psychiatrists and psychologists are often invited to give expert testimony. They testify what kind of psychosis the accused had or in what kind of emotional state the accused committed the crimes.

Let us assume these criminals advanced various philosophical theories. Some violent crimes as well as white-collar crimes require human intelligence, mind and will. Philosophers were invariably scholars who assumed reason alone or emotions alone would run in the desirable direction. Has it been proved scientifically one way or another? No answer can be drawn from human history. Certain socio-economic and political conditions drove the Germans, the best-educated and intelligent people, highly pious in Catholicism and Protestantism, to display the same violent, anti-social and inhuman impulses during World War II as any group of ignorant pagans.

The psychiatrists, too, have yet to answer whether or not religion as the ultimate value orientation can work as the inspiring and motivating force of human conduct. The great psychoanalysts of the modern era, Sigmund Freud (1856-1939) and Carl Jung (1875-1961), totally disagreed on this point: Freud considered religion as a neurosis and Jung recognized an important role of religion as the conscious and unconscious source of wisdom and a motivating force for the individual.

Are human beings unique because they can think or talk or because they are capable of believing and letting their belief be the pilot and guide of intelligence and emotions? One can answer either way because a controversial question has no clear-cut scientific answer.

Reason, mind and will are faculties of men. Can we single out reason as all-important or emotions as all-important? The unemployed intellectuals and the modern paper pushers tend to contribute nothing to the society but become parasitic by rejecting and undermining the established values simply because such values are not kind to them. In debating which faculty of men is all-important and why, the Enlightenment philosophers of the 18th century and the Romantic philosophers of the 19th century were in the same labyrinth as the Greek philosophers of the pre-Christian era.

Philosophical reasoning and scientific probes invariably come to the end of the road without being able to determine the ultimate value of life or the meaning of one's existence. The Bible, however, contains all aspects of ancient Hebrew life: human reason including righteousness, sophistry, fancy, treachery and cunning; a wide range of human feelings from depression and despair in the darkest hours to hope and exuberant joy; a reservoir of human will-power, resolute determination, senseless defiance, and stamina displayed in the historical and social context of the ancient Hebrew life. Above all one's spiritual view of life, which originated in religion, generates and guides his intelligence and emotions.

What the ancient Hebrews found worthy for pursuing as the ultimate meaning of life was directly tied to the search for righteous human conduct and evaluation of right or wrong in their historical and social circumstances. The ancient Hebrew value judgments were true to life even if they were not necessarily reasonable or logical. The Hebrew tradition of spiritualizing objective standards of proper and righteous conduct culminated in the Book of the Law and the teachings of Jesus.

Where are one's views of life situated? Although modern medical science discovered that an average person's brain contains fifteen billion nerve units, which enable a man to memorize, hear, see, smell, make speech, and so on, nobody knows where one's views of life are situated. The views of life seem to be distant from us most of the time and very near to us at other times.

It was the ancient Hebrew prophets, the writers of the Law and Jesus who were bent on translating abstract spiritual views of life into human conduct in the world of reality. The spiritual and moral yardsticks Jesus taught, however, present a few problems in modern society.

In modern society the mode of living varies considerably from one ethnic or social group to another. One's needs and desires seem quite different from those of his "neighbor." Can human wants and emotions be so different because of differences in the modes of living among various peoples? One's answer to the question will determine whether or not he can put back Christ and His yardsticks into modern life.

Modern society is different from the ancient world of Jesus' time in many ways. By way of example, one serious traffic accident involving only two parties brings in two insurance companies, their insurance adjusters and lawyers. Then come the lawyers representing the real parties. The real parties are driven to the periphery of the dispute.

In claiming or collecting the amount of one's damage each party will find it difficult to apply the yardstick to his decisions and actions because one no longer feels he is hurting any one personally but merely trying to collect from an impersonal insurance company; besides, the real parties do not make decisions but listen to the counsel of the lawyers.

In determining one's negligence, however, the final question comes down to whether one took "reasonable" care, the "standard" of what a "prudent" and "diligent" man would do under given circumstances. It would be impossible to interpret law, ancient and modern, or to determine one's negligence without about a dozen or so words such as "fair," "equitable," "conscientious," "reasonable," and so on, which invariably indicate that yardstick only vaguely.

Conversely, human institutions including law and the legal apparatus cannot function unless the people in a given society are willing to adhere to the yardstick.

There are no identical negligence cases if the varying degrees of negligence contributed by the parties involved, the individual characteristics of the parties involved, the circumstances, the degree to which God contributed to the accidents, and other variable factors are taken into consideration. Each individual case is different and the merits of such a case have to be examined in a public forum.

One's long- and short-term physical and emotional damages cannot be translated precisely into monetary amounts. The standards applicable at every step of the way are not clear. Unless there is a yardstick which the people in a given society adhere to, every negligence case has some merits which are worthy enough to be decided by the court and there is no reason for any one to miss the opportunity to exaggerate and claim as much as possible at every opportunity; accordingly, the only consideration is to balance what one might gain or lose by going to the court.

It is senseless for any one to sue someone who does not have any money, property, or some insurance coverage; otherwise, on the scale of justice, those who sue in negligence cases have relatively little to lose but much to gain whereas the defendants have little to gain but much to lose. This puts average middle-class people in fear of the possibility of losing what they have. Only the extreme rich or poor are immune to this sense of fear. A man lifts up a power lawnmower to trim the hedge in his yard, and instead cuts himself. In suing the manufacturer for not warning on the label of the danger of using the power mower as a hedge trimmer, could he win a six-figure or seven-figure award?

An invisible party is often involved in each accident. If God were allowed to be sued, the pile of paperwork of pleadings against God would match any mountain.

If one escapes a near tragic accident luckily, he should praise God and raise a joy-filled affirmation. If he is involved in a freakish accident, or has a tragedy in the family, he is supposed to attribute tragedies to the inscrutable and unfathomable will, purpose or reason of God. God wins always, either with love or His inscrutable will, and men lose no matter what. Men are, then, products of a schizophrenic existence–caught between no-win situations. Can we love God? Did Jesus think the question raised here is relevant to one's spiritual perspective?

Another obstacle to the yardstick is the fast-expanding areas of modern life governed by amoral norms: fibs in our social conduct, situation ethics, white lies to insure security or avoid embarrassment, flowery flattery, various interview techniques, intimidation techniques, sales techniques–the list today is almost endless.

Lying hundreds of times each day is considered even a sign

of modern educated sophistry and better social status. If one tells the truth he may be considered a humorless, witless or naive simpleton. The people often do not want to or do not know how to deal with the truth, especially when the truth is too good to be true, ugly, exciting, boring, or too sad. This kind of amoral modern attitude fosters the notion, "One may do anything one pleases as long as no one else is hurt."

Even the law governing procedures, evidence, antitrust and unfair trade practices are by and large such amoral rules of the games in which trial strategies and procedural maneuvers often outweigh substantive right or wrong. One side can harass the other side every step of the way; accordingly, interrogatories, depositions, requests for the top managers of the corporation to appear as witnesses or other techniques of harassment count.

The latitude in which one can make moral choices is shrinking fast. The Church also has been limiting rather than expanding man's freedom to make moral choices. No one can fault the churches for taking moral stands on social issues; nevertheless, it is a different matter for the church to pass judgments on an individual belief or each specific case of divorce, abortion, birth control, artificial insemination, in vitro fertilization, voluntary euthanasia, and so on.

It is necessary to impose limits on or check undesirable social changes brought about solely through customary changes; otherwise, every kind of self-indulgence and instant gratification will become justified as a new value. But if a legal stand does not work as limits on or as a check against such changes there must be enormous forces necessitating such transformation; likewise, a spiritual and moral stand does not work as a limit on or as a check against undesirable customary changes if such transformations are necessitated by variable social forces.

A moral stand as an inward message has a spiritual meaning but such a stand as an outward message on enforceable standards of conduct nullifies the spiritual meaning of moral choices for the individuals involved.

Furthermore, the people actually involved go through an agonizing emotional process. Would an average woman want an abortion as a matter of right? Should the church condemn her as a murderer? Would an average husband or wife want a divorce as a matter of right? Often, in sheer desperation, the people involved feel they no longer have choices. Should the Church pass judgments and aggravate the agonies of the people involved? Can such judgments be relevant to the people involved who no longer feel they have choices, moral or otherwise?

All human institutions eventually have to conform to the moral sense of the people or face disintegration. Readers may recall that about thirty years ago a husband and wife were encouraged to throw as much dirt as possible at the spouse of many years for a divorce in a public forum. In Massachusetts a minimum legal cost for a simple divorce then was three to four thousand dollars; however, many lawyers in Massachusetts handle a comparable simple divorce case for a few hundred dollars of today's money. Why this difference? No more theatrical drama is required to be staged in the court. Furthermore, a husband and wife of many years today often get separated and divorced amicably and "cuddly." Also, the scavenging atmosphere of a public forum is gradually disappearing.

One step further one will find a man and a woman living together without the benefits of civil or religious marriage. It is legally recognized, and socially tolerated. If this custom remains persistent for long, even religious recognition of such living arrangements in the future would not startle anybody.

On the other hand, some married couples, who have been living separately as strangers for years, do not bother going through a legal divorce. One can shred out the implications of this development endlessly. It is, however, a matter of fact that modern no-fault and easier divorce laws in Massachusetts developed in spite of the strong opposition from the churches. Is it against the will of God to eliminate the waste and unnecessary friction which tend to hinder enjoyment of living?

Not all social changes, of course, carried out through customs are morally justified. But rigid religious and legal stands on divorce created social forces leading the couples to live without the benefits of marriage, civil or religious. The fact underscores the importance of negotiating the reality honestly, and of not letting the spiritual stands create unnecessary complications in individual lives.

It is not for us to peer into the future and see the results of each moral choice. Recently a President of the United States wished to make public policies fair to the people. A three-martini business lunch is tax deductible, but a laborer's hot-dog or hamburger lunch is not. He said he would do away with privileged tax deductions, and his intent could not be more moral. Then he had to give up the idea. Waitresses and restaurant owners demonstrated against the announced policy of the President. Hotel owners and city mayors, who rely on convention business, and all businessmen simply did not take kindly to the moral tone of the President.

A moral choice necessitates a change, and a change in our complex modern society is like a spider's web in which the impact of one change runs into all directions. The possible adverse impact of each change leaves us to the illusion that most moral values and ideals are questionable, and that effective or drastic action is no longer possible because of the adverse effects in the complicated state of affairs in modern society.

More than ever in the Modern Age one must consider if his moral choice is likely to bring about results in conformance to his spiritual perspective. Often results are quite contrary to the original intent. Ezra contributed to unbearable sacrifices and sufferings on the part of Jews on account of Judaism, quite contrary to his original intent, and Jesus contributed to Christian persecution of the Jews contrary to his intent of peace and love. Napoleon, however, contributed to the formation of modern European nations contrary to his intent of world conquest and Marx contributed to the establishment of dictatorial states instead of perfect democratic societies without the need for states.

In our daily lives our best intent, love and affection often bring about results quite contrary to such intent and love. One's love is often repaid with hurt; consequently, one may become afraid to love any more in fear that a new love might turn into unbearable pain. One gives a ride to a stranger, who robs him. Some children, well-loved, tenderly nurtured with all socio-economic advantages, turn out to be estranged vegetables while other children turn out to be sound all-around persons in spite of no parents at all or parents who could provide little love. In the particular sense that the results of each moral choice are not for modern mortals as for the ancients and the medievals to see, the will of God is inscrutable and the human mind cannot fathom the workings of God.

In evaluating each of the alternatives and choices one faces an earnest, burdensome and effortful challenge even to arrive at each moral choice. The ancient Jews decided to shape their future instead of enduring their fate. Can the moderns afford to drag the feet over moral choices simply because the consequences of each choice is not for us to see? Indeed such humane efforts to arrive at a moral choice, to rise above the sense of fear, and to make a commitment make one conscious of the quality of life and living.

It is idle to talk about moral choices if the religious, socio-economic, legal and political systems affecting individual lives would leave little room for individuals to make moral choices.

Today we read and hear so much about "unbiased" statistical and scientific reports on abused children, abused wives, wives raped by husbands, abused husbands, abused parents, abused employees, abused students, abused teachers, and so on down the line. Assume such reports are not talking about isolated cases but general trends. Think of the experts on abused children, the experts on abused wives, and so on. Each law has to be enacted on each special abuse category, and Federal and State government agencies must be created to handle each abuse category. Imagine horrifying stories about various abuses. More lawyers and judges would be needed to interpret each law or decide on the cases. Getting confused? Are modern champions of causes finding the sense of fear to be the convenient instrument to promote their causes?

The case in point is a typical loving and untroubled family of four. A teenager son, without a license, takes a joy ride. The teenager looks at the world through his own carefree prism, and the father through his viewpoint of responsibility and liability. Love and reasoning may or may not work. A scream will invite screams, and tears and hurt will divide the family into hostile camps. A chain reaction is complicated enough. Think of the intervention of outside experts and state employees to simplify the matter.

Always the assumption is that scientific and statistical reports consist of facts. Psychological and other intangible factors are difficult to quantify, and scientific reports are subject to the interpretation of what is not in such reports. Therefore, in the modern world the facts are infinitely many, just as the ancients perceived about constantly changing worlds play-acted by little gods. Unless the spiritual and moral values are shared by the people there cannot be facts; nevertheless, a group of experts may wave statistical and scientific reports and try to impose on the people the sacrifices in spontaneous freedom to moral choices and family life by spreading an incredible sense of fear and horrors. Every one claims to be an "expert" who is entitled to plan and manage some aspect of others' affairs.

(Nearly all religious themes originated in the human sense of terror and fear in anticipation of unbearable and unpredictable miseries to come. The teaching of Jesus in urging his Jewish contemporaries to challenge and rise above fear and to have courage to love and interact the self with others has all the meanings today as ever.)

The socio-economic framework of our society affects our lives and our moral choices to a great extent. Money and property are essential elements for human existence, and one's self-esteem. Socio-economic and political issues are endless in order to make the world a better place to live. How do we apply the spiritual yardstick to the complex socio-economic problems? An example would be numerous people on public welfare rolls. Today the public welfare is a burden to the givers, and yet it cannot expect the receivers to retain the sense of self-esteem. It is no longer conducive to the spiritual and moral sense of sharing.

Should a society institutionalize welfare, public housing and foodstamps? The questions are manifold. Can the sense of economic insecurity drive men to work? Can one feel an incentive to earn the bare minimum? Can any socio-economic system afford to drive a segment of the population out of the mainstream of life and then extend institutionalized charity to them for an indefinite period of time?

No one today can claim he is creating material values all by himself. A truck driver did not invent a truck. A farmer did not invent a tractor. A TV newsman did not invent a TV system. Every one of us is getting the benefit of social values created in innumerable ways each day. However, there is no allocation formula at present to determine what is a "fair" share assignable to each individual or each occupational group except the old rule of supply and demand.

While an enormous transition is taking place from the pure

contractual system of supply and demand to the allocation system there is no clearcut allocation formula, i.e. a scientific formula. Social democracy, coupled with private property rights and political democracy, may or may not be the imperative of the new age; nevertheless, one's faith in what he considers to be the imperative for the coming age is inseparable from his religious perspective.

Alas! Look at another way. Now you see what you don't see. Absolute truths gone! Modern men came to believe in *absolute truths* of modern scientific principles. Modern social science principles are valid only within a given social framework. They become old-hat when the social framework itself makes a drastic change. In a society such as the United States, where dynamic social changes keep taking place from one decade to another, if not visibly one year to another, no social science principles can remain durable for long. Furthermore, absolute truths of modern relativism and scientism should represent "no sacrosanct principles," but in reality modern men tend to believe in eternal and unchangeable scientific principles. The law of supply and demand is one of those sacrosanct principles.

Industrial owners at the inception of capitalism used to take risks and get rewarded for taking risks. Today industrial owners do not take risks by holding bonds and stocks of many different corporations, and they win in some and lose in others. Industrial owners no longer work hard because operations of the corporations are left to hired professional managers. Whatever other reasons one may add every advanced nation employs today the allocation system as a measure to counter the growing side-effects of the social ills and dislocations that the natural law of supply and demand creates. (It should be noted that the human sense of fear can create havoc on the law of supply and demand as the moderns experience runaway inflation and depressions.)

The allocation system, unlike the law of supply and demand, is neither a self-operating and enforcing system nor a precise and exact formula. The allocation system entails a central planning, not for any productive purpose but for a negative purpose of distributing only. Accordingly, a government has to adjust and readjust diverse and conflicting interests for the good of the citizens and the nation. Every socio-economic group has a lobby to watch or influence legislation. Every state and every legislator has obligations to bring home Federal money as much as possible. Every socio-economic group battles for a slightly bigger share of the pie than the last.

Central planning in any country assumes social values created and to be created. The first step is to collect a portion of social values created as equitably as possible, but subject to lobbying, political pressures, abilities to pay, and so on. The second step is to distribute as equitably as possible, but also subject to lobbying, pressures, needs, and so on. Inevitably both collection and distribution become less than equitable each way. As noted already there is no scientific allocation formula. The pot in the interim belongs to everybody. It means everybody is entitled to the pot and nobody has to take care of it: the cost of delivery eats up substantially the money to be redistributed.

Some of the public apartment buildings built in every city were torn down after less than ten years of use. If our socio-economic framework were to enable each of the have-nots to buy into a housing unit each individual would take care of his own property. Nobody takes care of the property which belongs to everyone or to the State. A driving force is an individual thing and no governing elite can tell individuals what that should be by writing rules. Furthermore, fear, prejudices and hate are not free but very costly indeed.

Are money, property and other human needs and desires irrelevant to God and His attributes? Are we building a pantheon just like the ancient Romans did two thousand years ago? Should we consider scientism, various philosophical schools, contemporary laws, and economic theories as rivals to the monotheistic God? Not all but many scientific, philosophical, legal, and economic doctrines made contributions to human progress and humanity by fulfulling human wants and desires to a great extent. In that sense they have been great supporters of, rather than being rivals to, one God.

The fundamental conflict between Christianity and scientism would vanish as long as human existence and spiritual reality are fused, and existence and spiritual reality support each other. In this connection Marxism was nurtured in the Judeo-Christian tradition. One can neither become an atheist simply because he damns God for idly watching human sufferings and miseries and denies the existence of such God as seemingly indifferent to the meaning of human existence, nor can one become a Christian simply because he preaches God only in a mystic sense. It was the teaching of Jesus that one can have the Kingdom of God only when one can fuse morality and religion. In the parlance of today's language a man is free and alive only so long as one's perspective of life and the world he lives in interact. The pursuit of a religious perspective becomes a destructive bedlam when divorced from the life in the world. When human existence and spiritual reality are separated, then various philosophical schools, scientism, laws, and socio-economic theories become little gods and rivals to one God, because human existence, wants and desires in this world are irrelevant to the Pantheon of Heaven and Hell.

Once human existence and spiritual reality are separated one's existence is tragic: Either one has to live in complete absorption in a sort of make-believe mysticism that shuts out all the realities beyond or one is no more than a cog in a gigantic machine, and the world appears to him a mirage in which one's own needs and desires cannot interact with those of others. Each individual, totally naked spiritually, can create a little make-believe world of his own, instead of perceiving the Kingdom of God.

The virgin birth, resurrection, and miracles personified human warmth, love and hope, and were integral aspects of early and medieval Christianity, leading men to faith in the Greco-Roman world just as Santa Claus and Easter eggs enrich our thoughts in the form of dramatized images and symbols during the Christmas and Easter holiday seasons today.

As long as they are understood in the historical circumstances there is no reason for such beautiful yet powerful images to pose as obstacles to one's faith; nevertheless, such images as articles of faith tend to reduce grownups to the state of being children and render the church impotent to adapt to needs of industrial and scientific societies. With all the mystic symbols as articles of faith the churches cannot nurture the free will of the individual to distinguish right or wrong and make moral choices, but speak pathetically of "sins."

Jesus praised the innocence of children but certainly did not equate ignorance or wishful illusion with innocence. Furthermore a complete absorption in the religious images and mysticism of personal salvation, inner consolation of ecstasy, and apathy to the reality of the world, in the atmosphere of scientism and proliferation of information, not only deprives a Christian of individuality, personality and moral choices, but encourages individuals to delude or deceive themselves and shy away from realities and truths and also makes the traditional Judeo-Christian faith indistinguishable from the Eastern fatalistic mystics and some Christian sects which keep springing up by aspiring to bizarre views of the millennium, fear, unconditional submission, tax-free schemes, outright superstitions and frauds. One either substitutes the love of Jesus for some unattainable love in real life or takes the teachings of Jesus as a sort of consolation for unattainable goals in real life or as an excuse for avoiding the attainable goals: One denies the Judeo-Christian faith.

Mystic beliefs tend to represent absolute truths. Absolute and unquestionable truths are a congenial step to absolute power. The spiritual perspective elevated men to perform noble acts of love and service to others in the human history, but a slight distortion in such a spiritual perspective also turned men of single-minded devotion into paranoid leaders at the top and zombie-like fanatics at the bottom and became instrumental in the cruel human tragedy which happened in holy inquisitions, the holocaust during World War II, and Jonestown in Guyana. One may call it psychological illness or the devil or demon but it is nothing more than a slight deflection of the tendency for illusion to become reality. A slight distortion in the spiritual perspective can shatter the divider, fragile as glass, between religion and illusion.

The evil of "flesh" in medieval Christianity meant the supremacy of the spiritual power over secular rulers, but the evil of flesh today means the supremacy of spiritual truths over scientism and the material life of the real world. To many Christian cults springing up today, the evil of flesh is the outside world, including established churches, which offer alternatives to such cults.

All Christian creeds and dogmas are important so long as they enable individuals to perceive the spiritual and moral perspective of life. But such creeds and dogmas as articles of unchangeable and eternal truths artificially created "heretics" and "pagans" and perpetuated conformism, ignorance, helpless divisions and struggles among the believers throughout history. In fact that is what we have: All the ecumenical movements are led to the dead-end street of creeds and dogmas.

Ironically, unchangeable creeds and dogmas have caused divisions and are likely to cause further divisions within Christianity. A few divisions offer the people a choice and keep the churches on their toes for internal discipline within each hierarchy, but fragmentary divisions drive the people helplessly to confusion and agnosticism.

The Bible is clear enough not to require further creeds and dogmas. If creeds and dogmas are needed, why should they be considered as unchangeable and eternal truths binding upon every future generation of Christians to come? The Christmas tree, little dwarfs and giants and the red-nosed reindeer are neither creeds nor dogmas, yet they enrich our lives just the same. The question today is not whether or not creeds and dogmas help Christians interpret the teachings of Jesus in a uniform way, but whether or not such a uniform interpretation is essential to Christianity.

No one today can deny the melancholy fact that incredible harm had been done by creating heretics artificially on the basis of creeds and dogmas which were not even relevant to the teachings of Jesus. Perhaps there were some moral distinctions between "enemies" in the context of "love your enemies" and "enemies of God," but "heretics" persecuted throughout history were more terribly unfortunate political losers rather than religious ones. Only in hindsight were heretics persecuting the Christians.

Furthermore, the Church may let each generation of Christians go back to the teachings of Jesus and interpret his words in the light of the needs and desires of their time. The Bible is readily available and no one, including the Church, can tell the moderns that what one can read clearly in the Bible is erroneous in the light of creeds or dogmas. For practical purposes the Church cannot compete with the TV networks in presenting a mystery series; no institution, however, can compete with the church in educating the people on the magnificent and unique spiritual and moral messages of Jesus.

The Church authority to maintain creeds and dogmas should not entail the authority to pass judgments. Should the Church have the authority to absolve anyone from sins or excommunicate or issue a shunning order, or to refuse to admit certain members to sacraments or to sort out groups of heaven-bound and hell-bound Christians?

"Sins" in the teachings of Jesus relate to moral choices. If so, one can forgive oneself or refuse to do so. Jesus always said, "Your sins are forgiven," but never said, "I forgive you."

Enforceable standards of conduct relate to law, not moral choices. This distinction of law and moral choices differentiates correspondingly a church from a secular organization. One is not free to do whatever he wants according to his conscience or any other prism in a secular organization, or he must be ready to face the consequences even for spiritual and moral reasons.

One is, however, free to do whatever his spiritual perspective or conscience dictates within or without the religious organizaton of which he is a member. If one follows blindly specific values and teachings of the religious organization, he is forfeiting his own spiritual perspective or conscience and his own self.

There are no absolute truths or solutions involving moral choices on each issue. It is not that certain things are right or wrong but there are many rights on a single issue, and nobody knows in advance the consequences of each right.

"Sins," "repentance," "forgiveness," "judgments," and "faith" in the teachings of Jesus carried meanings different from the same words in the Old Testament context and also different from those of St. Augustine.

The fundamentalists and evangelists today almost invariably repeat a formula of the original sin. (A teenager's comment: "Why should I be damned for Adam's sin? Who was Adam? I remember only vaguely my own grandpa.") The formula sets forth: God as the moral judge dispensing penalties for sins; Jesus on the cross redeeming penalties for sins; repentance; and being born again and self-denial. This formula was perfectly suited to the anarchic European societies of the early Medieval Age and the early Modern Age when raw force replaced the orderly objective standards of human conduct. Such a formula of total self-denial and the evils of the flesh addressed to powerful elements of anarchic ages, such as general-kings, feudal lords, bands of brigands, and western gunmen certainly worked well to the benefit of societies and mankind. Can this mystic formula stir a moral fervor today?

To begin with, any statement that all men are depraved and sinful is as pointless as saying that all men are good and social. Any statement that flesh, money, and properties are irrelevant to one's spiritual life is as senseless as saying that the dignity of human existence is of no concern to one's spiritual life. Modern men are in general overburdened with laws which specify extensively objective standards of conduct and other foreclosure obligations that moderns have to discharge; consequently, moderns feel powerless and insignificant, and the mystic formula works as a great consolation to moderns by making repentance easy. Repenting and being forgiven in such a mystical sense, however, is irrelevant to moral choices and is oblivious of the real world: It is to forget about the real world rather than to interact with the world and to resign to the aimless life rather than to reshape our own future in the world.

The church has the authority to absolve sins or an individual can make moral choices according to his spiritual views of life, but it cannot be both ways. Why did Judaism as practiced during the Hasmonaean dynasty and Christianity as practiced during the medieval centralized papacy fall into degeneration? Not a single ecclesiastical legislation concerning relief of the poor was enacted at the zenith of its wealth during the medieval centralized papacy. Whenever spiritual authority was translated into secular power and wealth, moral choices were transformed into objective, enforceable standards of conduct, thus leaving no room for individuals to make moral choices.

Religious institutions were no different from other secular institutions vulnerable to abuses and degenerations. Religion and any kind of secular authority (instead of moral authority) is a fatal combination. Not only history has proven it, but also Jesus was particularly concerned with that fatal combination. (It cannot be within the spiritual and moral purview to worship a pope, a man, and allow him to be an infallible and indispensable moral legislator and judge of hundreds of millions of other men.)

Today more than ever, modern men are feeling the urge for faith to guide their lives and see the meaning of their lives. One's meaning of life enables him to reconcile his self with others, and he can bring a new outlook on life and regain self-esteem.

In the Kingdom of God one is ever willing to conform to customs, conventions and laws out of his willingness to do so in the moral and spiritual sense. But he refuses to be merely one of the crowd in ever conforming for the sake of conformity or in ever unconforming for the sake of unconformity.

In the Kingdom of God, in the process of making moral choices, the sense of social rejection or acceptance does not come into the picture because one leaves an estimation and meaning of his life to himself and not to anyone else.

In all other make-believe worlds the sense of social acceptance or rejection depends upon the estimation in which one thinks he is held, and the sense of social acceptance or popularity leads him to self-love; but the estimation is not up to himself but to others. In the make-believe worlds, the sense of social rejection or unpopularity is tragic for anyone: there is no room for self-esteem because he has left the estimation to others. In these make-believe worlds, whether one is popular or unpopular, he cannot do anything about his sense of insecurity because it appears to him that the changing circumstances and constantly changing human relationships bang up against him.

In the Kingdom of God there is no room for anyone to feel lonely or boring or lead a life of a hermit. It is a life capable of being loved as much as a life capable of loving. It is a life capable of forgiving itself as much as a life capable of forgiving others. It is a life capable of having self-respect as much as a life capable of recognizing self-esteem held by others as well. It is a life one would give all he can to as much as a life he would get the most out of.

In the Kingdom of God one's life is peace of mind and full of meanings, and he can rise above fear, pressures, tensions and cares of human existence. It is human for one to grieve over the death of a spouse, children, close relatives or friends or to go through a period of stress over divorce, personal illness or financial difficulties. The world would not be the same without someone whom one used to love dearly, and there ought to be some answer or cure for the unbearable pains of a terrible loss. Only one's meaning of life would tell him how to lose, heal emotional wounds, regain hope, and live and die. Each day is one's entire conscious life if he rises above fear, sadness, regret and anxiety. We should not ask ourselves the millennium-old questions which clearly have no answers.

Somehow men learned to think of death painfully and birth with joy. Yet death and birth are so alike; consciousness into unconsciousness or vice versa. Do any of us remember the pain or joy of being born? Would we feel any pain or joy in falling into a dreamless sleep? It is beyond anyone's ability to state what is to come after death. Everyone owes God and himself a death as well as a life worthy of living and dying. One's death is as meaningful as a life he lives through. The Kingdom of God is the same world seen or to be seen through the same spiritual perspective of the ancients, the moderns and the future generations and their common yearnings for ever a little better place in which to live.

In the Kingdom of God one will not allow fear, anxiety, disappointments, sadness, bitterness, defeats or any other negative feelings to eat up his vitality. One cannot afford to be too frightened while awake, too frightened to fall into sleep without pills or alcohol and yet too frightened to fall into a dreamless sleep.

In Christianity, the historical religion, one does not get disillusioned by institutions or systems which are not working as they should. Men yearned for, strived for and created a little better place to live in in the zigzagged course of the ever-imperfect world. The historical religion tells us the realistically attainable goals as well as the limitations of the best human efforts. In the Kingdom of God one strives for perfection in the institutional systems, one's own life, one's own marriage, love, job, entertainment, wealth, power, happiness, or sensual pleasure.

It is, however, an ironical aspect of modern affluent life in which everyone is looking for heightened possibilities for happiness and pleasure. Heightened possibilities are perceived as perfection. There is certain tragedy for one to *desperately* look for perfection in marriage, love, family life, wealth and power. One demands perfection of his or her spouse, children, public officials, churchmen, sportsmen, and so on; accordingly, one tends to wallow in the imperfections of the society, social institutions and every aspect of his life and justify his nihilistic, purposeless, and valueless life.

What is happiness? What is pleasure? What is perfection? No scientist, psychoanalyst, Madison Avenue or TV commercial can tell you what they are. No social scientist can tell you what are perfect economic systems or political systems. They are to a great extent the way one sees what they are for himself through the prism of his spiritual perspective or other prism. Only one's perspective of life can define for him the purpose of the wealth or power one seeks or the means to attain them. An elegant party-hopping from one to another, expensive vacations from one place to another, something new, something stronger, someone new—all turn out to be less than perfect because the seeker does not know or see what perfection is, without consulting with his spiritual perspective.

On the other hand, constant nagging, hounding, complaining, whining, fretting, crabbing, and an overdriving administrator's zeals stem from one's own fear of and impatience with his own imperfections and create terrible irritants for others. It is one's desperate attempt to evade responsibility by blaming someone else for the imperfections which he cannot even define, again without consulting with his spiritual perspective. The pride and joy of being a mother and the boredom and painfulness of being an over-qualified babysitter are two different portrayals of the identical motherhood.

In the Kingdom of God one does not get disappointed over imperfections or failures. What is imperfection, or failure? The fear of failure, the sense of one's own weakness and faults, the fear of commitments, the fear of society and the fear of interaction which lead one to a loss of self-esteem, inaction, withdrawal and escapism, which avoid challenges and the opportunities to learn human possibilities as well as limitations, are imperfections. The fear of establishing long-term goals worth striving for, the fear of sticking to the moral yardstick worth respecting and the fear of making a commitment to a moral choice lead many moderns to a loss of self, oblivion, self-deception, and unconsciousness in the dazed and desensitized "joys and pleasures" of getting by and instant gratification.

It is a terrible injustice to Jesus and his Church if the Kingdom is looked at in terms of Heaven and Hell. Heaven and Hell are the religion of senseless apocalytic terror and fear, not of love. It was the teaching of Jesus that fear, terror, horror, and insecurity on one hand and love on the other do not mix too well. One has to overcome the sense of fear and insecurity before he can love. If the church is to trump up fear and preach love from both sides of the mouth, then the teachings of Jesus are neither original nor unique, His teachings as the greatest spiritual and moral values are completely obscured, and the Church is no more than a heavenly travel agency.

For historical and other reasons gulfs have been created between church creeds and dogmas on one hand and the teachings of Jesus on the other, between mysticism and scientism, and between secular values and morals required in the real world on one hand and the superficial and illusory values on the other. Such rifts are ever-widening. The churches as well as modern people merely inherited these problems; accordingly, the enormous challenges to bridge such gaps face modern people and the churches, and needless to say, they are not overnight tasks.

In the dehumanization process of the industrial and scientific age modern man is bidding for humanization more than ever in the history of mankind. The moderns as well as the churches no longer can afford to indulge in the will not to believe. What confronts us and the modern churches is the age-old question of Buridan's mule which depicts a stubborn ass starving to death between alluring bundles of hay simply because he cannot make up his mind which one to eat.